Understanding Tourism Mobilities in Japan

The total number of foreign tourists received in countries throughout the world was 530 million in 1995. That number broke through the 1 billion mark for the first time in 2012, at 1,035,000,000. In 2015, it reached 1,180,000,000. According to Anthony Elliott and John Urry, modern society has been characterized as being "mobile", and within that we are also living "mobile lives".

In modern society, flows of people, things, capital, information, ideas and technologies are constantly occurring, and as they are merging like a violently rushing stream, what could be termed a landscape of mobilities has appeared. Social realities are in flux and are transforming to become different than they were before. This volume will expand the inquiry of tourism mobilities comprehensively and clearly from the fields of humanities and social sciences. In particular, tourism mobilities has been actively investigated up to now in the UK, US, Europe and Australia, but even though the Japanese body of literature contains a great many excellent studies of Japanese examples, there are almost no English-language articles presenting their results.

Publishing examples of Japanese tourism mobilities will not only foster new and exciting lines of inquiry for existing and future research on tourism mobilities, but will also have implications for humanities and social sciences throughout the world.

Hideki Endo is a Professor in Tourism Research in the Faculty of Letters and Executive Director of the Institute of Humanities, Human and Social Sciences at Ritsumeikan University, Japan. He has studied the sociology of tourism, especially the social transformation that mobility and tourism bring. Among his publications are *Tourism Mobilities* (2017), *Media and Culture* (2017), *Space and Media* (2015), *Tourism and Media* (2014), *Contemporary Cultural Studies* (2011) and *Actualities in Sociology of Tourism* (2010).

ANTINOMIES
Innovations in the Humanities, Social Sciences and Creative Arts

Series Editor: Anthony Elliott
Hawke Research Institute, University of South Australia

This Series addresses the importance of innovative contemporary, comparative and conceptual research on the cultural and institutional contradictions of our times and our lives in these times. *Antinomies* publishes theoretically innovative work that critically examines the ways in which social, cultural, political and aesthetic change is rendered visible in the global age, and that is attentive to novel contradictions arising from global transformations. Books in the Series are from authors both well-established and early careers researchers. Authors will be recruited from many, diverse countries – but a particular feature of the Series will be its strong focus on research from Asia and Australasia. The Series addresses the diverse signatures of contemporary global contradictions, and as such seeks to promote novel transdisciplinary understandings in the humanities, social sciences and creative arts.

The Series Editor is especially interested in publishing books in the following areas that fit with the broad remit of the series:

- New architectures of subjectivity
- Cultural sociology
- Reinvention of cities and urban transformations
- Digital life and the post-human
- Emerging forms of global creative practice
- Culture and the aesthetic

Subverting Consumerism
Reuse in an Accelerated World
Edited by Robert Crocker and Keri Chiveralls

Understanding Tourism Mobilities in Japan
Edited by Hideki Endo

For a full list of titles in this series, please visit www.routledge.com/Antinomies/book-series/ANTIMN.

Understanding Tourism Mobilities in Japan

Edited by Hideki Endo

Routledge
Taylor & Francis Group

LONDON AND NEW YORK

First published 2021
by Routledge
2 Park Square, Milton Park, Abingdon, Oxon OX14 4RN

and by Routledge
52 Vanderbilt Avenue, New York, NY 10017

Routledge is an imprint of the Taylor & Francis Group, an informa business

British Library Cataloguing-in-Publication Data
A catalogue record for this book is available from the British
Library

Library of Congress Cataloging-in-Publication Data
A catalog record has been requested for this book

ISBN: 978-1-138-38775-1 (hbk)
ISBN: 978-0-429-42608-7 (ebk)

Typeset in Times New Roman
by Wearset Ltd, Boldon, Tyne and Wear

Contents

Illustrations

Figures

Tables

Contributors

Adam Doering is an Associate Professor of Tourism at Wakayama University, Japan. He has published widely on a range of topics, including critical tourism studies, lifestyle sports in East Asia, destination marketing organization (DMOs) and sustainable tourism and transportation. His current research examines the role of surf tourism in Fukushima's post-disaster recovery.

Tim Edensor is Professor of Human Geography at Manchester Metropolitan University and a Research Fellow in Geography at Melbourne University. He is the author of *Tourists at the Taj* (1998), *National Identity, Popular Culture and Everyday Life* (2002), *Industrial Ruins: Space, Aesthetics and Materiality* (2005), *From Light to Dark: Daylight, Illumination and Gloom* (2017) and *Stone: Stories of Urban Materiality* (2020). He is also the editor of *Geographies of Rhythm* (2010) and co-editor of *The Routledge Handbook of Place* (2020), *Rethinking Darkness: Cultures, Histories, Practices* (2020) and *Weather: Spaces, Mobilities and Affects* (2020).

Hideki Endo is a sociologist, Professor/Vice Dean at the "College of Letters", Executive Director of the Institute of Humanities, Human and Social Sciences and Vice President of "Research Organization to manage and support Research Institutes and Research Centers" at Ritsumeikan University, Kyoto, Japan. Endo is also editor-in-chief of *The Tourism Studies* published by the Japan Institute of Tourism Research, and served on the editorial board of the *Asian Journal of Tourism Research* which was one of the international academic journals on tourism studies. He has a wide range of research interests in the sociology of tourism, and has published many books and research articles on various aspects of the sociology of tourism. His current main research interest is "tourism mobilities", especially focusing on (1) the relationships between tourism, media, popular culture and social communications in a mobile digital age, and (2) the mobilization of social risks concerning "human and natural disaster", including pandemic viruses such as COVID-19.

Koji Kanda is a cultural geographer and Professor at the "College of Letters", Ritsumeikan University, Kyoto, Japan. His main research interest is the relations between the production of tourism places and mobilities, especially focusing on assemblage, media, imagination, gender and hospitality. He is editor-in-chief of *Tourism Studies Review* published by the Japan Society of Tourism Studies.

Tsz Hei Kong (Terrence) is a junior research fellow at the Center for Tourism Research (CTR) at Wakayama University, Japan. Terrence received his master's degree in tourism from the same school in 2020. His research interests include visual methodologies, representations, destination marketing and management.

Jonas Larsen is Professor in Mobility and Urban Studies at Roskilde University, Denmark and PhD programme leader for Society, Space and Technology. He has a long-standing interest in tourist photography, tourism and mobility more broadly. More recently, he has also written extensively about urban cycling and running. He is currently writing a book on urban marathons and is the key academic expert in a new large research project on urban walkability. His work has been translated into Chinese (both in China and Taiwan), Japanese, Polish, Portuguese, Czech, Korean (in process) and Turkish (in process), and he is on the editorial board of *Mobilities, Tourist Studies and Photographies*.

Masato Mori is Professor of Faculty of Humanities and Law and Economics, Mie University. His current research is focused on post-humanist approaches to cultural geographies, visual culture and everyday material culture.

Richard Sharpley is Professor of Tourism and Development at the University of Central Lancashire, UK. He is co-editor of *Tourism Planning & Development* and on the editorial board of a number of other journals. His research interests lie primarily within the areas of the relationship between tourism and sustainable development and the tourist experience.

Hiroshi Sudo is a sociologist and Professor at the Graduate School of Regional Policy Design at Hosei University in Tokyo, Japan. He has studied postmodern theories on sociology of tourism, and researched especially in fields in the Asian Pacific.

Ryotaro Suzuki is a Professor in the Department of Tourism and Transnational Studies at Dokkyo University, Japan. With an academic background in anthropology, he has research interests in the intersection of culture and tourism, especially in Vietnamese handicrafts, Japanese souvenir "omiyage" and folk performing arts.

Fumiaki Takaoka is a sociologist and a Professor at the College of Tourism, Rikkyo University, Japan. His research interests lie in the sociology of tourism and urban sociology. He has published research papers on the authenticity of tourism, travel routes and travel connections.

Shingo Teraoka is a sociologist and Professor in the "Faculty of Letters" at National University Corporation, Nara Women's University, Nara, Japan. His research areas include community revitalization, rural tourism, food and agriculture and local media in Japan. He is co-editor of *Kanko media Ron (Tourism and Media)*.

Makoto Yamaguchi is a Professor at Dokkyo University, Japan. His research interests lie in the history and culture of tourism in modern Japan. He has published several books including *Guam and Japanese* (2007), *Overseas Tourism of Japan* (2010) and *Birth of "Cabin Attendant" in Japan* (2020).

Series editor foreword

I regard this book as of the upmost importance. *Understanding Tourism Mobilities in Japan* provides, for the first time, an accessible overview of developments in tourism and mobility research, with a central focus on Japanese tourism studies. To date, such research has mostly only appeared in Japanese-language publications. I am delighted to have Professor Endo's edited collection appear in *Antinomies*, again breaking new ground for the Series.

The mobilities paradigm – as developed by authors such as Adey, Thrift, Urry and Elliott, Sheller and Kesselring – has made a major contribution to the development of the social sciences and humanities in these early decades of the 21st century. Never before has "life on the move" been so widespread across the planet – as travel, transport and tourism reconfigure our lives and our lives in these times. From automobility to aeromobility, and from communicative mobility to virtual mobility, women and men today are travelling further, faster and arguably more frequently than at any time previously in human history. Mobilities has become especially important in the broader context of Japanese society, largely because of the changing geopolitical presence globally of the country and of the importance of tourists to the region as well as the wider significance of various media icons and cultural trends (such as Manga and Pokémon GO) which link to the mass appeal of "life on the move".

Understanding Tourism Mobilities is a book that deals with extensive and hugely contested mobility processes in the broader context of Japanese society, and the various contributors to this book look at the intersecting implications of mobilities for – amongst others – social and cultural relations, social inequality, social networks, the nature of places, changing dimensions of time and space, and alternative mobility futures.

Professor Hideki Endo has himself emerged not only as a major theorist of mobilities in Japan, but also as a contributing force to mobilities on a worldwide scale. As the Executive Director of the Institute of Humanities, Human and Social Sciences, as well as the Vice President of the Kinugasa Research Organization, at Ritsumeikan University, Professor Endo appears magically everywhere: from conducting fieldwork in Seoul to delivering research presentations in Adelaide. His looping of the planet – at once physical, communicative, virtual and imaginative – has been inspirational to scholars and students in the emerging field of mobility studies, and it has been my good fortune to get to know him well, both at his Institute in Japan and at the Jean Monnet Centre of Excellence at the University of South Australia.

Hideki Endo's authority as an editor of this brilliant work on mobilities comes in no small part from his own experience of "life on the move", both intellectually and practically. *Understanding Tourism Mobilities in Japan* is fresh and provocative, casting new light on topics of crucial importance to the analysis of travel, transport and tourism across Japan in particular and the world more generally. The volume offers a set of beguiling essays.

Anthony Elliott
Adelaide, May 2020

The significance of research on tourism mobilities and related issues

Hideki Endo

The age of mobilities[1]

People, things, capital, information, ideas and technologies are constantly on the move in contemporary society. Across the globe, business people fly through the sky, immigrants leave their homelands, exchange students travel to other countries to study and professional athletes move between Europe, America and Asia. According to the International Organization for Migration (IOM)'s *World Migration Report 2020* (https://publications.iom.int/system/files/pdf/ wmr_2020_en_ch_2.pdf; accessed December 31, 2019), the number of people who migrated to another country increased from 192 million in 2000 to 272 million in 2019.

According to Anthony Elliott and John Urry, contemporary society has become characterised by *mobility*, and we too are living 'mobile lives'. Flows of people, things, capital, information, ideas and technologies constantly arise and converge into a torrent to create what might be called 'landscapes of mobilities'. This has shaken up our social reality, giving it an entirely new form. Elliott and Urry describe this change in the following way:

> People today are 'on the move', and arguably as never before. Massive social changes – globalization, mobile technologies, intensive consumerism and climate change – are implicated in the ever-increasing movement of people, things, capital, information and ideas around the globe. It is estimated that people today travel 23 billion kilometres each year. By 2050 it is predicted that, if resource constraints do not intervene, this will increase fourfold to 106 billion kilometres each year. Travel and tourism make up the largest industry in the world, worth in excess of $7 trillion annually. The number of international flight arrivals nears one billion. People today are travelling further, faster and (for some at least) more frequently. While many choose to travel, others are forced to be 'on the move'. Asylum seekers, refugees and forced migration also proliferate. Add to this a rapid explosion in communicative and virtual mobilities, with more mobile phones than landline phones and over one billion internet users, and it is clear that a

golden age of mobility has truly arrived – bringing with it dizzying possibilities and terrifying risks.

(Elliott & Urry 2010: iv)

It is precisely within this context that *the real* is being restructured and re-realised. Rather than 'stabilising' or 'positivising' our existing realities, however, mobility constantly shakes it up and alters it to create *new* realities.

The 'mobility turn' in the human and social sciences

Alongside this transition to an 'age of mobility', the human and social societies are under pressure to develop new forms as well (Endo 2017).

Of course, the human and social sciences have always questioned their *raison d'être* and reformed themselves, undergoing several turns in response to societal transformations. Among these is the so-called 'linguistic turn', which came about in the 1960s when society began to be restructured around information, symbols and images. Proponents of the linguistic turn believe that social realities are constructed through discourse. For them, language is not a 'transparent mirror' that merely *reflects* social realities; rather, it *builds* social realities.

This idea by no means takes social institutions and culture as given; it makes it clear that they are always formed in close connection to linguistic and symbolic discourse. Another aspect of the linguistic turn is the semiotic perspective of culture. Though semiotics was advocated by Swiss linguist Ferdinand de Saussure, figures like Roland Barthes used it to decipher popular culture and reveal the ideological nature inherent in its content.

Later on, from the 1980s to the 2000s, social conflicts that were hidden behind information, symbols and images erupted in a variety of ways. This is when the *cultural turn* in the human and social studies began to be discussed. The cultural turn was developed largely in the field of cultural studies, which had been influenced by structuralism and post-structuralism.

As with the linguistic turn, the cultural turn regards our social realities as being constructed from discourse, composed of symbols and interpreted as such. However, the cultural turn stipulates that behind this symbolism exist various kinds of inequality, discrimination and exclusion, differentiating it considerably from the linguistic turn. While the linguistic turn places importance on clarifying the ideological nature inherent in social realities in relation to languages, symbols and images, the cultural turn goes further, emphasising what it sees as a 'battlefield of representation' upon which diverse social positions negotiate politically to construct social realities.

Though the human and social sciences have undergone the linguistic turn and the cultural turn, there is arguably a call for another new turn. The ideological nature of symbols (which the linguistic turn sought to capture) and the social negotiations behind the ideological nature (which the cultural turn sought to capture) are no longer connected to the movements of people, things, capital, information, ideas or technologies, but are manifested in those movements. Elliott and Urry call this perspective the 'mobilities paradigm', which they have outlined as follows (see Elliott & Urry 2010: 15–21, or Urry 2007: 44–60):

1   Every social relationship involves diverse 'connections' that are more or less 'at a distance', more or less fast, more or less intense, and more or less involving physical movement. Historically, the social sciences have overly focused upon geographically propinquitous communities. They have been based on more or less face-to-face social interactions with those present at the same location. However, most connections with peoples and social groupings are not based on propinquity anymore.

2   These processes stem from five interdependent mobilities of: human beings, material, capital, information, images and ideas. Examples of these are provided below.
   •   The corporeal travel of people for tourism, work, migration and escape.
   •   The physical movement of objects to producers, consumers and retailers; as well as the sending and receiving of presents.
   •   The imaginative travel effected through the images of places and peoples appearing on and moving across multiple print and visual media.
   •   The communicative travel through messages exchanged via letters, telegraph, fax and mobile telephone.

3   Mobility is not identical for everyone, but uneven and linked to age, gender, race and social class.

4   The fact every social relationship is 'at a distance' does not mean that there are no face-to-face connections. Face-to-face connections are made only occasionally and for specific periods.

5   Complex groupings of human beings, material, capital, information, images and ideas (assemblages) are seen as a result of mobility in the present age.

6   Forms of government in the present age are not concerned with a single 'territory', but with mobile populations moving across and beyond 'territory'.

7   While social science has treated social life as a social realm independent of and separated from the worlds of 'nature' and 'objects', this viewpoint is challenged here.

8   The concept of 'affordance' is crucial to analysing these relationships. For example, the technologies of automobility and aeroplanes provide people with affordances, and such couplings between human beings and the environment are important.

9   Because mobility uses energy that releases carbon dioxide, the dependence of society on carbon dioxide will unavoidably become an issue.

10   Mobility-systems are organised around the processes that circulate people, objects and information in diverse spaces at various speeds.

11   These various mobility-systems and routeways linger over time.

12 Mobility-systems, such as computer-controlled cars, are based on increasingly expert forms of knowledge.
13 Interdependent systems of 'immobile' material worlds, and especially exceptionally immobile platforms (roads, garages, stations, airports, docks), are necessary to give structure to mobility experiences.

Significance of research on tourism mobilities

Based on this discussion, Urry advocates the idea of 'the social as mobility', arguing that *the social* is shifting from 'society' (which is based on immobility) to 'mobilities'. He writes:

> Much twentieth-century sociology has been based upon the study of occupational, income, educational and social mobility. This literature regarded society as a uniform surface and failed to register the geographical intersections of region, city and place, with the social categories of class, gender and ethnicity. Further, there are crucial flows of people within, but especially beyond, the territory of each society, and these flows relate to many different desires, for work, housing, leisure, religion, family relationships, criminal gain, asylum seeking and so on. Moreover, not only people are mobile, but so too are many 'objects', 'images', 'informations' and 'wastes'. Mobility is thus to be understood in a horizontal rather than a vertical sense, and it applies to a variety of actants and not just to humans.
>
> (Urry 2000: 186)

Of course, Urry's argument here requires more thoughtful examination. For example, we ought to think carefully about whether it is appropriate to contrast 'society' and 'mobilities'. At the dawn of the modern era, sociology discovered 'society' by setting out to understand aspects of *the social*, and sociology was institutionalised as a discipline along the way (Sato 2011). If we suppose that what 'society' encompasses – that is, 'the connotation of society' – now includes mobilities, which exhibit new, dynamic stirrings, then 'society' and 'mobilities' ought to be understood to be closely intertwined, rather than opposed to each other.

Taking all of that into account, a more detailed critical analysis of Urry is needed in the future. If we follow Urry's line of reasoning, however, then *the social* must appear most clearly in tourism, even in the context of mobility. One can no longer consider mobilities in the contemporary world without thinking about tourism and travelling.

Even though tourism numbers sometimes fall because of a variety of events, such as terrorist attacks in the US, Europe and other countries around the world; infectious diseases like COVID-19 or SARS; natural disasters like the Great East Japan Earthquake; and economic conditions like the financial crisis of 2008, hundreds of millions of people around the world continue to travel to other countries. In relation to mobilities, Jószef Böröcz states that such travel continually creates mass 'leisure migration' (Böröcz 1996). Tourism has become a social phenomenon that creates mobilities and rocks the very foundations of our societies and cultures (Hannam & Knox 2010). This is spelled out explicitly in the concept of 'tourism mobilities'.

As society becomes increasingly mobile, traditional objects of study in the humanities and social sciences are undergoing considerable change: realities, identities, cultures, local communities, cities, nations, the media, religious sacredness, gender, labour, the environment and more. Tourism is the *topos* upon which the figures of mobile contemporary society come sharply into view, and as such, research on tourism mobilities has the hidden potential to revolutionise existing discussions in the human and social sciences. The significance of research on tourism mobilities arguably lies in its ability to capture societal shifts.

Issues in research on tourism mobilities

In advancing such research on tourism mobilities, what kinds of issues should we pay attention to? In this volume, I would like to focus on two aspects of tourism called *locality* and *performativity*.[2]

Locality

In the present day, places are not things that have always existed, but are rather constantly being created in their relationship to tourism mobilities. A given place is not a tourist destination because it has always been one; rather, we travel to a place because it has been constructed as and transformed into a destination. Sheller and Urry (2004: 5) discuss this as follows:

> Conventionally there are presumed to be 'tourist' or 'potential tourists' on the one hand, and 'places' that constitute potential 'tourist destinations' on the other. The tourism researcher then examines those forces that propel individual tourists or groups of tourists to travel to one or other such destination place. Psychologists or economists normally see the 'factors' that induce such travel as individual, while sociologists or anthropologists look for more social factors. But in either case there is an ontology of separate events, where places and indeed cultures are presumed to be relatively fixed and given, and that happen to push or pull discrete tourists from place to place and from time to time. [...] This book by contrast presumes that tourists' activities are not so separate from the places that are visited. Those places are moreover not fixed and unchanging but depend in part upon what happens to be practiced within them.

They go on to argue that in contemporary society, places that were created and altered for the purpose of travelling as a leisure activity are 'living' places. It is becoming more and more difficult to positivise places as fixed things, as globalisation has primarily been driven by mobilities. Thrown into the vortex of mobilities, places have become constantly exposed to change amid the multi-layered struggle between globalisation and localisation. Places are reconstructed and transformed by tourism, and these transformed places, in turn, cause tourism to take on new forms as well.

I would like to cite tours to Hashima, Nagasaki Prefecture, as an example of this. Hashima is an island that spans 480m from north to south and 160m from west to east, with a circumference of 1,200m and an area of 63,000m². Coal was discovered on the island at the beginning of the first decade of the 1800s, and in 1890, Mitsubishi began full-scale deep-sea mining operations. Along with an increase in coal output, this led to the construction of high-rise housing complexes to house laborers and their families. During the peak of coal mining on Hashima, there were as many as 5,300 people living on the small island. The sight of the housing complexes, which were made of reinforced concrete and built in a way that juts out of the island's precipices, resembles the battleship *Tosa*, which is why the island became commonly known by the name *Gunkanjima* (Battleship Island). In 1974, the mine closed because of the shift in energy demand from coal to oil, and Hashima became a deserted island, reduced to ruins.

Starting in the 2000s, the island found itself in the limelight as a touristic resource. In 2015, it was inscribed as a UNESCO World Heritage site, as part of *Sites of Japan's Meiji Industrial Revolution: Iron and Steel, Shipbuilding and*

Figure 1.1 View of *Gunkanjima* (Battleship Island).
Source: photo by the author.

Figure I.2 Tourists visiting the once-abandoned Battleship Island.
Source: photo by the author.

Coal Mining, which began to change the meaning of a place that used to be nothing more than an abandoned island. Hashima started to attract tourists from around the world and various travel agencies began offering tours there, which further increased the number of people enjoying tourism on the once-abandoned island. This resulted in the emergence of a form of tourism that could be called 'tourism in abandoned places' (Figures I.1 and I.2).

Tourists travelling to Battleship Island find it important that this place, destined to gradually fall into ruin, tells the story of the coal industry's boom and bust. Hashima probably would not have piqued the interest of so many tourists if operations were still going on there and the island showed signs of activity. The high-rise housing complexes are deteriorating little by little and it might not be possible to see them the same way on a subsequent visit. This place attracts so many tourists precisely because it has fallen into ruin. However, after the 'ruination' reaches a point at which most of the buildings have deteriorated, tourists will move on to another location. Even so, if the high-rise housing complexes were 'restored' or 'saved', they would cease to be these ruins. For this reason, Battleship Island is arguably a place that people want to be preserved in its state of ruin (i.e. they want the ruins to be preserved). When tourism reconstructs a place and changes its meaning, giving it new life as a destination for 'tourism in abandoned places', this can put it in the ironic position of having its ruins 'preserved'. This is the process that can be seen on Battleship Island.

Performativity

Recent research on tourism mobilities has made ample reference to sociologist Erving Goffman's argument that our everyday world is formed through the process of performance. Of course, references to Goffman's argument can be found from a fairly early stage in the field of sociology of tourism. Actually, in *The Tourist*, the first edition of which was published in 1976, Dean MacCannell borrows Goffman's terms *front region* (i.e. stage, as in performance stage) and *back region* (i.e. backstage) to discuss the 'authenticity of tourism' (MacCannell, 1999: 91–107).

According to MacCannell, tourists are not looking for tacky, made-up tourist spaces; they are driven by the desire to see the authentic – they want to see the real lives of the people living at their destinations and to experience absolutely untouched and authentic original culture. Yet what they see is 'staged authenticity', which they are allowed to see.

However, MacCannell limits his discussion to certain points concerning the authenticity of tourism and does not go as far as explicitly stating that tourism is closely connected to our everyday world through performance. That connection is exactly why performativity has been a focal point of recent researches on tourism mobilities, which have explored attempts to re-examine the boundary between the everyday and the non-everyday.

These points are also extremely important in emphasising the physicality that tourism mobilities entail. For example, when Urry, a researcher who has furthered sociological research on tourism mobilities, applied Michel Foucault's notion of 'gaze' to tourism in his *The Tourist Gaze*, published in 1990, he went no further than stating that the tourist gaze is socially formed. However, 20 years later, in 2011, after tourism mobilities had started to have a considerable effect on society and gained greater breadth and depth, Urry revised the entirety of *The Tourist Gaze* in collaboration with Jonas Larsen and published *The Tourist Gaze 3.0*, which amply incorporates perspectives that focus on performance and emphasises the physicality of tourists. Urry and Larsen state that 'tourism demands new metaphors based more on being, doing, touching, and seeing rather than just "seeing" ' (Urry & Larsen 2011: 190). This spurred discussions about the relationship between physicality and modes of mobility such as airplanes, automobiles and bicycles (Featherstone, Thrift & Urry 2005; Larsen 2017).

Tourism can only exist when the physical performances of people such as tourists 'on the move', employees working in the tourism industry and local residents who welcome the tourists connect to the everyday world. Furthermore, when a place 'is a tourist destination', it is supported by the physical performances of these actors. Recent research on tourism mobilities attempts to throw these points into relief.

This becomes clear if we consider, for example, Abbey Road in London, where the cover photo for the rock band The Beatles' album *Abbey Road* was taken. The album cover depicts the members of The Beatles crossing Abbey Road on a

Figure I.3 Tourists trying to imitate the way The Beatles crossed Abbey Road.
Source: photo by the author.

crosswalk, which has led many tourists to visit the street and cross it in the same way. Tourists travel from all over the world to visit this place, and their performances of crossing the crosswalk, posing like The Beatles and taking a snapshot of it have changed the meaning of Abbey Road and have had an effect on the local community. Their performances have transformed Abbey Road into a tourist destination and continue to call new tourists there as a result (Figure I.3).

Overview of this volume

This volume will comprehensively and clearly expand the inquiry of tourism mobilities in the fields of human and social sciences. Tourism mobilities have been actively investigated in the UK, US, Europe and Australia, but even though the Japanese body of literature contains a great many excellent studies of Japanese examples, there are almost no English-language articles presenting these results.[3]

Publishing examples of Japanese tourism mobilities in English will not only foster new and exciting lines of inquiry for existing and future research on tourism mobilities, but also have implications for human and social sciences throughout the world.

The first four chapters depict the theoretical framework of tourism mobilities for the purpose of discussing Japanese case studies. 'Seeking sensuous mobilities: tourist quests for familiarity and alterity' (Tim Edensor) will explore the multi-sensory qualities of mobile tourist experiences. This chapter will focus on the divergence between tourist mobilities that satisfy desires for comfort, convenience and predictability, and those that offer a vigorous enlivening of corporeal and affective experience.

The purpose of the chapter 'Tourism, "nowstalgia" and the (non)experience of place' (Richard Sharpley) is to explore in particular the relationship between the use of smartphone cameras and the significance of place to the tourist experience. More specifically, drawing on the notion of 'nowstalgia' – as opposed to nostalgia – it sets out to propose that although tourists are by definition in place, the tourist experience is becoming disentangled from place.

'New tourism and social transformation in postmodernity: sociological examination of Japanese new tourism' (Hiroshi Sudo) will focus on the ideas of mass tourism and new tourism. This chapter will insist that tourism is becoming a liquid, self-organic system open to local living areas outside the traditional market.

The next chapter, 'Late tourism and "boomerang" mobility in Japan' (Makoto Yamaguchi), will discuss the centrality of experience of mobility itself, and the ways in which the performances peculiar to mobile and social media depart from experiencing the authenticity of photographic subjects and enable tourists to extract authenticity from their own performances in a self-directed and engaged manner.

Chapters 5 to 8 will take a fresh look at the relationship between regional studies and tourism mobilities, with Japanese regions as case studies. 'Mobility turn in rural districts in Japan: from "Kanko (tourism)" to "Kankei (relationships)"' (Shingo Teraoka) will study 'Kankē Jinko (relationship population)', which has taken the place of 'Koryu Jinko (temporary visitors, mainly tourists)'. 'Kankei Jinko' is a term indicating people with diverse mobility situations between tourism and residence, as expressed by the phrase 'more than tourism, less than residence'.

'The new mobile assemblages created by *Pokémon GO*' (Koji Kanda) will inquire into the new forms of movement created by this highly popular and influential smartphone game application and the unique features of the mobilities of *Pokémon GO* players.

'The roots and routes of Matryoshka: souvenirs and tourist mobility in Russia, Japan, and the world' (Ryotaro Suzuki) will examine the relationship between human mobility and objects, discussing a case of Russian folk crafts, such as Matryoshka dolls that are sold as souvenirs in many tourist spots in Japan.

'"Transference of traditions" in tourism: local identities as images reflected in infinity mirrors' (Hideki Endo) will discuss the transference of tradition with reference to a specific case study of the Yosakoi Festival in Kochi Prefecture, Japan, arguing that local identities have become fluidised.

Finally, Chapters 9 to 13 will consider tourism mobilities in terms of their association with performativity, while introducing case studies of tourism phenomena in Japan. 'Marathon mobilities: a western tourist perspective on Japanese marathons' (Jonas Larsen) contributes to the (tourism) mobilities literature by giving an embodied tourist perspective on the Tokyo Marathon and the Kyoto Marathon. This chapter explores why Westerners travel to and experience these faraway events and cities.

'Performative nationalism in Japan's inbound tourism television programmes: *YOU, Sekai!* (The world), and the tourism nation' (Adam Doering and Tsz Hei Kong) will consider how inbound tourism offers a familiar yet new context for understanding the complexities and contradictions of national identity and nationalism in the context of Japan's tourism nation-building efforts, by examining the performative Japanese/non-Japanese social relations that enact and reinforce well-established national cultural boundaries within the context of Japan's inbound tourism television programmes.

'Shibuya Crossing as a non-tourist site: performative participation and re-staging' (Fumiaki Takaoka) will analyse the strange tourist site of Shibuya Crossing from the perspective of the sociology of tourism. In doing so, this chapter focuses on tourists' participatory practice.

'Mobilising pilgrim bodily space: the contest between authentic and folk pilgrimage in the interwar period' (Masato Mori) studies the mobility of Japanese pilgrimage 'Henro'. This chapter will stress that the intersection of speed, transportation technology, representations of pilgrim movement and experience all combine to mould pilgrim bodily space, which Duncan (1996) termed 'Body Space'.

'Digital media as "social spaces" of tourism: the Japanese cases of travelling material things' (Hideki Endo) will investigate how a close connection between 'social spaces' in tourism and digital media has changed the nature of tourism by examining the travel of stuffed animals. In conclusion, this chapter will pose a new question arising from the fact that tourism mobility has started to give rise to phenomena that could not have existed before.

Notes

1 The modes, directions, meanings and intensities that people, things, capital, information, ideas and technologies travel by, in, for and with are diverse and multi-layered. For this reason, this volume primarily discusses 'mobilities' in the plural in order to reflect the diversity and multi-layeredness of mobility.
2 While the points of discussion with regard to tourism mobilities have been limited to locality and performativity in this volume, there are of course many other points being discussed in such research. Going forward, these points need to be organised thoughtfully so that they can be discussed further.

3 For example, in Europe, the journal *Mobilities* is edited by K. Hannam, M. Sheller and others (www.tandfonline.com/rmob; accessed June 1, 2020). In Japan, the symposium Tourism Mobility was held jointly by the Japan Society for Tourism Studies and the Ritsumeikan University Institute of Humanities, Human, and Social Sciences in July 2016. The symposium featured Larsen as the keynote speaker, who collaborated with Urry on *The Tourist Gaze 3.0* and also contributes to *Mobilities*, and its findings were printed in the academic journal *Tourism Studies Review*, vol. 5, no. 1.

References

Appadurai, A. (1996). *Modernity at large*, Minneapolis, MN: University of Minnesota.

Duncan, N. (1996). *Body space: Destabilising geographies of gender and sexuality*, London: Routledge.

Böröcz, J. (1996). *Leisure migration: A sociological study on tourism*, Oxford: Pergamon Press.

Edensor, T. (2000). Staging tourism: Tourists as performers. *Annals of Tourism Research*. 27(2): 322–344.

Elliott, A., & Urry, J. (2010). *Mobile lives*, Oxford: Routledge.

Endo, H. (2017). *Tsurizumu Mobirities: Kanko to ido no shakai riron [Tourism mobilities: Social theory of tourism and mobility]*, Kyoto: Minerva Publishing.

Featherstone, M., Thrift, N., & Urry, J. (2005). *Automobilities*, London: Sage.

Goffman, E. (1959). *The presentation of self in everyday life*, New York: Doubleday & Company Inc.

Hannam, K., & Knox, D. (2010). *Understanding tourism: A critical introduction*, London: Sage.

Larsen, J. (2017). Leisure, bicycle mobilities and cities, in J. Rickly, K. Hannamm & M. Mostafanezhad (eds.), *Tourism and leisure mobilities: Politics, work and play*, London: Routledge. pp. 39–54.

MacCannell, D. (1999). *The tourist: A new theory of the leisure class*, Los Angeles, CA: University of California Press.

Sato, T. (2011). *Shakaigaku no houhou [Method for sociology: Its histories and structures]*, Kyoto: Minerva Publishing.

Sheller, M., & Urry, J. (2004). *Tourism mobilities: Places to play, places in play*, London: Routledge.

Urry, J. (1990). *The tourist gaze: Leisure and travel in contemporary societies*, London: Sage.

Urry, J. (2000). Mobile sociology. *British Journal of Sociology*. 51(1): 185–201.

Urry, J. (2007). *Mobilities*, Cambridge: Polity Press.

Urry, J., & Larsen, J. (2011). *The tourist gaze 3.0*, London: Sage.

Chapter 1

Seeking sensuous mobilities

Tourist quests for familiarity and alterity

Tim Edensor

Introduction

As the tourist industry continues to expand, its sheer diversity can be bewildering, as can the range of mobile practices being undertaken by tourists. The variety of travel modes, adopted to get to and from destinations, to explore surroundings or as a practice in and for itself, involve an abundance of mobile experiences. Tourists become mobile on aeroplane flights, road trips and organised coach tours; they organise their journeys around train and bus timetables, cruise on canal boats or giant ships, and cycle, walk and run to and around tourist attractions. Some tourists undertake journeys at their own speed, perhaps contingently composing the route as they move. Some engage in competitive races or challenging physical journeys, while others make long pilgrimages to esteemed destinations. Many stitch key destinations together in itineraries organised according to different temporal arrangements and geographical scales. Some follow established tour schedules while others prefer the 'road less travelled'. There are also considerable variations in who can travel widely and frequently as a tourist and who may only make sporadic journeys for pleasure, geographical inequalities in access to mobility that are reflected in the history of travel writing, where accounts by western travellers hugely predominate. Indeed, ethnocentrism continues to pervade most academic enquiry into tourism and this includes accounts of tourist mobility (though see Cohen and Cohen, 2015, for a critique, and Edensor and Kothari, 2018, for a counter-example). Such ethnocentric distortions will surely change in the context of expanding tourism from Asia, Africa and South America, where travel to elsewhere is increasingly conceived as a right by a burgeoning middle class, as noted in T. C. Chang's (2015) important paper.

Despite this plethora of mobile tourist experiences, as Tim Cresswell (2006) contends, until recently, studies of travel and mobility have often ignored the qualitative experience of journeys. Accordingly, in this chapter, I explore the multisensory qualities of mobile tourist experiences to disavow assumptions that they merely comprise uneventful travel from A to B – the locations between journeys at which tourism really takes place. Instead, I contend that the extremely varied sensorial qualities of such journeys are integral to tourist experience. The bulk of the chapter will focus on the divergence between tourist mobilities that satisfy desires for comfort, convenience and predictability, and those that offer a vigorous enlivening of corporeal and affective experience. I will primarily draw on examples from Asia, and particularly Japan, in elucidating the discussion. Beforehand, though, I discuss how we might further contextualise forms of tourist mobility.

First, I want to emphasise the enormous inequalities in mobility and the persistence of endemic forms of immobility which shape who is able to move and to where. For it is estimated that the percentage of the world's population participating in international flight is a mere 2–3%, even though these people constitute half of all international travel; 'hypermobile' frequent travellers (Hall, 2015). This is not solely a matter of wealth, for there are vastly unequal restrictions on citizens from different nations who are permitted to travel. This current situation bears comparison to the accessibility to travel granted by possession of a British passport during colonial times and the contrasting possibility for mobility for those whom were colonised.

Second, the rise of the internet has prompted a huge increase in virtual mobilities. As Hannam *et al.* (2014) discuss, as information and communication technologies become more advanced and integrated into corporeal travel practices, there is increasing spillover between the everyday and the holiday. While travelling, tourists are able to access multiple networks and become immersed in hybrid spaces of in-betweenness, fluidly switching between corporeal co-presence with fellow travellers and virtual co-presence with others simultaneously connected to distant social networks. Through blogging, mailing and other social media, mobile connections are newly forged and continuously sustained, while such technologies also provide instant information about the spaces through which tourists move.

Third, as mentioned above, an enduring problem in much academic tourist literature is the figuring of the tourist as a single, lone traveller, usually male and white. Yet the absurdity of this preoccupation is revealed when we realise that most tourism is undertaken with other people, with family and friends. Though recent accounts have foregrounded the social and familial relations in tourism more generally (Schanzel *et al.*, 2012; Baerenholdt *et al.*, 2017), this also inflects experiences of mobility. A brief consideration draws attention to the ways in which tourists endeavour to ensure that long journeys are tailored to the needs and demands of children. We might also acknowledge how forms of mobile intimacy can emerge with friends and family, and more transiently, with strangers. For instance, travel on a compartment of an Indian train involves encounters with mobile traders and beggars, and a temporary intimacy often devolves amongst fellow travellers who share food and stories. Such harmony may not always eventuate. On a 36-hour bus journey through Himachal Pradesh, an American tourist who wearied of the consecutively screened Bollywood films throughout the journey was asked to leave the bus following his loud and persistent protestations.

Fourth, I consider the centrality of particular mobile experiences to particular tourist adventures. For instance, for those travelling on the Trans-Siberian Express, the journey itself seems fundamental, whereas a flight to an airport adjacent to a tourist resort may be less central to a two-week vacation. Nevertheless, I submit that all journeys are integral to tourist experience, for they are part of the experiences of all forms of tourism. The familiar reliability of 'dwelling-in-motion' (Sheller and Urry, 2006: 214) may induce a comfortable sense of being in and knowing a place, and such journeys might afford opportunities for reverie, listening to music, conversation with others or computer game-playing, modes of moving away from mundane everyday experience, or indeed, part of quotidian life. Yet even the most apparently functional journey is a time of transition, replete with anticipation and moving from one state to the next, a sense of release, of surrendering to the motion of the vehicle, boat or plane. Moreover, mobile experience is not simply unchanging but contains different phases. For instance, a walk through a scenic landscape might commence with a lively, sprightly gait and an openness to surroundings, during unremarkable stretches might solicit withdrawal into interior circumspection, and towards the end might become overwhelmingly focused on physical pain and exhaustion (Edensor, 2010).

Sensing while mobile

In considering the multiple forms of tourist mobility, I foreground how the body feels during travel, for all spaces in which we are accommodated and move through have the potential to generate sensory experiences. The affordances of 'tourist space', like other spaces, constitute 'the materialities and sensibilities with which we act and sense' (Rose and Wylie, 2006: 478). While mobile, we apprehend the affordances of the vehicles, ships and aeroplanes we move in, and mobile experience is also conditioned by the ways in which the forms of transport on which we travel respond to the landscapes we pass through as well as the ways these landscapes shape our experience of this space. Rail, automobile and air travel (Budd, 2011) have all radically transformed our apprehension of the world. The interior textures, windows, roominess, degree of insulation, smells and temperatures of travel technologies afford particular sensations, as do the materialities, surfaces, contours and gradients of the routes along which we travel. They encourage us to follow particular courses of action, and solicit a multi-sensory, more-than-visual apprehension of place, space and landscape. Indeed, many of these experiences of distinctive forms of tourist mobility and place become quite familiar to us, contributing to what David Crouch (2000) calls 'lay geographical knowledge', a knowing that is discursive, practical and sensual. Claudio Minca and Tim Oakes (2006: 20) underline how mobile experience is integral to the formation of such understandings: '[p]laces are at once the sedimented layers of historical experience, cultural habit, and personal and collective memory and continually remade by lived bodily movement'. These diverse forms of movement open up and close down possibilities for engaging with place, vehicle and other people as we move through space.

Given its importance to tourist theory over the past three decades, I briefly consider the salience of John Urry's (Urry and Larsen, 2011) seminal notion of the tourist gaze as the central sense through which tourist place and space is experienced. Elsewhere, I have critiqued an insistence on this visual centrality, arguing that in many kinds of tourist endeavour, non-visual sensations come to the fore as touching, smelling and listening are mobilised. Caroline Scarles (2009: 466) maintains that since the visual tourist experience of place 'exists as a series of embodied practices as tourists encounter the world multisensually and multidimensionally', the gaze continuously 'emerges via the materiality and corporeality of the body'. More specifically, Katrin Lund (2005: 40) asserts that whilst climbing, 'the sense of vision and the mountaineer's gaze cannot be separated from examining the body that moves and touches the ground'. These contentions reveal that tourism cannot be captured by one dominant sensation such as the gaze, but changes continuously according to context and contingency, for 'there is no beginning and no end, but a series of rhythms, flows and fluxes, in-between points and stages that tourists move in and around' (Scarles, 2009: 466). This is especially pertinent with regard to the unfolding experience of mobility, during which a 'static pictorialism' (Merriman *et al.*, 2008: 192) is not possible. Yet in focusing on the ways in which a mobile gaze is enacted, it is evident that different kinds of tourists focus their attention according to specific imperatives: a birdwatcher will scan the landscape for signs of avian movement and then direct sole focus to that spot, while a photographer will review broad swathes of space (Büscher, 2006).

In mobile tourist pursuits such as swimming, motorcycling and walking, we can similarly apprehend 'the multiplicity and the interaction between different internally felt and outwardly orientated senses' (Paterson, 2009: 768) beyond the visual, which include smell, sound and tactility as well as kinaesthesia (the sense of movement), proprioception (felt muscular position and stance) and the vestibular system (sense of balance). As Merriman points out, 'pedestrians, cyclists and motorcyclists ... have very different embodied engagements with and experiences of inhabiting the spaces of streets and roads' (2009: 590). To emphasise, then, the multiple forms of mobility experienced by tourists stimulate an equally multiple range of sensations.

I now turn to the main theme of this chapter: the contrasting forms of sensory mobile tourist experiences. On one hand, these are characterised by predictable, ordered and comfortable passage through space. On the other, they seek mobilities that produce enlivening, unpredictable and powerful sensations. These resonate with larger contrasting modern impulses and exist in tension with each other. In their contemporary incarnation, they originate in the growth of cities in the west at the turn of the 20th century, articulated by Georg Simmel's (1995: 31) account of how these urban settings solicited powerful new sensory experiences, an 'intensification of nervous stimulation' that assailed the city dweller in an 'accelerated city life'. The only response of the urban inhabitant, Simmel argues, was to adopt a blasé attitude to form a shield against overwhelming sensory onslaught. However, this very dynamism and the perceived sensory disorder that accompanied it also subsequently encouraged intensive efforts to regulate the urban environment in order to enable more orderly sensory experiences. Consequently, a host of technological developments and political measures were adopted to regulate these supposedly unruly environments, from extensive policing, waste management and traffic control to the rational and respectable recreation made available in parks and libraries. While certainly producing more orderly cities, such regulatory strategies have eventuated in the sterile, homogeneous and sensorially deprived 'blandscapes' that proliferate in many settings.

These contradictory modern desires for sensory order and sensory alterity are also discussed in tourist theories that seek to explain the motivations for much tourism. For instance, Chris Rojek (1995: 80) identifies what he refers to as an 'Apollonian' modernity that affirms 'structure, order and self-discipline', and the contrasting qualities of Dionysian modernity, productive of 'sensuality, abandon and intoxication'. Whilst the dominant modern urge might be to seek spatial and sensory order, the desire to transcend regulated environments and seek to become immersed in powerful and unfamiliar sensations has constantly bubbled below the disciplined surface of everyday life and stimulated a growing range of 'escape attempts' (Cohen and Taylor, 1992). Contemporary expressions might be the radical sensory alterity offered by a range of hallucinogenic and stimulant drugs, the intense sounds and moments generated at large rock festivals, and the many kinds of themed experiences offered in the 'experience economy' (Lorentzen, 2009). As I will discuss, peak experiences and immersive environments of many kinds are well provided for by the tourist economy, and many of them involve technologies and spaces of mobility that offer unfamiliar and intense sensory experiences.

Comfortable and predictable sensations

In contemplating how tourism provides predictable and orderly forms of mobility that are eagerly sought as an escape, I emphasise that such experiences should not be lazily critiqued as mindless escapism. For in affording opportunities for bodies to be released from the often onerous duties and toils of everyday life, technologies that facilitate seamless, comfortable movement are part of a vast complex in which infrastructures and networks have been developed to minimise effort, anxiety and strain for tourists. Everything is taken care of by others for a week or two.

Judith Adler (1989) demonstrates how travel programmes, brochures, accounts and guidebooks are 'a means of preparation, aid, documentation and vicarious participation' for the western culture of sightseeing. Such technologies prepare tourists to carry out a range of practices that are governed for many by a shared 'common sense'. Similar observations could be made about the promises made by travel companies about smooth transit via air and coach on the way to the air-conditioned tourist enclave, such as those that proliferate on the island of Okinawa, and that follow a typically standardised format of plush furnishing, pools, sea-based activities and high-end cuisine.

Problematically, tourist literature has overwhelmingly focused upon spatially extensive movements rather than the more modest, everyday mobilities that take place in comfortable, familiar surroundings, as tourists walk from beach to pool, from bar to shop, ambling slowly between amenities. Paying attention to these ordinary routine pleasures further highlights a broader deficiency in the recent upsurge in writing about mobilities. Here, scholars have similarly ignored the most common forms of mobile experience, namely the walk to the shop to buy daily provisions, the short journey to work or school (though see Bissell, 2018), and even the much shorter movements in and around home and garden, where we organise domestic space to facilitate smooth transit between one room and another. Such mobilities are akin to many of the quotidian practices of tourists. For in tourist enclaves, resorts, heritage districts and cultural quarters are similarly organised to facilitate ease of movement, with legible routes clearly marked to enable swift passage, personnel available to guide visitors along preferred routes and the familiar organisation of recognisable patterns making movement through space easily manoeuvrable. Smooth floor tiles and carpeting coerce the body into silent, regular movement and pathways are polished and cleansed to ensure that the body is undisturbed in its unhindered progress towards destinations. In moving through these spaces of continuity and stability, the tourist body is cajoled into enacting regular, well-rehearsed movements and cossetted into sensing familiar experiences of ease and comfort (Edensor, 2007a). Such designs affirm Jennifer Craik's contention that the production of large-scale, customised, themed tourist developments 'entail[s] a convergence or blurring between tourist and everyday leisure activities' (1997: 125). Similarly, travel on the tour bus provides a familiar, mundane rhythm wherein a tourist's body is seated in comfortable seating, calmed by the soft purr of the engine, shielded from glaring sunlight by tinted windows and often informed by the commentary of the tour guide about the sights outside, a smooth rhythm that is interrupted by intermittent movement outside the bus to gaze, photograph, eat and shop.

In Japan, for instance, many rail tours have recently been developed to cater for those who are content to sit on trains and view the scenery and have been described as 'train nerds' or *densha otaku*. The seven-kilometre Sagano Scenic Railway near to Kyoto runs slowly alongside the banks of the Hozugawa River and its accompanying ravine and is especially popular during the autumn months for *koyo*: viewing the reds and greens of the trees. Similarly, the Koruba Gorge Railway, originally constructed to aid in the building of the Kurobe Da, is now a 20-kilometre sightseeing track that passes through over 40 tunnels and 20 bridges. Such mobile experiences take away any effortful forms of mobility.

Tourist experiences such as these are organised by tour managers, guides, hotel staff and travel agents who usher tourists along particular routes, organise their photographic performances along the way and meet expectations in providing the requisite standards of comfort, cleanliness and refreshment. Nevertheless, though these personnel go to great lengths to produce predictable and uninterrupted travel, they cannot plan for the disruptions of unpredictable bodily effects, such as travel sickness, indigestion, jetlag – itself caused by long-distance mobile tourist experience – and attendant cultural and spatial disorientation (Anderson, 2015), tiredness or illness. In certain circumstances, insulated attempts cannot wholly exclude the begging children who may approach at traffic lights, scenes of poverty or peculiar behaviour by fellow passengers from tourist experience. The unbroken, regular rhythms anticipated on a highly structured coach tour around the Ring of Kerry on the west coast of Ireland may not always eventuate, for unforeseen events, disturbances along the route and one's own body might interfere with the promises of seamless mobility (Edensor and Holloway, 2008).

Enlivening

Though much mobile tourism involves a retreat into relaxing comfort and familiarity, many other kinds of tourist practice move away from predictability and seek out unfamiliar sensations – often by looking for distinctive kinds of sensory mobile experiences.

In contradistinction to the inhabitation of and movement through highly regulated enclavic spaces, other tourists, notably backpackers, seek to move through realms where they expect to encounter a sensual otherness, to experience sensory provocations and delights outside ordered tourist destinations. Opening their bodies to receive pleasurable and jolting sensations on the move, such tourists choose forms of transport that are not insulated from the environments through which they pass. In accommodating their bodies to these mobile sensory alterities, backpackers must adapt to squeezing into smaller spaces on cheap local buses, tolerate the heat or cold that blasts through opened windows, inhale the swirling dust and accept the sharp intrusions of acrid aromas. They may undertake journeys of rickety tuk-tuks, rickshaws or motorcycles that weave through roads that teem with diverse, cross-cutting vehicles and animals, and endure the effects of the potholed surfaces that convulse vehicles with shuddering jolts. They may take local trains with cramped carriages and abide the other sweating, swaying bodies that press against them in crowded conditions.

Besides these sensorially rich forms of transport where tourists are at the whim of the practices of drivers and subject to the affordances of mechanised travel and the conditions of routeways, tourists also make their own paths through multisensory spaces on foot, by bicycle or by motorbike. I have written elsewhere (Edensor, 2000) about the sensory thrills that bazaar and market areas in India offer to tourists who are happy to become immersed in their vibrant mix of social activities, and similar conditions pertain in similar settings in Vietnam, Thailand and Indonesia. Walking through such unfamiliar spaces is to confront a wealth of different sensations: the noise made by people and animals, religious sounds and loud music; the uneven, possibly slippery textures underfoot, and the need to weave a path through a press of other human bodies, animals and traffic; a proliferation of powerful smells, including fruit, alcohol, fried food, body odour, sewage and animal excreta, incense and smoke; and a range of unfamiliar sights that include the heterodox artefacts that accumulate on market stalls, the luminous colours of fabric and the curious juxtapositions that emerge as divergent vehicles, people and material elements come into momentary conjunction. In exemplifying these issues, Jamie Gillen (2016) discusses the motorbike guides who provide tours on the back of the bike for visitors to Saigon. As well as soliciting a friendly conviviality with the riders, the tours provide what many tourists referred to as an enthralling sensory overload: riders confidently weaving a path through the traffic, the unaccustomed smells and tastes at the food stops, the drenched neon landscape, and the unfamiliar sounds of the city contributing to a giddy encounter with the parts of the city often avoided by package tourists. While encounters with such spaces may provide a sensory overload that disturbs those unused to moving through them, they can also cause many tourists to reflect on the comparatively sterile, highly regulated environments through which they typically move, besides finding the sensory stimulation exhilarating.

These modes of moving that afford a more extensive experience of the sensations of place are also germane to the emergent practices of 'slow tourism', a mode of inhabiting and moving through space in which time is taken to savour food, movement and conviviality and absorb environmental qualities. Such practices include the increasing popularity of taking cruises along the Mekong River in Laos, Thailand, Cambodia and Vietnam, and the tourist endeavours that arrest movement in meditation, yoga or mindfulness techniques that seek to solicit a greater awareness of the self and be mindful of environs 'in the moment'. In addition, rural areas are characteristically marketed as destinations in which to escape the frenzied pace of life in the city – recalling Simmel's contentions discussed above – a realm in which to slow down, take notice of surroundings and 'get back in touch' with oneself. In Japan, Murayama and Parker (2012) contend that slow tourism is historically grounded in earlier traditions of undertaking pilgrimages to shrines and temples, and such trails remain popular in a more secular era. A more recent promotion of slow tourism has emerged in Japan with, for instance, Kyoto endorsing the virtues of walking in its 2010 slogan 'Slow Life Kyoto' and the rural area of Yamaguchi promoting the slow, sensory practices of dining, shopping and walking. Indeed, the popular tourist pursuit of visiting the zen gardens in cities such as Kyoto demands a more sustained temporal engagement that chimes with the meditative practices of the creators and spiritual devotees of these sites. Swiftly undertaken tours of such places cannot gain a sense of the subtle aesthetics of arrangements, different textures and delicate sounds; these impressions can only be grasped by a lingering engagement.

These slower practices resonate with walking holidays where a sustained immersion in landscape solicits a deeper knowing of the sensory qualities of wind and rain, the stony and springy textures underfoot, changing gradients, and the smells and sounds of place. This is especially evident in Japan in the growing popularity of walking along the thousand-year-old Kumano Kodo, a network of pilgrimage trails that stretches south from the Kansai cities of Osaka, Nara and Kyoto. The routes chosen are usually shaped by the three key shrines of Kumano Hongu Taisha, Kumano Nachi Taisha and Hayatama Taisha, and the diverse scenic pleasures of deep valleys, mountains and small villages. Aching bodies are apt to join fellow walkers in the steaming *onsen*, a large communal bath. Walkers in Tokyo may head for the strenuous, steeper challenges of Mounts Takao and Mitake. Such walking tours entice bodies into becoming accustomed to long periods of physical effort, and the pace of movement allows them to become attuned to the sounds, smells, textures and sights of the landscape they move through.

These slow immersive mobile engagements diverge from a wealth of tourist pursuits, also usually carried out in rural space, in which more vigorous corporeal engagements are sought to solicit 'peak experiences'. There are an increasing range of adventure sports on offer through which tourists themselves take responsibility for progress. Sapporo is a key destination for skiers and snowboarders to become (re)acquainted with the distinctive sensations of negotiating cold, icy downhill slopes at speed. Canoeists must learn to steer and stay afloat amidst the surge of wild water, while mountain bikers must negotiate steep, rough and muddy ground. These vigorous pursuits entail the development of an intimate sensing of these affordances that are part of the acquisition of skill. In Japan, adherents learn how to move along the watery affordances of the Nagano region in the hot spot of Hakuba, where the energetic practice of white-water rafting (Cloke and Perkins, 1998) is also practised, along with the more extreme buzz offered by bungee jumping. Other sensuous watery encounters include scuba and deep-sea diving (Merchant, 2011), and enthusiasts of both are drawn to the oceanic environment in Okinawa. More organised encounters with wild water are provided by boats that offer tourists the opportunity to experience the vigorous spinning of the crafts along the edges of the Naruto Whirlpools, as sea water moves back and forth between Japan's Seto Inland Sea and the Pacific Ocean. In addition to these forms of larger commercial provision, other subcultural forms of adventure tourism are staged at destinations that possess the affordances with which they seek to sensorially engage. Climbers travel to clamber up the rocky surfaces of Nagano, sand-boarders congregate to hurtle down the slopes of the immense sand dunes in Tottori Prefecture and zipliners career across Lake Biwa.

In a more structured format, thousands of people travel across the world to join locals in participating in sporting challenges, notably in the city marathons, held in Kyoto, Tokyo and many other Japanese cities, where a focus on the running body's capacity to manage the physical trials that must be endured will have been honed in repeated training beforehand. Here there is a turning in on the body, in which the runner attends 'directly to his or her breathing, blood circulation, heartbeat, muscles and visceral rhythms' (Larsen, 2019). The often intense sensations generated by pain and exhaustion diverge from many of the other mobile experiences discussed here in that a sensing of the surroundings is somewhat incidental, though runners attend to gradients and surfaces underfoot. Equally immersive are the more communally oriented occasions, frequently the object of tourist participation, that focus around dance and music. For instance,

Arun Saldanha (2002) explores how Goan beach raves combine the inward focus on the sensations provoked by dancing, the feel of the grainy textures of sand and the saturating humidity with more external sensory stimuli, including the tactilities of other moving bodies, sounds of music, smells of sweat, kerosene and cannabis, sight of the moon, and swaying coconut trees. Together with the varied effects of sensory-enhancing drugs taken by many participants, such events offer intensely powerful experiences in which ravers feel and sense together, enhancing communitas.

A similar sharing of intense sensation is found in the increasingly popular rollercoasters, log flumes and other white-knuckle rides that compete to offer a range of sensory thrills, whirling, plummeting and disorienting bodies that move in all directions at rapid speeds. Lynn Sally (2006: 295) describes how during the early 20th century, amusement parks at New York's renowned holiday resort of Coney Island 'capitalized on sensorial experience and escalated it to monumental proportions, transformed spectacle as total-body sensations and invited thrill seekers to experience amusement with and through their entire bodies'. This legacy persists and is continually advanced technologically in the ongoing development of ways to kinaesthetically enliven moving bodies. Attractions include spinning flat rides like carousels, drop towers that plunge riders from a high point, dark rides and simulator rides where seats and containers move in correspondence to the events that unfold on a moving screen to convey more extensive passenger movement. The ongoing innovation in the attractions designed to immerse visitors in thrilling, disorienting movement on ever-more intense mechanical rides is well exemplified in the development of recent thrill rides in Japan. Nagashima Spa Land offers the *Steel Dragon*, the world's longest rollercoaster and the second fastest in the country, peaking at 153 kilometres per hour and rising to a height of 97 metres, from which it subsequently plunges down. Fuji-Q Highlands theme park in Yamanashi Prefecture features *Dondonpa*, where a soundtrack is played throughout the ride that mimics the beating of the average heartbeat. Claimed to be the world's fastest launch acceleration, riders experience a top speed of 172 kilometres per hour in a mere 1.8 seconds while sensing a corporeal resonance with the sounds being played. *Bandit*, installed at Yomiuriland near Tokyo, is designed to pass through the treetops of hundreds of cherry trees, and proves especially popular during the annual cherry blossom *Sakura* Festival, thereby combining the visual sensing of scenic beauty and the kinaesthetic experience of high speed. Equally unusual is *Vanish*, at Yokohama's Cosmoland, which triggers a dynamic spray of water as it plummets into a hole in the middle of a pool. These increasingly diverse rides offer a range of sensory experiences that augment and enhance the rapid movement of the body through vertical and horizontal space and, critically, decentre the visual, further undermining academic preoccupation with the tourist gaze.

This decentring of the visual is fundamental to a range of dark tourist attractions that I have visited – and by dark, I mean literally those bereft of illumination.

Such sites include dark walks through 'haunted' corridors such as the *Fear Factory* in Queenstown, New Zealand (Edensor, 2018), restaurants where visitors can 'dine in the dark' (Edensor and Falconer, 2015), and concerts and plays staged in the dark. In *Dialogue in the Dark* (Edensor, 2013), which has formerly been staged in Osaka and Tokyo, a visitor is guided through a series of rooms that simulate archetypal settings or iconic urban sites, using only a walking cane to navigate. In gaining some insight into the ways in which blind people experience the world, participants are encouraged to attend to touch, sound and smell to orient themselves to the qualities of the particular spaces through which they move.

The foregrounding of darkness is integral to other experiences that are not conditioned by total blackout, but rather by a pervasive gloom. Most pertinent here is Dark Sky tourism (Edensor, 2013), especially popular amongst astronomers in search of clear views of the night sky, but which also offers tourists the chance to walk through nocturnal spaces untainted by artificial light, further advancing the non-visual apprehension of nature. Iriomote-Ishigaki National Park, located in Okinawa Prefecture, Japan, has been designated an International Dark Sky Park, the first location in Japan to receive international accreditation. The national park sprawls over a land area of about 406.53 square kilometres (157 square miles) of the Yaeyama Islands, extending over several islands, areas of sea and adjacent coastal areas. Rather more unique to Japan is the recent craze for what has become known as factory love, or *Kojo Moe*, which is particularly popular in the Yokohama and Kawasaki areas. Tourists take boat tours after dark across stretches of water from which can be viewed a range of illuminated industrial sites, such as chemical plants, oil refineries and large dockside cranes, reconfigured as sublime rather than abject. As Hilary Orange (2017: 63–64) details, the 'proximity of other bodies in a confined space, the unfamiliar rocking motion and movement of the boat, the sound and smell of the diesel engine, and the dark' produce a potent, highly unusual sensory experience that is especially conditioned by the visual thrill of the galaxy of illuminations radiating from the industrial sites and reflecting in the water.

Finally, another rather unorthodox kind of industrial site that offers an intense sensual experience as well as stimulating affective impressions of melancholy, memory and haunting is the ruin. As I have explored in earlier research (for instance, Edensor, 2007b), at decaying former industrial sites there are opportunities for multiple haptic encounters with excessive and unconfined materialities, including great scope for lively mobile adventures. Moving through the ruin, the archetypal disordered place and manifold textures, aromas and sounds are confronted. Tourists have been drawn to particular 'celebrity' ruin sites such as in the American city of Detroit and Pripyat, the Ukrainian village abandoned after the Chernobyl nuclear disaster. At these locations, where once unofficial, underground tours could be sought, now more organised businesses offer tours. Hashima Island (commonly referred to as 'Battleship Island') has become especially popular in Japan, its extraordinary shape, structure and location drawing tourists who roam freely along its heterogeneous stairs, walkways and balconies, experiencing powerful affective and sensory entanglements with the site (Kasemets, 2015).

Conclusion

In this chapter, I have drawn attention to the wealth of mobile experiences that are integral to tourism and contribute to the tourist's quest for sensory familiarity and alterity. In seeking to decentre academic preoccupations with the tourist gaze, I have focused on visual experiences apprehended while mobile as well as particularly foregrounding those numerous occasions on which tourists apprehend rich non-visual sensations. Clearly, forms of mobility are especially salient to the production of such tactile, kinaesthetic and sonic impressions. To conclude, I want to underline how distinctively different tourist practices and values can coincide, intersect and clash at particular sites, and this is no less the case with regards to mobile experience and practice. This underlines how tourist mobilities are socially and culturally shaped, not simply pragmatic modes of moving between and towards attractions.

At India's globally renowned, iconic Taj Mahal, different tourists move around the site, experiencing different elements and various spaces, carrying out diverse practices, sometimes bumping into each other as they pursue contrasting objectives and desires. European and American package tourists are typically ushered around the grounds of the memorial in rapid stop-start motion, encouraged to take photographs at particular points, stopped and delivered selective short narratives about the site's history, discouraged from independently ranging across the space at their own speed and direction, and after some while, marshalled back towards their tour bus. Backpackers, by contrast, tend to wander at will, unhurriedly seeking out less populated corners and unorthodox spaces from which to gain alternative photographic views of the mausoleum. They intersperse walking around with lounging on walls and lawns. To many Indian Muslim visitors, the site is a sacred space, and they are apt to walk directly to the mosque that lies adjacent to the domed monument or scrutinise the Quranic script that is inscribed across the walls of the site. Finally, crowds of domestic tourists, in family or village groups, noisily proceed down the site's central path, stopping to chat, laugh and rest. These more informal movements and dispositions are apt to disturb the progress of certain western package tourists who complain that they are blocking paths, are not sufficiently reverent towards the monument itself and are not moving in ways that acknowledge the centrality of the aesthetic qualities of the Taj. These different tourists all experience the Taj Mahal in diverse ways, not least in apprehending the site according to the diverse sensations solicited by their mobile practices.

References

Adler, J. (1989) 'Origins of sightseeing', *Annals of Tourism Research*, 16: 7–29.
Anderson (2015) 'Exploring the consequences of mobility: reclaiming jet lag as the state of travel disorientation', *Mobilities*, 10(1): 1–16.

Bærenholdt, J.O., Haldrup, M. and Urry, J. (2017) *Performing Tourist Places*. London: Routledge.

Bissell, D. (2018) *Transit Life: How Commuting Is Transforming Our Cities*. Cambridge, MA: MIT Press.

Budd, L. (2011) 'On being aeromobile: airline passengers and the affective experiences of flight', *Journal of Transport Geography*, 19(5): 1010–1016.

Büscher, M. (2006) 'Vision in motion', *Environment and Planning A*, 38: 281–299.

Chang, T.C. (2015) 'The Asian wave and critical tourism scholarship', *International Journal of Asia-Pacific Studies*, 11(1): 83–101.

Cloke, P. and Perkins, H. (1998) '"Cracking the canyon with the awesome foursome": representations of adventure tourism in New Zealand', *Environment and Planning D: Society and Space*, 16(2): 185–218.

Cohen, E. and Cohen, S. (2015) 'A mobilities approach to tourism from emerging world regions', *Current Issues in Tourism*, 18(1): 11–43.

Cohen, S. and Taylor, L. (1992) *Escape Attempts*. London: Routledge.

Craik, J. (1997) 'The culture of tourism', in C. Rojek and J. Urry (eds) *Touring Cultures: Transformations of Travel and Theory*. London: Routledge.

Cresswell, T. (2006) *On the Move: Mobility in the Modern Western World*. London: Routledge.

Crouch, D. (2000) 'Places around us: embodied lay geographies in leisure and tourism', *Leisure Studies*, 19(2): 63–76.

Edensor, T. (1998) *Tourists at the Taj*. London: Routledge.

Edensor, T. (2000) 'Moving through the city', in D. Bell and A. Haddour (eds) *City Visions*. London: Routledge.

Edensor, T. (2006) 'Sensing tourist spaces', in C. Minca and T. Oakes (eds) *Travels in Paradox: Remapping Tourism*. London: Rowman and Littlefield.

Edensor, T. (2007a) 'Mundane mobilities, performances and spaces of tourism', *Social and Cultural Geography*, 8(2): 199–215.

Edensor, T. (2007b) 'Sensing the ruin', *The Senses and Society*, 2(2): 217–232.

Edensor, T. (2010) 'Walking in rhythms: place, regulation, style and the flow of experience', *Visual Studies*, 25(1): 69–79.

Edensor, T. (2013) 'Reconnecting with darkness: experiencing landscapes and sites of gloom', *Social and Cultural Geography*, 14(4): 446–465.

Edensor, T. (2018) 'The sensory pleasures of the disoriented tourist', in M. Sheller, S. Kesselring and O. Jensen (eds) *Mobilities and Complexities: Reflections on Post-Carbon Social Science*. London: Routledge.

Edensor, T. and Holloway, J. (2008) 'Rhythmanalysing the coach tour: the Ring of Kerry, Ireland', *Transactions of the Institute of British Geographers*, 33(4): 483–501.

Edensor, T. and Falconer, E. (2015) 'Dans le Noir: eating in the dark – sensation and conviviality in a lightless place', *Cultural Geographies*, 22(4): 601–618.

Edensor, T. and Kothari, U. (2018) 'Consuming colonial imaginaries and forging post-colonial networks: on the road with Indian travellers in the 1950s', *Mobilities*, 13(5): 702–716.

Gillen, J. (2016) 'Urbanizing existential authenticity: motorbike tourism in Ho Chi Minh City, Vietnam', *Tourist Studies*, 16(3): 258–275.

Hall, C. (2015) 'On the mobility of tourism mobilities', *Current Issues in Tourism*, 18(1): 7–10.

Hannam, K., Butler, G. and Paris, C. (2014) 'Developments and key issues in tourism mobilities', *Annals of Tourism Research*, 44: 171–185.

Kasemets, K. (2015) 'Affect, rupture and heritage on Hashima Island, Japan', in H. Sooväli-Sepping, H. Reinert and J. Miles-Watson (eds) *Ruptured Landscapes*. Dordrecht: Springer.

Larsen, J. (2019) ' "Running on sandcastles": energising the rhythmanalyst through non-representational ethnography of a running event', *Mobilities*, https://doi.org/10.1080/17 450101.2019.1651092.

Lorentzen, A. (2009) 'Cities in the experience economy', *European Planning Studies*, 17(6): 829–845.

Lund, K. (2005) 'Seeing in motion and the touching eye: walking over Scotland's mountains', *Etnofoor*, 181: 27–42.

Merchant, S. (2011) 'Negotiating underwater space: the sensorium, the body and the practice of scuba-diving', *Tourist Studies*, 11(3): 215–234.

Merriman, P. (2009) 'Automobility and the geographies of the car', *Geography Compass*, 3(2): 586–599.

Merriman, P., Revill, G., Cresswell, T., Lorimer, H., Matless, D., Rose, G. and Wylie, J. (2008) 'Landscape, mobility, practice', *Social and Cultural Geography*, 9(2): 191–212.

Minca, C. and Oakes, T. (2006) 'Introduction: travelling paradoxes', in C. Minca and T. Oakes (eds) *Travels in Paradox*. Oxford: Rowman and Littlefield, 1–22.

Murayama, M. and Parker, G. (2012) ' "Fast Japan, slow Japan": shifting to slow tourism as a rural regeneration tool in Japan', in S. Fullagar, K. Markwell and E. Wilson (eds) *Slow Tourism: Experiences and Mobilities*. Bristol: Channel View.

Orange, H. (2017) 'Flaming smokestacks: Kojo Moe and night-time factory tourism in Japan', *Journal of Contemporary Archaeology*, 4(1): 59–72.

Paterson, M. (2009) 'Haptic geographies: ethnography, haptic knowledges and sensuous dispositions', *Progress in Human Geography*, 33(6): 766–788.

Rojek, C. (1995) *Decentring Leisure*. London: Sage.

Rose, M. and Wylie, J. (2006) 'Animating landscape', *Environment and Planning D: Society and Space*, 24: 475–479.

Saldanha, A. (2002) 'Music tourism and factions of bodies in Goa', *Tourist Studies*, 2(1): 43–62.

Sally, L. (2006) 'Fantasy lands and kinesthetic thrills sensorial consumption, the shock of modernity and spectacle as total-body experience at Coney Island', *Senses and Society*, 3(1): 293–310.

Scarles, C. (2009) 'Becoming tourist: renegotiating the visual in the tourist experience', *Environment and Planning D: Society and Space*, 27: 465–488.

Schanzel, H., Schänzel, H., Yeoman, I. and Backer, E. (eds) (2012) *Family Tourism: Multidisciplinary Perspectives*. Bristol: Channel View.

Sheller, M. and Urry, J. (2006) 'The new mobilities paradigm', *Environment and Planning A: Environment and Planning*, 38: 207–226.

Simmel, G. (1995) 'The metropolis and mental life', in P. Kasinitz (ed.) *Metropolis: Centre and Symbol of Our Times*. London: Macmillan, 3–45.

Urry, J. and Larsen, J. (2011) *The Tourist Gaze 3.0*. London: Sage.

Chapter 2

Tourism, 'nowstalgia' and the (non)experience of place

Richard Sharpley

Introduction

Tourism and place are inextricably linked. That is, as an increasingly evident manifestation of contemporary mobilities, 'tourism is, above all, a spatial phenomenon' (Minca, 2000: 389); it involves the movement of people from one meaningful place or 'centre' to another place or centre 'out there' (Cohen, 1979: 180), typically in pursuit of new, meaningful experiences. More simply stated, the 'very idea of a "holiday" is ... based on the opportunity to shift or change spatial context' (Minca, 2000: 390), in particular to experience something different or 'other' (Urry, 2005). In turn, this suggests that tourists purposely seek out specific places in the expectation of satisfying and distinctive experiences that such places promise (Suvantola, 2002) and, hence, that tourism can only be understood in terms of 'the social, cultural and psychological interactions that visitors have with the place' (Jepson & Sharpley, 2015: 1159).

For much of the history of the modern phenomenon of tourism, this has undoubtedly remained the case. The UK's seaside resorts of the nineteenth century, for example, offered experiences that not only occurred in non-ordinary, differentiated time and place but that also emanated from the performances of tourists themselves in those places (Walton, 1983); moreover, these seaside resorts, attracting early mass tourists, were also culturally distinct in that they challenged the prevailing 'bourgeois culture with its concerts, museums, galleries, and so on' (Urry, 1994: 234). Similarly, during the twentieth century, although tourism increasingly came to reflect cultural change with the emergence of a culture based upon mass production and consumption in general becoming evident in the development of mass forms of tourism in particular, tourism typically remained defined by destination-related experiences that were temporally and spatially distinct. The flight to the sun was a flight to the 'Other'.

More recently, however, two transformations have occurred that arguably have served to weaken, if not break, the link between the tourist and the place as a basis for understanding the tourist experience. First, just as tourism or, more precisely, tourist travel is but one phenomenon within a social world that has come to be increasingly viewed and explained through the conceptual lens of mobilities, so too are tourist places (destinations) in a sense mobile. As Sheller and Urry (2004: 1) suggest, places are 'always "on the move". Places are "performed" ... and in these performances they are put into play in relation to other places, becoming more or less desirable, more or less visited'. As a result of this process, underpinned by the 'networked mobilities of capital, persons, objects, signs and information' (Sheller & Urry, 2004: 6), new destinations and new tourist practices have emerged to the extent that tourism places and tourism time have become de-differentiated (Lash, 1990: 11) from other social practices. Tourism has, in a sense, simply become cultural (Urry, 1994) and, consequently, although people still travel to places as tourists, everywhere (as opposed to 'somewhere else') has become a destination. Tourist places have become indistinct from non-tourist places; as destinations, they have become what Auge (1995) refers to as 'non-places'. Hence, it can be argued that the relationship between specific places and meaningful tourist experiences is diminishing or, at least, becoming less significant.

Second, and more significantly, the nature of the tourist experience has been transformed by another element of contemporary mobilities, namely rapid advances in information and communication technologies in general and the advent and affordances of the smartphone in particular. The impact of information technology on tourism has been increasingly explored in the literature (for example, Benckendorff, Sheldon & Fesenmaier, 2014; Egger & Buhalis, 2008), although the focus is primarily on the supply of tourism services rather than on tourists' experiences (but see Sharpley, 2018; Tribe & Mkono, 2017). Notably, with some exceptions (Wang & Fesenmaier, 2013), the widespread use of smartphones amongst tourists, particularly as a medium for taking and sharing photographs, has attracted more limited attention, surprisingly so given the fundamental change this has brought about in that most traditional of tourist practices – photography – and what this reveals with regards to the interaction between tourist and place.

The purpose of this chapter, then, is to explore in particular the relationship between the use of smartphone cameras and the significance of place to the tourist experience. More specifically, drawing on the notion of 'nowstalgia' (Korin, 2016) – as opposed to nostalgia – it sets out to propose that although tourists are by definition in place, the tourist experience is becoming disentangled from place. That is, it will be suggested that through the increasingly ubiquitous use of smartphone technology for taking and sharing images, including 'selfies', the tourist experience is defined less by being in place and more by the production of images for the future consumption of experience. The first task, then, is to review briefly the concept of space and place as a basis for understanding the established significance of place to the tourist experience. The chapter then goes on to consider the evolving practice of tourist photography and the changing relationship between the tourist-photographer and place resulting from the increasing use of smartphones in order to lead into the argument that tourism can now increasingly be understood not as the experience of place, but as the production and sharing of 'nowstalgic' experiences.

Space, place and the tourist experience

In his book *Being and Time* (in the German original *Zein und Zeit*), first published in 1927, the philosopher Martin Heidegger refers to human existence as *dasein*, literally 'being there' or being in the world. More specifically, he famously argues that place 'places man in such a way that it reveals the external bonds of his existence and at the same time the depths of his freedom and reality' (Heidegger, 1958: 19, cited in Tsatsou, 2009: 24). In other words, Heidegger is suggesting that place is fundamental to the human experience; that the human condition of being necessarily requires a spatial context. Alternatively stated, 'to exist at all ... is to have a place – to be implaced ... To "be" is to be in place' (Casey, 1993: 13).

Following Heidegger, the study of place was taken on by human geographers who, adopting a phenomenological approach, reconceptualised it on the basis of human awareness and knowledge (Unwin, 1992). Subsequently, the concept of place became the focus of research within a variety of disciplines across the humanities, arts and social sciences, resulting in numerous perspectives and a recognised lack of definitional consensus. Nevertheless, a common theme linking most definitions and disciplinary perspectives is that human existence is defined by the relationships that people have with place; that places can be understood in terms of the meaning that people accord them. Indeed, Cresswell (2015: 12) usefully suggests that 'the most straightforward and common definition of place is a meaningful location'. And that meaning, or the relationship that people have with place, is described by a variety of terms including place attachment, place identity, place dependence, place bonding and sense of place, the latter arguably being the most recognised and utilised term (Stedman, 2003). At the same time, and reflecting the argument above that the de-differentiation of tourism from other cultural practices has resulted in the emergence of 'non-places', it is argued by some that the (post)modern world is increasingly defined by a condition of placelessness whereby people's relationships with place are becoming diminished through time-space compression (Harvey, 1990, 2012) or what Giddens (1994) refers to as 'distanciation', both of which are the outcome of technological and other globalising transformations, most notably in the context of this chapter the advances in media and communication technologies (Tsatsou, 2009). Interestingly, it was also the notion of placelessness, manifested in uncertainty, instability and a sense of alienation in modern societies, that inspired MacCannell's (1976) proposal that tourists are contemporary secular pilgrims seeking meaning or connectedness in other places; yet, as this chapter will suggest, that search for meaning is being undermined by the contemporary focus on 'nowstalgic' experiences.

To return to the concept of place and its traditional significance to the tourist experience, however, irrespective of definitions and terminology, key to understanding the significance of place is its relationship with space or, more precisely, the distinction between space and place. Space is a common term applied in numerous contexts, but it is generally understood to imply emptiness or a void (Lefebvre, 1991); hence, space is, in a sense, meaningless whereas places have meaning or, as Bremer (2006: 26) suggests, the distinction lies in the 'particularity of places [compared] to the homogeneity of space'. Put another way, 'What begins as undifferentiated space becomes place as we get to know it better and endow it with value' (Tuan, 1977: 6) or, as Gieryn (2000: 465) suggests, 'place would revert to space if we vacuumed out the distinct collection of values, meanings and objects that created it'. Similarly, Relph (1976: 43) conceptualises place as space that is accorded meaning through human involvement, but adds the dimension of human intentionality into the creation of place: 'The essence of place lies in the largely unselfconscious intentionality that defines places as profound centres of human existence', a perspective that is of direct relevance to the assumed intentional selection of places (destinations) by tourists in the expectation of meaningful experiences. Hence, as Bærenholdt et al. (2004: 3) observe, tourism spaces become tourism places only 'when they are appropriated, used and made part of the living memory and accumulated life narratives of people performing tourism'. This relationship between space and place is conceptualised in Figure 2.1.

Importantly, space and place are not independent. Place cannot exist without space (Agnew, 2011) and, moreover, space is defined by movement from place to place (Tuan, 1977). Hence, the existence of place is dependent on space, as is the case in tourism inasmuch as the significance of two meaningful places (home and the destination) is defined by the movement (travel) through the space between them.

If place is indeed a 'centre of meaning' (Relph, 1976: 2), the question then to be addressed is: what factors establish or constitute that meaning or, more precisely, how are places socially constructed? A variety of perspectives are proposed in the literature (see, for example, Manzo, 2003), though generally place is considered to comprise three components, namely the physical/objective environment or, more broadly, the physical attributes of a particular place; the social or cultural significance attached to place; and people's experiences or behaviours – that is, the manner in which they interact with place.

Addressing each of these in turn, first it is evident that the very basis of a place is the tangible physical features that distinguish it from other places. For tourists, of course, it is such features, whether the combination of sun-sea-sand for summer holidays, mountains for winter sports or the built heritage environment for cultural tourism, that represent the 'pull' of the destination (Uysal & Jurowski, 1994).

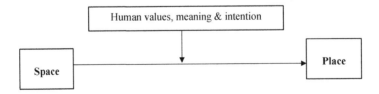

Figure 2.1 From space to place.

Second, however, places are endowed with cultural meaning or, as Gieryn (2000: 473) puts it, 'meanings that individuals and groups assign to places are more or less embedded in historical contingent and shared cultural understandings of the terrain'. For example, rural tourism destinations may be understood through a cultural lens of 'rurality', representing a bygone, arcadian yet imagined era (Short, 1991); equally, destinations in less developed countries may, perhaps, be viewed by Western tourists through culturally determined understandings of tradition and modernity. The point is, any one place may be subject to different cultural interpretations; 'any physical place has the potential to embody multiple landscapes, each of which is grounded in the cultural definitions of those who encounter that place' (Greider & Garkovich, 1994: 2). And third, the way in which people experience, use or interact with a place, either in the past or the present, also ascribes meaning or significance to that place. Certainly, for example, childhood memories of family holidays may contribute to a sense of belonging or connection to a particular place, whilst the opportunity to engage in what Urry (1992) describes as either a romantic (alone or with significant others) or collective (shared with many others) gaze may determine the significance attached to different places. More specifically, 'place social bonding' is increasingly considered a dominant factor in place attachment (Ramkissoon, Weiler & Smith, 2012: 264); that is, the significance or sense of a place reflects the communal bonds developed between people in (or as tourists, visiting) that place (Hammit, Backlund & Bixler, 2006).

There remains considerable debate in the literature with regards to the relative significance of each of these three components to the construction of place. Some, for example, suggest that the contribution of the physical environment to a sense of place remains underestimated (Stedman, 2003), an argument that is of particular relevance to tourism, although a distinction must be made between the physical environment as an attraction and as a catalyst of place attachment. However, it is generally accepted that it is how people understand and interact with place, or in touristic terms how they 'perform' places (Bærenholdt *et al.*, 2004; Coleman & Crang, 2002; Edensor, 2001), that is a key factor in the establishment of place; without such interaction, meaning may not be ascribed and place may revert to space. Indeed, as observed earlier, the significance of tourism places in particular has long been defined by the manner in which tourists interact with or perform them whilst, of particular relevance to this chapter, photography has long been a specific activity through which tourists have connected with and experienced place (Scarles, 2009). Not only are tourists drawn to destinations by the opportunity, in Urry's (2002) much-cited terminology, to 'gaze' on places, but also to record or capture them – or culturally determined images of them (Caton & Santos, 2008) – in photographs. And importantly, as is now discussed, tourists' photographic practices have evolved over time, most recently through the advent of smartphone photography, to the extent that it can be argued that tourists no longer directly interact with destinations; that a key link between the tourist experience and place has been broken.

Tourist photography: from cameras to smartphones

Since sightseeing first emerged as a social practice (Adler, 1989), travellers and tourists have not only visually consumed places but also sought to record them in images. Initially, this was achieved through the medium of painting or drawing (Taylor, 1994) but, since its invention in the early nineteenth century, photography has been so intertwined with tourism that it is difficult to separate them (Teymur, 1993). Not only do the 'emergence of mass tourism and popular photography owe a great deal to one another' (Belk & Yeh, 201: 345) but also, as Haldrup and Larsen (2003: 24) emphasise, 'taking photographs is an emblematic tourist practice; it is almost unthinkable to travel for pleasure without bringing the light-weight camera along and returning home without snapshot memories'.

Not surprisingly, then, tourist photography has long been considered from a variety of perspectives, not least with regards to the relationship between tourists and their subjects (Garlick, 2002; Sontag, 1977). In addition, how and why tourists take photographs, the influence of technological innovation (Larsen & Sandbye, 2014; Lo et al., 2011) and the significance of photography to the overall tourist experience have been subject to academic scrutiny. Nevertheless, two themes that broadly reflect the evolution of tourist photographic practices are evident in the literature (Stylianou-Lambert, 2012).

On the one hand, it is suggested that, traditionally, tourists have adopted a passive role when practising photography. That is, they are seen as typically attempting to seek out and reproduce images they have encountered in postcards, guidebooks, marketing materials and, perhaps, online (Jenkins, 2003), in so doing not only verifying their anticipated experience as well as gaining tangible evidence to show others of having been there through sharing the ubiquitous 'holiday photos', but also completing what Albers and James (1988: 36) describe as 'a hermeneutic circle, which begins with the photographic appearances that advertise and anticipate a trip ... and ends up with travelers certifying and sealing the very same images in their photographic production'. Inevitably, such images will, as noted above, be culturally influenced – that is, just as places are subject to interpretations that vary according to the cultural grounding of those encountering them, so too will photographs of places be similarly culturally determined. Others, conversely, are more ambivalent about the hermeneutic circle concept (Garrod, 2008), not least because as old as the practice of tourist photography itself is the tradition of tourists placing themselves in the photograph; the passive tourist photographer, having sought out the image they wish to reproduce, becomes doubly passive through requesting others to take over the role of photographer in the production of the indisputable evidence that 'I was here' (Bell & Lyall, 2005). Generally, however, this perspective on tourist photography confirms the meaningful relationship between the tourist and the place, not only through the desire to record it in images but also through confirmation of being 'in place' through positioning the self in photographs of the place. In other words, the tourist experience is directly linked to the place; the place is experienced 'in situ' and also subsequently, perhaps as a manifestation of what Marschall (2012) refers to as 'personal memory tourism', through the recorded image of being there.

On the other hand, more recently it has been suggested that tourist photography has become a more proactive, embodied activity, reflecting the argument that tourism more generally is now being performed by tourists (Bærenholdt *et al.*, 2004). Rather than being a passive form of consumption whereby tourists capture predetermined images of places and people, some argue that photography is becoming a performance that 'lights up the tourist experience' (Scarles, 2009: 465). Tourist photography is now 'less concerned with spectatorship and "consuming places" than with *producing* place myths, social roles, and social relationships' (Larsen, 2005: 417, emphasis in original). As Scarles (2009: 471) explains, tourist photography has not only become a 'reflexive performance [in which] only desirable or aesthetically pleasing experiences that reinforce desired experience and place narratives' are captured, but also one based on imposing imagination on reality, overlaying 'physical space with imagined space' (Scarles, 2009: 472–3) to create images that represent the lived and experienced moment, combining reality and imagination and the self and the other, when the photograph is taken. Again, however, the place and the tourist-photographer's interpretation of it remains the basis for understanding the tourist experience.

Most recently, however, the advent of digital photography and, specifically, of smartphones has brought about a fundamental transformation not only in the role and function of photography in society more broadly, but also in the practice and significance of tourist photography in particular (Van House, 2011). As argued shortly, this is in turn disconnecting place from the tourist experience or, more precisely, contributing to tourist experiences that are independent of place (and, in a sense, also of time). First, however, it is useful to explore briefly the consequences of the digital revolution in photography.

The digitalisation of photography

For over 150 years, although it became progressively simpler, cheaper and more convenient, photography – as a social practice – remained film-based. As a result, people tended to take relatively few photographs, limited by the number of frames on a film and the costs of films and of processing and printing. Moreover, with the exception of Polaroid 'instant film' cameras which were particularly popular in the 1970s, a time-lag existed between taking the photograph and seeing the resultant print; for many tourists, part of the holiday experience was receiving, with some anticipation, the pack of prints from the processors after returning home. Hence, taking photographs was typically reserved for special occasions such as birthdays, weddings, family gatherings and, of course, holidays; the social function of photography was essentially to record special or non-ordinary events (Bourdieu, 1996).

Following the introduction of the digital photography and latterly the smartphone camera, however, this function did not disappear but dissolved into the increasingly voluminous production of images of the everyday; that is, as digital cameras served to 'elevate otherwise ordinary objects and events to photo-worthy occurrences' (Okabe & Ito, 2003: 26), the traditional purpose of taking pictures was transformed. Originally (and ironically) developed by Kodak, over the last two decades digital cameras have become increasingly widely used and, particularly with the introduction of the smartphone (the first such device, the 'Simon Personal Communicator', was launched by IBM in the mid-1990s, and the Apple iPhone in 2007), the taking and sharing of photographs on a variety of Web 2.0-supported social media platforms has become not only widespread but, for many people, an integral element of contemporary social life.

The popularity of smartphones with their picture-taking affordances lies in both their convenience, removing the need to carry a separate and perhaps bulky camera, and their technological functionality. Tourist-photographers are now able to take innumerable images, inspecting them instantaneously on screen and discarding/deleting (and if necessary re-taking) 'unsuccessful' pictures; the risk of disappointment no longer exists. Hence, not only has the significance of the practice of photography been transformed, with the often immediate consumption or viewing of images becoming an essential element of producing photographs, but also the tourist has much more control over the manner in which people and places are represented (Haldrup & Larsen, 2010). At the same time, the practice of photography has become playful, the shared viewing of images (usually of the self and others) on-screen contributing to group social experiences (Li, Sharpley & Gammon, 2017) whilst, of particular relevance to this chapter, images produced by/in smartphones are now mobile. In other words, also increasingly integral to tourist smartphone photography is the practice of uploading images onto social media sites. And it is this, along with other functions and capabilities of smartphones, that suggests that tourist photography is increasingly driven by the desire for 'nowstalgic' experiences that are not place-bound.

Smartphone photography and 'nowstalgic' tourist experiences

There is no doubt that, in many respects, smartphone technology is having a transformative influence on tourist behaviour and experiences; broadly, it is 'changing travel planning, constructing and destructing one's sense of tourism, and reconfiguring the relationship amongst tourists, places and others' (Wang & Fesenmaier, 2013: 58). In a practical sense, constant and wide access to relevant information provides tourists with richer knowledge and, hence, more confidence in their travel purchase decisions (Wang, Park & Fesenmaier, 2012). At the same time, travel planning has become more flexible; no longer constrained by pre-planned decisions, people are now able to construct or alter their experiences whilst being a tourist, in effect making it up as they go along. As a result, they are now more empowered; more in control of the holiday experience.

In addition, smartphones enable tourists more generally to remain connected (subject, of course, to the availability of wi-fi and other connection services). On the one hand, this may be considered to be beneficial to the tourist experience, not least through, for example, people being able to share novel experiences with 'absent others' whilst on holiday as well as knowing that they can be easily contacted if necessary – although the latter might be considered a disbenefit, hence the increasing popularity of 'digital detox' holidays in places with limited or no internet/phone connectivity (Dickinson, Hibbert & Filimonau, 2016). More specifically, the connectivity offered by smartphones enhances tourists' sense of security, reducing the uncertainty or challenge of travelling in unfamiliar places and cultures. On the other hand, however, such connectivity is deconstructing the traditional significance of the tourist experience (Sharpley, 2018: 179–81). Tourists' use of and increasing dependence on smartphones not only challenges the notion of the experience of the 'Other', of being away – the tourist might physically be in the destination but they remain socially/psychologically rooted 'at home' – but also reduces the sense of adventure, excitement or serendipity associated with travel. Moreover, the use of, for example, 'sat-nav' facilities or so-called 'augmented reality' applications (Yovcheva, Buhalis & Gatzidis, 2012) serves to limit tourists' visual and emotional engagement with places; they may easily navigate the destination or be informed about a particular place, but do they see or 'feel' that place? In short, the connectivity affordances of smartphone disconnect the tourist from the destination; the tourist experience is becoming less place-defined.

This disconnection process is amplified in particular by the use of smartphones for the taking and online sharing of photographs, not least through the increasing ubiquity of the 'selfie' (Holiday *et al.*, 2016), a practice that is coming to define people's experiences both as tourists and more generally. As Korin (2016: 50–1) laments:

> … the preoccupation with recording rather than the experiencing is a staple in videos and photographs that plague social media sites and streams in the contemporary world … [tourists] … are increasingly invested in producing user-centred self-executed visual narratives, frequently sacrificing an engaged participation in the situation that they work so hard to preserve.

Providing examples of tourists capturing adventurous experiences on their smartphones for instantaneous upload or attendees at music events turning their backs to the stage both to record the performance and to confirm their being there, Korin (2016) describes perhaps more frivolous versions of a practice that can be increasingly witnessed at tourism and leisure destinations and events around the world. And it is a practice that also has a darker side as commentators increasingly consider, for example, the ethical dimensions of tourist selfies at disaster sites (Ibrahim, 2015) or what Hodalska (2017: 405) refers to as 'ghoulish souvenirs providing emotional detachment'. A discussion of this particular issue is beyond the scope of this chapter but, more generally, given that often significant financial and other resources are invested in the consumption of tourist experiences, Korin (2016: 51) logically goes on to ask 'how such a seemingly contradictory practice has gained preponderance and become a dominant cultural practice'. The answer, he proposes, lies in 'nowstalgia', a contemporary culturally defined condition which encourages people, through their photographic practices, to detach themselves from present action and situations; in short, to detach themselves from being in place.

In order to understand the concept of 'nowstalgia', it is first necessary to review briefly that of nostalgia from which it derives. Although 'nostalgia has probably always been part of the human condition' (Gammon & Ramshaw, 2013: 201), the actual term first emerged in the late seventeenth century. Derived from the Greek words 'nostos' (meaning homecoming) and 'algos' (pain), it was coined to describe a form of homesickness so extreme that it was considered to be a neurological disease (Sekikides, Wildschut & Basen, 2004: 200–1). Over the next two centuries it became more widely seen as a condition of depression or melancholy, though often still associated with homesickness, loss or grief, but by the twentieth century it had acquired its contemporary and more positive interpretation as a form of wistful longing for happy (or happier) past times or places. In other words, nostalgia can be thought of as an arguably rose-tinted 'yearning to return to or relive a past period' (Fairly & Gammon, 2005: 183) that is, implicitly, better or more desirable than the present.

Nostalgia, then, is inextricably linked to memory; something cannot be yearned for if it is not remembered. However, this immediately raises the distinction between individual and collective memory and its association with nostalgia, with some arguing that it is only possible for people to be nostalgic about a period that they have actually lived through (Davis, 1979). Others, conversely, consider it possible to be nostalgic towards periods experienced by previous generations but maintained as a collective – if not entirely accurate – memory (Goulding, 2002). For example, reference was made earlier in this chapter to the notion of 'rurality', a socially constructed, nostalgic vision of an arcadian, pre-modern countryside that, for some, continues to motivate participation in rural tourism. Either way, the important point here is that although nostalgia is concerned with the past, the nostalgic past is becoming ever closer to the present in a world defined by rapid technological advance and socio-cultural change and a pervasive postmodern anomie that encourages people to seek identity and meaning in what might be described as a 'present-past'. As a consequence, in circumstances facilitated by contemporary technology – specifically smartphones – nostalgia is becoming replaced by 'nowstalgia'.

According to Korin (2016: 52–3), 'nowstalgia' can be defined as:

> ... the production and distribution of visual documents with potential future nostalgic value by an individual who become increasingly engaged in its

documentation and sacrifices her participation in the activity or situation deemed likely memorable in a time to come.

In other words, by focusing entirely on the photographing of places or events on a smartphone and, in the particular case of 'selfies', locating the self in that recording, thereby directing the viewer (the self or an other) towards the photographer, the significance of the experience lies not in the place or event but in the expectation of nostalgic feelings in the future when viewing the photograph. Putting it another way, rather than experiencing the place or event itself, the tourist-photographer experiences in the present the anticipation of nostalgic yearnings in the future to relive the place or event; they experience the process of 'nowstalgia'. And in so doing, the tourist is no longer 'in place' and their experience in no longer defined by place; rather, they become, in a sense, a conduit for the experience of the place by others viewing uploaded images and for their own future nostalgic satisfaction.

Conclusion

It would be incorrect to suggest that the concept of 'nowstalgia' can be applied to all touristic contexts and experiences. Undoubtedly, many tourists are still drawn to particular places by the tangible characteristics and culturally constructed significance of those places, and enjoy experiences that are defined by their interaction with them; indeed, it would be a simple task to identify numerous examples. However, as the use of and greater dependence on smartphone technology for planning, negotiating and recording tourist experiences becomes more widespread, that technology is resulting in the non-experience of place as tourists become increasingly psychologically or emotionally detached from the physical place. Not only does constant connectivity with the 'outside world' deflect engagement with the destination, in the extreme manifested in what Tribe and Mkono (2017) refer to as 'e-lienation', but also smartphone-based 'nowstalgic' photographic practices in particular emphasise the disconnect between the tourist experience and place. That is, the recording in images of the place and the self in anticipation of nostalgic yearning represents a curious fusion of past and future that occurs in the present, but that denies tourists the experience of the present time and present place. And as the use of mobile information and communication technologies becomes more pervasive, with all that implies in a socio-cultural context, it must be asked whether contemporary conceptualisations of place more generally are becoming less relevant.

References

Adler, J. (1989) Origins of sightseeing, *Annals of Tourism Research*, 16(1), 7–29.
Agnew, J. (2011) Space and place, in J. Agnew and D. Livingstone (Eds), *Handbook of Geographical Knowledge*, London: Sage Publications, pp. 316–30.

Albers, P. and James, W. (1988) Travel photography: a methodological approach, *Annals of Tourism Research*, 15(1), 134–58.

Auge, M. (1995) *Non-Places: Introduction to an Anthropology of Supermodernity*, London: Verso.

Bærenholdt, J., Haldrup, M. and Urry, J. (2004) *Performing Tourist Places*, London: Routledge.

Belk, R. and Yeh, J. (2011) Tourist photographs: signs of self, *International Journal of Culture, Tourism and Hospitality Research*, 5(4), 345–53.

Bell, C. and Lyall, J. (2005) 'I was here': pixilated evidence, in D. Crouch, R. Jackson and F. Thompson (Eds), *The Media and the Tourist Imagination: Converging Cultures*, Abingdon: Routledge, pp. 135–42.

Benckendorff, P., Sheldon, P. and Fesenmaier, D. (2014) *Tourism Information Technology, 2nd Edition*, Wallingford: CABI.

Bourdieu, P. (1996) *Photography: A Middle-Brow Art*, Cambridge: Polity Press.

Bremer, T. (2006) Sacred spaces and tourist places, in D. Timothy and D. Olsen (Eds), *Tourism, Religion and Spiritual Journeys*, Abingdon: Routledge, pp. 25–35.

Casey, E. (1993) *Getting Back into Place: Toward a Renewed Understanding of the Place-World*, Bloomington, IN: Indiana University Press.

Caton, K. and Santos, C. (2008) Closing the hermeneutic circle? Photographic encounters with the other, *Annals of Tourism Research*, 35(1), 7–26.

Cohen, E. (1979) A phenomenology of tourist experiences, *Sociology*, 13(2), 179–201.

Coleman, S. and Crang, M. (Eds) (2002) *Tourism: Between Place and Performance*, Oxford: Berghahn Books.

Cresswell, T. (2015) *Place: An Introduction, 2nd Edition*, Chichester: John Wiley & Sons.

Davis, F. (1979) *A Yearning for Yesterday: A Sociology of Nostalgia*, New York: Free Press.

Dickinson, J., Hibbert, J. and Filimonau, V. (2016) Mobile technology and the tourist experience: (dis)connection at the campsite, *Tourism Management*, 57, 193–201.

Edensor, T. (2001) Performing tourism, staging tourism: (re)producing tourist space and practice, *Tourist Studies*, 1(1), 59–81.

Egger, R. and Buhalis, D. (2008) *eTourism: Case Studies*, Oxford: Butterworth Heinemann.

Fairly, S. and Gammon, S. (2005) Something lived, something learned: nostalgia's expanding role in sport tourism, *Sport in Society*, 8(2), 182–97.

Gammon, S. and Ramshaw, G. (2013) Nostalgia and sport, in B. Garrod and A. Fyall (Eds) *Contemporary Cases in Sport*, Oxford: Goodfellow Publishers, pp. 201–19.

Garlick, S. (2002) Revealing the unseen: tourism, art and photography, *Cultural Studies*, 16(2), 289–305.

Garrod, B. (2008) Understanding the relationship between tourism destination imagery and tourist photography, *Journal of Travel Research*, 47(3), 346–58.

Giddens, A. (1994) *Beyond Left and Right: The Future of Radical Politics*, Cambridge: Polity Press.

Gieryn, T. (2000) A space for place in sociology, *Annual Review of Sociology*, 26(1), 463–96.

Goulding, C. (2002) An exploratory study of age related vicarious nostalgia and aesthetic consumption, *Advances in Consumer Research*, 29(1), 542–6.

Greider, T. and Garkovich, L. (1994) Landscapes: The social construction of nature and the environment, *Rural Sociology*, 59(1), 1–24.

Haldrup, M. and Larsen, J. (2003) The family gaze, *Tourist Studies*, 3(1), 23–45.

Haldrup, M. and Larsen, J. (2010) *Tourism, Performance and the Everyday: Consuming the Orient*, Abingdon: Routledge.

Hammitt, W., Backlund, E. and Bixler, R. (2006) Place bonding for recreation place: conceptual and empirical development, *Leisure Studies*, 25(1), 7–41.

Harvey, D. (1990) *The Condition of Postmodernity*, Oxford: Blackwell.

Harvey, D. (2012) From space to place and back again: reflections on the condition of postmodernity, in J. Bird, B. Curtis, T. Putnam and L. Tickner (Eds), *Mapping the Futures: Local Cultures, Global Change*, Abingdon: Routledge, pp. 17–44.

Hodalska, M. (2017) Selfies at horror sites: dark tourism, ghoulish souvenirs and digital narcissism, *Zeszyty Prasoznawcze*, 60(2), 405–23.

Holiday, S., Lewis, M.J., Nielsen, R., Anderson, H.D. and Elinzano, M. (2016) The selfie study: archetypes and motivations in modern self-photography, *Visual Communication Quarterly*, 23(3), 175–87.

Ibrahim, Y. (2015) Self-representation and the disaster event: self-imaging, morality and immortality, *Journal of Media Practice*, 16(3), 211–27.

Jenkins, O. (2003) Photography and travel brochures: the circle of representation, *Tourism Geographies*, 5(3), 305–28.

Jepson, D. and Sharpley, R. (2015) More than sense of place? Exploring the emotional dimension of rural tourism experiences, *Journal of Sustainable Tourism*, 23(8–9), 1157–78.

Korin, E. (2016) Nowstalgia: articulating future pasts through selfies and GoPro-ing, *Meiden & Zeit*, 31(4), 50–60. Available at: https://medienundzeit.at/wp-content/uploads/2017/02/MZ-2016-4-online-ed.pdf#page=52 (accessed 23 November 2018).

Larsen, J. (2005) Families seen sightseeing: performativity of tourist photography, *Space and Culture*, 8(4), 416–34.

Larsen, J. and Sandbye, M. (2014) *Digital Snaps: The New Face of Photography*, London: I.B. Taurus.

Lash, S. (1990) *Sociology of Postmodernism*, London: Routledge.

Lefebvre, H. (1991) *The Production of Space*, Oxford: Blackwell.

Li, M., Sharpley, R. and Gammon, S. (2017) Towards an understanding of Chinese tourist photography: evidence from the UK, *Current Issues in Tourism* (DOI: 10.1080/13683500.2017.1377690).

Lo, I., McKercher, B., Lo, A., Cheung, C. and Law, R. (2011) Tourism and online photography, *Tourism Management*, 32(4), 725–31.

MacCannell, D. (1976) *The Tourist: A New Theory of the Leisure Class*, New York: Schocken Books.

Manzo, L. (2003) Beyond house and heaven: towards a revisioning of emotional relationships with places, *Journal of Environmental Psychology*, 23(1), 47–61.

Marschall, S. (2012) 'Personal memory tourism' and a wider exploration of the tourism–memory nexus, *Journal of Tourism and Cultural Change*, 10(4), 321–35.

Minca, C. (2000) 'The Bali Syndrome': the explosion an implosion of 'exotic' tourist spaces, *Tourism Geographies*, 2(4), 389–403.

Okabe, D. and Ito, M. (2003) *Personal, Portable, Pedestrian: Mobile Phones in Japanese Life*, Cambridge, MA: MIT Press.

Ramkissoon, H., Weiler, B. and Smith, L. (2012) Place attachment and pro-environmental behaviour in national parks: the development of a conceptual framework, *Journal of Sustainable Tourism*, 20(2), 257–76.

Relph, E. (1976) *Place and Placelessness*, London: Pion.

Scarles, C. (2009) Becoming tourist: renegotiating the visual in the tourist experience, *Environment and Planning D: Society and Space*, 27(3), 465–88.

Sekikides, C., Wildschut, T. and Basen, D. (2004) Nostalgia: conceptual issues and existential functions, in L. Greenberg, J. Koole and T. Pyszczynski, T. (Eds) *Handbook of Experimental Existential Psychology*, New York: The Guilford Press, pp. 200–14.

Sharpley, R. (2018) *Tourism, Tourists and Society, 5th Edition*, Abingdon: Routledge.

Sheller, M. and Urry, J. (2004) *Tourism Mobilities: Places to Play, Places in Play*, London: Routledge.

Short, J. (1991) *Imagined Country: Society, Culture and Environment*, London: Routledge.

Sontag, S. (1977) *On Photography*, London: Penguin Books.

Stedman, R. (2003) Is it really just a social construction? The contribution of the physical environment to sense of place, *Society & Natural Resources*, 16(8), 671–85.

Stylianou-Lambert, T. (2012) Tourists with cameras: Reproducing or producing? *Annals of Tourism Research*, 39(4), 1817–38.

Suvantola, J. (2002) *Tourist Experience of Place*, Aldershot: Ashgate.

Taylor, J. (1994) *A Dream of England: Landscape, Photography and the Tourist's Imagination*, Manchester: Manchester University Press.

Teymur, N. (1993) Phototourism – or the epistemology of photography in tourism, *Tourism in Focus*, 6, 6 and 16.

Tribe, J. and Mkono, M. (2017) Not such smart tourism? The concept of e-lienation, *Annals of Tourism Research*, 66, 105–15.

Tsatsou, P. (2009) Reconceptualising 'time' and 'space' in the era of electronic media and communications, *Platform: Journal of Media and Communication*, 1, 11–32. Available at: https://lra.le.ac.uk/bitstream/2381/31479/4/PlatformVol.1_Tsatsou.pdf (accessed 25 November 2018).

Tuan, Y. (1977) *Space and Place: The Perspective of Experience*, Minneapolis, MN: University of Minnesota.

Unwin, T. (1992) *The Place of Geography*, Harlow: Longman.

Urry, J. (1992) The tourist gaze 'revisited', *American Behavioral Scientist*, 36(2), 172–86.

Urry, J. (1994) Cultural change and contemporary tourism, *Leisure Studies*, 13(4), 233–8.

Urry, J. (2002) *The Tourist Gaze, 2nd Edition*, London: Sage Publications.

Urry, J. (2005) *Consuming Places*, London: Routledge.

Uysal, M. and Jurowski, C. (1994) Testing the push and pull factors, *Annals of Tourism Research*, 21(4), 844–6.

Van House, N. (2011) Personal photography, digital technologies and the uses of the visual, *Visual Studies*, 26(2), 125–34.

Walton, J. (1983) *The English Seaside Resort: A Social History, 1750–1914*, Leicester: Leicester University Press.

Wang, D. and Fesenmaier, D. (2013) Transforming the travel experience: the use of smartphones for travel, in L. Cantoni and Z. Xiang (Eds), *Information and Communication Technologies in Tourism 2013*, Berlin/Heidelberg: Springer, pp. 58–69.

Wang, D., Park, S. and Fesenmaier, D. (2012) The role of smartphones in mediating the touristic experience, *Journal of Travel Research*, 54(4), 371–87.

Yovcheva, Z., Buhalis, D. and Gatzidis, C. (2012) Smartphone augmented reality applications for tourism, *E-review of Tourism Research*, 10(2), 63–6.

Chapter 3

New tourism and social transformation in postmodernity

Sociological examination of Japanese new tourism

Hiroshi Sudo

Introduction

Tourism does not reside completely within the tourism industry market. Instead, it utilises everyday lives, culture and the human relations of local people in tourist sites. Such utilisation cannot be counted according to economic market values. Besides that, it contains various fields (nature or culture) utilised not only for industrial production but also for its own preservation and reproduction.

As tourism extends outside the market, its industry emerges from old territory to create new markets. Japanese tourism studies have expended a great deal of effort on how best to address new demands and supplies in these expanding markets. Furthermore, tourism studies have attempted to depict such changes as "new tourism" and conducted much research on practical ways to contribute to new and rapidly expanding tourist markets.

Moreover, Japanese tourism studies have depicted tourism positively to include local people's social identities and ties in addition to expanding the market into their everyday lives to activate their economies. Tourism studies have also considered political measures that create a new order of post-industrial capitalism's discovering – or making and remaking – consumers' desires, probably because tourism study has been rather a positivist science for politics and economics.

Therefore, most tourism studies lack critical viewpoints towards relationships between changes in tourism and people's social backgrounds, even though some have addressed the continuity from new Japanese tourism to mass tourism (Yamaguchi, 2017; Hamano, 2017; Takaoka, 2019). Exploring new tourism to promote marketing or policy making is not my concern here, however. Rather, this chapter focuses on how tourism became connected to global, disorganised, "liquid" capitalism and describes tourism's relationship to social and cultural change. After that, the chapter describes tourism's limited possibility of initiating cultural innovations and, in the end, affecting especially the human sense of solidarity.

Pseudo-event and staged authenticity

To begin, we examine Daniel J. Boorstin's pseudo-event theory, which has been the best target for criticism by new tourism theorists, who pit the simple point of view against modern tourists. Boorstin (1992: 96) criticises mass tourism as meaning "the decline of the traveller and the rise of the tourist"; that is, "travel ceased to be an activity – an experience, an undertaking – and instead became a commodity" (ibid.: 85). Boorstin argues that tourism cultures "are not spontaneous cultural products but only those made carefully for tourists' consumption, for foreign customers" (ibid.: 114–115). His theory is simple enough that Dean MacCannell (1999: 104) easily indicates its defects: It "lacks adequate technical perspectives".

MacCannell (1999: 105) counters Boorstin, arguing that his "pseudo" means that tourism objects are "insubstantial and transitory" and that "somewhere in tourist settings there are real events accessible to intellectual elites" (ibid.: 105). MacCannell insists, "rather, tourists demand authenticity just as Boorstin does" (ibid.: 104). MacCannell denies differences in viewpoints among tourists, travellers and anthropologists because the tourist gaze reaches beyond the tourist setting.

MacCannell further maintains that modern – usually meaning postmodern – tourists are fully reflexive actors. Additionally, he knows that tourist settings constitute various layers from deep "pseudo-events" (back region) to shallow "pseudo-events" (front region), and these simply represent "pseudo-realities" different from the real one. MacCannell asserts that modern tourist spots can not only connect values of tourism and culture, but also function to achieve cohesion and social integration. Therefore, "modern" tourists cannot be "mass tourists" contented with experiences of front-region tourist settings; instead, their acts positively and reflexively relate to the back region. Each tourist has both perspectives and can penetrate both because tourists are travellers and vice versa. Thus does MacCannell obviously deny any difference between mass tourists and new tourists. Any mass tourist is a traveller commonly wanting to see the back region. MacCannell seems to maintain that even an adventurous traveller who knows all the "settings of staged authenticity" and wants to enter these settings' "back regions" is simply a mass tourist or a new tourist acting as a traveller.

Although MacCannell points out tourists' profound attitudes towards settings' objects, his view is not entirely satisfactory because he does not explain sensory and behavioural changes that stem from their shift in lifestyle. When we focus on change, apart from tourists and local people's common ability to sympathise, MacCannell's tourists who go deep into settings seem to overlap with postmodern "new tourists". I define tourism that escapes mass tourism as "new tourism". Here, I attempt to describe background of changes in tourism and to discover whether new tourism goes beyond mass tourism, whether new tourism's characteristics just follow mass tourism, whether they differ and, if so, how.

The next section depicts typical characteristics of mass tourists acting as travellers who look down on the tourist from a viewpoint opposite MacCannell's view of a tourist, as compared with Auliana Poon's (1993) views of new tourism's characteristics.

Ironies of *The Beach* and new tourism

Are young travellers of **The Beach** *new tourists?*

The film *The Beach* (Boyle, 2000), adapted from but quite faithful to Alex Garland's 1996 novel of the same title, depicts the paradoxical theme of tourists who criticise Western mass tourists in Thailand. The film's protagonist Richard, an American (British in the novel) youth, does not like the typical backpackers in Thailand and aspires to "alternative" backpacking. Soon after arriving at the Bangkok airport, he heads to Khao San Road, the famous backpacker enclave. The film suggests that an alternative tourist is no more than a mass backpacker succeeding mass tourists and ends with the conclusion that their commune/enclave, isolated from mass tourists, is nothing more than tourists' "3S" (Sun Sand Sea) "paradise" (Eden) long pursued by Western mass tourists. The backpacker commune has no 1970s New Age philosophy denying Western civilisation – it is an image socially constructed through Orientalism. Also, the film constitutes several criticisms against new, alternative, mass tourists, and its ending depicts a fight between increasing numbers of tourists and armed farmers who illegally grow hemp. In the last scene (a departure from the novel), after barely escaping to his home country, Richard is shown sitting in an urban internet café, thus suggesting that Richard's alternative tourist image has been constructed through information technologies that emerged in the 1990s. Overall, *The Beach* portrays the lifestyle of a tourist attempting to avoid mass tourism. Perhaps tourism studies are stuck in the same attempt.

Characteristics of new tourism

In 1993, three years before publication of Garland's novel *The Beach*, Auliana Poon addressed new tourism theory in *Tourism Technology and Competitive Strategies* on tourism management. In its first chapter, "Tourism in Crisis" (3–25), Poon asserts, "The crisis of the tourism industry is a crisis of mass tourism" (ibid.: 3). She recounts mass tourism as beginning with commercial jets, assisted by cheap oil, charter flights, liberal spending on vacations and peace and economic growth from post-World War II to the mid-1970s. In fact, Poon believes that mass tourism has followed the assembly-line principle and mass force of scale production in other industries (ibid.: 4). Poon further argues that mass tourism destroys not only landscapes, pure waters, intact reefs, sea turtles, virgin forests and traditional cultures, but also the pristine solace of traditionally quiet cultures. At the time, Poon's mass tourism theory focused attention on mass tourism's negative

Table 3.1 Old and new tourists compared

Old (mass) tourist	New tourist
Search for the sun	Experience something different
Follow the mass	Want to be in charge
Here today, gone tomorrow	See and enjoy but do not destroy
Just to show that you had been	Just for the fun of it
Having	Being
Superiority	Understanding
Like attractions	Like sports
Precautious	Adventurous
Eat in hotel dining room	Try out local fare
Homogeneous	Hybrid

Source: Poon (1993: 10).

impacts caused by standard, rigidly packaged mass tours (ibid.: 6–10). Arising to cope with these negative impacts were the internal forces of new consumers and technologies and the outside forces that pushed environmental limits. As a result of such reflection and repentance, flexible, sustainable and individual-oriented tourism production emerged. At least, that is how Poon summarises the emergence of new tourism.

Consequently, after the mid-1970s, radical changes were required from inside and outside tourism industries to match new tourists' needs and desires. Consumers from developed countries became more experienced, more flexible, more independent, more quality conscious, greener and harder to please. They wanted to be different from the crowd. Poon catalogues differences between "old tourists" (meaning "mass tourists") and "new tourists" in Table 3.1.

Similarity between The Beach's new tourists and new tourism

In *The Beach* (film), Richard sees the backpackers in Khao San Road watching movies and mutters, "The only downer is, everyone's got the same idea. We all travel thousands of miles just to watch TV and have the comforts of home. And you gotta ask yourself" (Boyle, 2000). He looks down on Western tourists travelling within the "environmental bubble". In Garland's novel, Etienne, Richard's fellow traveller, mocks his own previous travel to Cheng Mai, saying, "Raft, trek, I want to do something different. But we all do the same thing" (2011: 19). These fictional characters become bored with mass tourism and lust for "more experience, more green (or blue)"; they become "harder to please" and "want to differ from the crowd". Their mentalities are relatively excessive, but they fit Poon's description of new tourists. Although they are in the same stream as new tourists who do not like mass tourism, Poon's new tourists hope for a new travel style away from mass tourism. However, like *The Beach*'s young characters, although they pursue deep back regions, they cannot, after all, imagine a path leading away from mass tourism's beaten track. Both novelist Garland and film director Boyle focus on the irony of new tourism being only a variation of mass tourism.

In addition, *The Beach* (film) suggests that their image of paradise includes getting rid of their daily lives' complexity and noise. Although they look disappointed that Ko Pha Ngan, just next to the isolated island where they stay, has been spoiled, they sometimes go there to buy commodities imported from Western countries. The parties held in their unpolluted paradise resemble Ko Pha Ngan's full moon party (Figure 3.1), which exemplifies John Urry's (2002) "collective gaze", while life on their isolated island exemplifies the "romantic gaze" (ibid.). Fundamentally, however, both are the same. Of course, Poon's new tourist, constructed by information technology, differs from romantic-gaze tourists whose consciousness is based on social class. Still, we can understand that romantic tourists of *The Beach* are just successors of mass tourists in the collective gaze. Especially after 2000, new tourists are defined by new bidirectional information tools and might be termed individualised mass tourists.

However, the film's expression of conflict between tourists and local people is also a stereotype lacking reality. Impacts of tourism mobility on local people's daily lives are more reflexive and complex than a fictional movie can show.

Figure 3.1 Full moon party in Ko Pha Ngan.
Source: photo by the author.

Images of tourists, in actual fact, often influence local residents at tourist sites. In many cases, people construct their identities under tourists' gaze and behave according to tourists' image. Thus, illusions of paradise are shared, finally, by both tourists and local people. Especially the "aesthetic reflexivity" (Beck, Giddens & Lash, 1994: 110–173) that tourism brings often combines with that of locals' everyday lives at a tourist site. Although new tourism, while wishing to go beyond mass tourism, is just its variant (as previously mentioned), we can also see its many, rapid positive and negative impacts on culture. Now, for instance, for tourists and residents' safety and public order, the local government controls even the full moon party at Ko Pha Ngan.

Nevertheless, local people's background of "reflexibility", along with its "substructure" of economic interest that accompanies tourism, sometimes has negative effects on cultural, social and political integration, leading to local communities' fragmentation as well as to positive effects of solidarity. Although *The Beach* (film) depicts a clear-cut conflict between tourists and residents, at most tourist sites, local people's attitudes are not homogeneous, and, indeed, we often see conflicts (Sudo, 2012; Sudo & Endo, 2018). Thus, modern tourism's impacts cannot be listed simply, so the next section describes Japanese tourism policy and the society constructed partly by complex modern tourism.

Change of Japanese tourism and the vision of new tourism

Modernisation of tourism and new tourism's political meaning in Japan

According to Alfred Shutz, our daily lives' reality is layered; for instance, the reality of science, of a dream, of a novel. Each has a semantic world built by people (Shutz, 1967). The reality of tourism is one of these worlds, socially constructed through devices of transportation or media. Tourism's reality is also constructed through tourists' experiences, so images and actualities collide and are blended into experiences of tourism.

Because the reality of tourism is socially constructed through tourists and local people's experiences, it often varies according to age or social change. While societies continuously make and change traditions, traditional guardians based on religious authority (e.g. a Shinto priest in pilgrimage to Ise) build holy sites, fixed as sacred spaces; that is, places of "formulaic truth" (Beck, Giddens & Lash, 1994: 82–83).

In Japan, Buddhism and Shintoism, accompanied by many rituals, have helped construct the realities of tourism (Kamata, 2013). The Ise pilgrimage, a tour around the 88-site Shikoku circuit, the Zenkoji pilgrimage, the Oyama pilgrimage and the Fuji pilgrimage, among others, are well known as traditional Buddhist and Shinto pilgrimages. These were originally sustained by the local financial system "Ko (講)" and performed systematically. However, the "hot-spring cure" performed on the pretext of medical treatment was actually practised as tourism based on religious tradition (Sekido, 2007). These traditional tourisms continued until the First World War. Thus, early Japanese tourism was embedded in the tradition and mores of premodern Japanese society.

As in every developed country, Japan's modern tourism emerged along with transportation systems, and the realities of Japanese tourism changed as transportation systems developed. First, railways and buses superseded walking. About 50 years after England's, Japan's first railway from Shinbashi (in Tokyo) to Yokohama was completed in 1872, and by around 1900, railroad networks were constructed throughout Japan. In other words, railroad companies' networks formed Japanese tourist spots (Oikawa, 2017). Traditional pilgrimages and hot-spring cure destinations, for instance Narita-San, Nikko, Kusatsu and Atami, were connected to Tokyo by railroad systems. Although these modern tourism destinations were still traditional, tourism developments led by railroad companies made new traditional "places" (or touristic "spaces"), and the realities of sacred places were gradually desecrated and disembedded from traditional Japanese lives. Traditions were "re-traditionalised" under national leadership and the transportation industries.

Furthermore, after the 1970s – postmodernity's starting point in Japanese society – (declining) places' value, along with tourists and local people's participation and performance, were rediscovered from the bottom up, in addition to tourism development from the top down. Sacred places that functioned as "creators of meaning" or "of identities" were re-created by tourists and local people in spite of the nation's direct control (Okamoto, 2015). This is one of the disembedding consequences of "abstract systems" (Beck, Giddens & Lash, 1994: 96) in tourism.

The prototype of Japan's postmodern tourism seems to be the Discover Japan campaign after the 1970 Osaka Exposition, with which a railroad company and an advertising agency were greatly concerned (Mori, 2007). The rather narcissistic message of "discover yourself", "discover Japanese culture" and "rediscovery of self", "rediscovery of Japanese culture" spread rapidly throughout Japan, either intentionally or unconsciously by media collaboration, for instance by a magazine and a television programme. The reflexive characteristic in rediscovery of individual and/or traditional culture and nature might have then been suitable to the formation of tourism mobility. "Disembedded" reinterpretation of tradition was shared through nostalgia in the postmodern sense, which actually means re-embedding traditions and identities. This behaviour became prominent in the mobile-media society after 2000. Tourism's participation in and rediscovery of cultural values are postmodern characteristics in which "socially created uncertainness looms large" (Beck, Giddens & Lash, 1994: 107).

After Japan's period of rapid economic growth ended, concurrent with the first oil crisis in 1973, Japanese society lost its "grand narrative" of productivity, equality and development, which had been promoted through manufacturing. After the oil crisis, Galbraith's (1979) unstable, restive Age of Uncertainty was left behind. After the 1985 Plaza Accord among advanced nations (Saeki, 1989: 4–5), "globalism" spread as a coordinated international policy. The Age of Uncertainty, linked with globalisation, changed the Japanese economy's base from manufacturing to service. To this mix was added the Japanese government's policy of increasing domestic demand and regional revitalisation. Saeki reports that "informatisation" and the softening service-based economy are "a result of having pulled the fields of information and service that used to be outside the market largely into its domain" (ibid.: 5–6). As a result of culture, knowledge and politics, formerly outside the economic market, now entering it, planning a policy simply through unmixed, simple economic-interest calculation became difficult. In "consumption of culture", interests other than (previously) strictly economic interests entered the economic domain. Furthermore, production trended to consumption, and the rise of "reflexive modernisation" did not necessarily indicate society's reflection controlled by economic mechanisms. Rather, the market absorbed culture combined with policy, and the world where we live was re-mythologised or re-enchanted. In Japanese policy making, tourism culture was especially intended to create national identity, and later, Japan's tourism policy advocated new tourism.

Japanese tourism policy after the Second World War

In 1960s Japan, as previously mentioned, tourism was organised by travel agencies as tour parties or packaged tours in which individuals took part. Their destinations were usually rigidly fixed, as in the premodern age: shrines, temples, spa tourism, etc. Additionally, railroad companies continued their prewar tourist resort development during the postwar period. Although by 1948 the government was organising small projects, for example the five-year tourism construction plan and, in 1956, the tourism project promotion plan, no big projects were undertaken. In other words, postwar Japan's government did not assume that tourism should be part of national policy (Oikawa, 2017). Only after the 1960s was full-scale tourism policy set. Based on the 1963 Basic Law on Tourism, the first White Paper on Tourism came out in 1964.

By this time, national development projects were mainly concerned with development of specific areas, such as industrial zones. Although rural areas criticised industrial projects that excluded them, the government seemed unable to counter the criticism (Teramae, 2009). Finally, in response, the Comprehensive National Development Plan was enacted in 1962, bringing the concept of "balanced development of country" to the fore; thereafter, development of districts forsaken by heavily industrial development policy was emphasised. In the 1970s, when the "leisure boom" began in earnest, the government concentrated its efforts on leisure policy. Not only Leisure Industry sections and the Economic Planning Agency, but also the Ministry of Construction, and the Environment Agency at the Prime Minister's office, constructed public leisure facilities.[1] This meant that tourism policy gained a position in Japan's post-industrialised social structure based on the value shift from producing goods to consuming services. Moreover, this seemed a national identity policy to provide people with social identity in the mobilised postmodernity bereft of grand narrative. In short, postwar Japan's tourism policy focused on "balanced development of a country" and "regional revitalisation" of areas left behind during industrial development; nowadays, the government's new tourism policies can be understood along the same line.

The "failure" of Resort Law and structural reflexivity

The policy of regional revitalisation through balanced development of national land from the 1960s underwent several iterations: A Plan for Remodelling the Japanese Archipelago during the Tanaka cabinet in the 1970s; and the Furusato (Regional) Creation Project during the Takeshita administration and then the Fourth Comprehensive Development Plan under the Nakasone cabinet, both in the 1980s. These seemed to converge in the Law for Development of Comprehensive Resort Areas ("Resort Law"). Especially the latter two acts accepted the proposal to expand domestic demand as economic measures for the strong yen policy, as agreed by the 1985 Plaza Accord and for the following economic depression due to yen appreciation. Consequently, these policies rapidly increased the money supply and generated unusual asset bubbles in land, stock and golf memberships. As we know, the asset bubble collapsed along with the sudden fall of stock prices in 1991. Important to observe in the changing economy and corresponding policies is that development shifted from hard construction to soft preservation or cultural rediscoveries. So far as tourism was concerned, local tourist spots were symbolised, refined and branded. In particular, mass leisure – as a break from the labour of mass production related to the grand narrative of progress through manufacturing – lost power because of the bubble's collapse and subsequent losses of the 1990s. Additionally, specialised tourism's development was supposed to occur regionally, while values shifted from production to consumption. Rural areas' symbols came to be expressed more artificially in the colour of each district.

However, as mentioned previously, tourism as small production of multiple products had begun in the 1970s, as in the Discover Japan campaign, for instance. In addition, the economic bubble's collapse in the 1990s added criticism to tourism projects' random development based on the Resort Law in its mild form.[2] As a result, tourism projects required encouraging regional leaders to establish endogenous organisations; that is, changing from external to endogenous development or from departing-point to landing-point tourism.

This movement led to creating regional images and generating local people's identity and pride even though these actions functioned as a reply to big cities' gaze.[3] Moreover, endogenous (as compared with city) tourism still held the merit of, for instance, "ossetai" or traditional hospitality, missing from the market. Thus was new tourism accepted in a Japanese manner.

Launching of the Tourism Agency and new tourism

In response to the stream of policy delineated above, the Tourism Nation Promoting Basic Plan was enacted in 2006, and the Japan Tourism Agency was established as a bureau of the Ministry of Land, Infrastructure, Transport and Tourism in 2008. In addition to promoting international tourism, the Japan Tourism Agency adopted the catchphrase "new tourism promotion". In the 2018 White Paper, it became, essentially, "district enterprise by tourism theme", but overall, the new tourism plan has persisted to the present (2019). (Here, I do not discuss attracting foreign visitors.) The term "new tourism" was used as "[a tourism] measure" in the White Paper on Tourism (Japan Tourism Agency, 2007) in 2007, the year previous to implementation of the Japan Tourism Agency.[4]

This measure aims to promote creation and circulation of "new tourism" based on new customer needs and characteristics of regional tourism resources, to revitalise the region through tourism, to create a new lifestyle that leads to development of a tourism industry with future high growth possibility, and to help people realise true affluence. To promote creation and circulation of "new tourism", such as long-stay tourism, eco-tourism and health tourism that efficiently employs original regional charm, a "new tourism" market is expounded by constructing databases and implementing a demonstration project, etc. (Japan Tourism Agency, 2007: 172).

As for types of new tourism, in addition to those mentioned above, industrial tourism, green tourism, cultural tourism and sea trips are specified. To combine all these into a Japanese national policy, the concept of new tourism promotes regional landing-type tourism instead of small production of multiple-products tourism based on changing individual desires and lifestyle, which Poon described along with the background of electronic communication technology development.

Indeed, this policy was employed as a "magic wand" for economic revitalisation in declining local areas (Sadakane, 2015). In fact, although merit attributed to local people other than self-employed workers, building constructors, transportation companies and hotel industries cannot be expected, the policy is a move forward politically (ibid.: 123–136). On one hand, tourists' arrival contributes positively to local politics and identity as proof of the land's charm. On the other hand, increasing tourism conceals "the reality of declining local areas" (ibid.: 132).

Although the fundamental new tourism policy's name was succeeded by "district enterprise by tourism theme" in 2018, the latter includes tourists' more personalised and specialised desires.[5] Thus, tourism as an identity policy in a post-modern society that seeks people's lost identities has been consistent with industrial development policy for abandoned areas from the 1960s.

New tourism led by consumers

While national policy addressed new tourism, there emerged also a new tourism of consumer initiatives; manga-anime, volunteer, art, old district, rock festival and dark tourism were spreading.[6] Common in Asian cities' tourism is old district tourism, in which tourists visit old but improved streets with a nostalgic atmosphere of local life. Old districts, including the Shilin night market in Taipei, Tahien street in Hanoi and Yanaka in Tokyo, draw tourists' attention independent of top-down development plans. These locations are easy to visit from city centres or on the way to the airport. In the Tokyo Yanaka area, for example, newly settled residents are increasingly participating in reorganising efforts, along with established residents and external volunteers. Another relatively recent example, manga-anime tourism, seems unique to Japan. Tourists, or fans, visit locations where manga (comics) or animation is produced. Manga-anime tourism deserves attention as a bottom-up, new tourism under Internet information-sharing conditions. The Washimiya area in Kuki city, for instance, became famous after *Raki☆Suta* (*Lucky☆Star*) was aired in 2007. The declining town recovered somewhat because manga and animation fans visited there on "pilgrimages". Then, the "pilgrims" began volunteering in the town's revitalisation by working with local residents, especially at festivals. Although more than five years have passed since the manga and animation projects were completed, despite some problems, cooperation in revitalising the town has survived.[7]

Common to old district and manga-anime tourism is regional, bottom-up reorganisation; new tourists, old residents and volunteers in Yanaka and fans and residents in Washimiya formed communities. Manga-anime tourists need especially strong ties because they believe in manga and animation realities, knowing that they are pretending, so they form communities of belief and sympathy between fans and residents. This situation sometimes causes differences in enthusiasm, commitment and interest in the economy, the mentality or politics (Sudo, 2008).

Although these new tourisms can form bases for new communities, such subcultural or hobbyists' ties do not usually build regional unity but form divided communities in a "micro utopia" (Bishop, 2004). In explaining the practice of relational art, Claire Bishop (ibid.; Sudo, 2017) asserts that artists and tourists do not connect in an overall community but in a small, closed area, forming a "micro utopia". Manga-anime or other hobby-oriented subculture tourisms seem to have the same characteristics.

Regional revitalisation policies using manga-anime pilgrimages or regional art festivals are now becoming a national top-down approach, with successes and limitations expected. Nevertheless, I have discussed how tourism connects with symbolisation of value and leads to endless relativization of value. After the oil crisis in the 1970s, we experienced value formation's disorganisation and the cultural market's symbolisation, especially distinct after the 1985 Plaza Accord. Japanese postmodern tourism proceeded under the conditions explained above. Using the concept of mobilities, the following section describes social changes related to new tourism after the oil crisis.

Social change and new tourism

Sociocultural change

While modernisation is a process of horizontal and vertical differentiation, Scott Lash (1990) describes the culture of postmodernity as a process of de-differentiation; the cultural paradigm shift from modern to postmodern happened beginning in the 1970s. About tourism culture, John Urry (2002: 77) says, "Many tourist practices, even in the past, prefigure some of the postmodern characteristics".[8] For example, tourist spots in Britain were represented as resembling Italian scenery like "simulacra" of postmodern culture that reverse the relationship between representation and reality. Tourism itself has characteristics of postmodern culture. New tourism also has the same cultural paradigm, for instance horizontal and vertical de-differentiation as well as inversion of representation and reality. However, such radical tourisms are termed "post-tourism"; here, I would like to describe one of the new "new tourisms", but I consider here only new tourism in general. I describe the relationship between new tourism and postmodernity by positing postmodernity as the social background producing a culture of new tourism, including "post-tourism".

Before the term postmodern became common, "post-industrial" was often used (Toffler, 1980; Bell, 1973). According to the famous post-industrial theorist Daniel Bell (1973), information technology development and the trend from material production towards the 1980s service economy radically changed social values. He predicted that as knowledge and the worth of information increased, the technocrat with knowledge and technology based on the market would have decisive public power. Although Bell first positively emphasised society's progress and control through knowledge and information, he later foresaw conflicts between an economy based on the ethics of labour and a culture aiming at consumptive pleasure. However, Toffler and Bell's viewpoints were basically optimistic about changing values from ethics of production to ethics of consumption.

The point is not just a direction change of desire from things to signs in the logic of the value shift from ethics of production to consumptive pleasure. Key is desire as created by signs of consumption (Yamazaki, 1984). Consumptive desire does not essentially exist internally but is produced externally. The Seibu Department Store's famous 1980s catchphrase exemplifies desires a priori nonexistence: "I want to know what I want (*Hoshii mono ga hoshiiwa*)". In a society that produces desire, its objects move from useful to symbolic value. To put it another way, self and desire have become socially constructed.

Giddens (1991: 198) pointed out the transformation of the "project of self" to lifestyle package in consumer culture. From this viewpoint, the self in high modernity is not the rational self in modernity, but a liquid self changed by consumer choices (Lyon, 1999: 76). Theories explaining these social situations are not only Toffler and Bell's post-industrial theory but also Jean-François

Lyotard (1984) and Jean Baudrillard's (1981, 1984) postmodern theories that deny cultural essentialism (see also Beck, 1992; Lash, 1990; Giddens, 1990; Lyon, 1999; Bauman, 2000). In particular, tourism realities without use value suit these theories, which have guessed right about the rise in new tourism. As Yamazaki (1984) emphasises, new tourism is consumption as aesthetics. Culture did not overcome the marketplace. Instead, the marketplace co-opted culture as an important element and is developing and/or transforming it.

Postmodernity, as defined by postmodern theory, is based on the Enlightenment project, for instance "progress" through technology, the "providence" of truth and beauty, and furthermore, the "analytic device" towards "exhaustion of modernity" and "forsaking of foundationalism" (Lyon, 1999: 10). However, modern premises have not been exhausted by challenging and defeating modernisation. As a feature of modernity, the nature of reflexivity obviously produces postmodernity. According to Giddens (1990: 39), "What is characteristic of modernity is not an embracing of the new for its own sake, but the presumption of wholesale reflexivity – which of course includes reflection upon the nature of reflection itself". That is, postmodernity is modernity "coming to understand itself rather than overcoming modernity" (ibid.: 48) as a consequence of modernistic reflexivity. Modernity's radicalisation and globalisation were required to produce postmodernity. Radicalisation of modernity in advanced nations brought doubt about modernity's development and progress and changed its lifestyles and values. Zygmunt Bauman (2000) emphasises loss of identity in "fluid (liquid) modernity" after the collapse of modern "solid (hard) modernity". As he observes, "The passage from heavy to light capitalism, from solid to fluid modernity, may yet prove to be a departure more radical and seminal than the advent of capitalism and modernity" (ibid.: 126). And just the condition of identity is questioned here. Individualisation in "fluid modernisation" is transformation of identity from a given into a task (or a gain) (ibid.: 31). Bauman further asserts, "It is the self-identity that becomes the straw at which the shipwrecked seeking rescue are more likely to clutch once the interest-navigated boats have foundered" (ibid.: 108). Tourism can be said to be this straw.

Postmodern theory rolls between being "a cultural reflex of late capitalism" and "bespeak[ing] a new social order beyond capitalism" (Lyon, 1999: 71). *The Beach* (film) exposed the new trend of a backpacker who pretends to have a new value but who finally proves to be just a consumer from a capitalistic country. Bauman accents the former theory, while Giddens and Lash embrace both. Urry (2014) also seems to embrace both even though he emphasised the former in the dystopian *Offshoring*. In spite of postmodernity, in particular, Giddens (1990: 149) seeks the possibility of "radicalised modernity".

Anyway, the former is the condition of latter, and the former creates the latter. Postmodernity functions ambiguously as capitalistic modernity. Nowadays, a prominent combination of consumerism and new information technology is creating a new order of capitalism.

Sociocultural change and new tourism

Here, mentioning briefly five points about the ambiguous social situation called postmodernity might be desirable: (1) The grand narrative (in this case, reliance for progress on development, equality and a reasonable subject) declines or is invalidated (Lyotard, 1984). (2) While modernity is a process of differentiation, postmodernity is a process of de-differentiation (Lash, 1990). (3) Reflexivity, particularly aesthetic reflexivity, progresses simultaneously with the spread of uncertainty (Lash & Urry, 1994). (4) Concern about the ecological system increases, to be taken up as a socio-political agenda (Giddens, 1990; Urry, 2014). (5) People begin to be widely conscious of the artificial nature of reality simultaneously with dilution of identity and recognise the possibility of reconstructing a reality artificially.

How does such a situation change the form of tourism mobility? Standard-oriented (packaged) tourism is reduced, and original, high-quality, aesthetic and green-oriented tourisms gain power. These are the features of new tourism that Poon (1993) mentions. Other expressions of postmodernity based on artificial creation of reality are MacCannell's "staged authenticity" theory as applied from Goffman's (1959) "front/back region theory" that emphasises tourists' autonomy. In postmodernity, the difference between labour and leisure, high and low culture, beautiful and ugly, male and female, production and consumption, or even front and back, by which modernity was characterised, is de-differentiated.

Both Poon and MacCannell's tourism theories imply that contemporary tourists have the reflexive nature that leads people to social reintegration. Indeed, the development of information technology, in particular bidirectional interactive communication technologies after 2000, greatly strengthened this trend's characteristics.[9]

Although tourism originally materialised in the hybrid of fictional and real objects, it generally enhances inversion of representation and the original object. Generally speaking, tourism culture is the kind of simulation that Baudrillard assigns to postmodernity. Aesthetic fiction becomes the tourist gaze's self-sufficient main object. Within the relationship of original reality and representation, the inversion phenomenon is becoming a pattern in new tourism, for instance in manga-anime tourism and art tourism.[10] The reflexive nature (structure) of tourist culture will form new, soft communities differing from old, rigid ones and will create identities and pride by re-embedding "new" traditions. In this manner, tourist agents, tourists themselves, local residents at tourist resorts and even tourism researchers are involved in the reflexive structure mechanism, regardless of right or wrong.

Socioeconomic change and tourism: post-Fordism and new tourism

Notably, changing conditions in the capitalistic "regime of regulation in economic development (modes of social integration)" serve as a backdrop to the tourism conditions discussed above. When we make an issue of mobility in contemporary society, most important is that capital, person, thing and information move beyond national borders, and this brings about capitalism's disorganisation (Lash & Urry, 1994). The condition of flexible and fragmentary production/consumption in the disorganised reflex of capitalism, accompanied by specialised consumption, is characteristic of post-Fordism.

Post-Fordism refers to the system of specialised small-batch production accompanied by flexible social and cultural values. In contrast, Fordism, the system of mass production and mass consumption based on the labour of Taylor system factories, is accompanied by rigid social and cultural values. Beck, Giddens and Lash (1994: 110–173) observe the new individualism in post-Fordism.

Beck, Giddens and Lash (1994) also describe modernisation's process in three stages from (1) traditional to (2) simple modern and then to (3) reflexive modern:

> Reflexive modernity is attained only with the crisis of the nuclear family and the concomitant self-organisation of life narratives; with the decline of influence on agents of class structure in voting behaviour, consumption patterns, trade union membership; with displacement of role-bound production through flexibility at work; with the new ecological distrust and critique of institutionalised science.
>
> (ibid.: 115)

Furthermore, for Lash, late modernity's reflexivity is aesthetic, so instead of a mass-production, mass-consumption system, consumers in a flexible production and marketing system, possible through information technology, form a community (or network) based on individualised and specialised aesthetic consumption.

Obviously, Poon's new tourism applies to this reflexive modernity in a post-Fordist, flexible production–consumption system. In post-Fordism, the market institutionalises consumers' disorganised "individual" desires into diversified capitalism made possible by information technology. New tourism, Poon says, is post-Fordist consumption that can include such fundamental diversities. Consumption is being created "aesthetically" and also becoming a political measure so that consumptive diversity may be felt as an individual's original "desire". New versions of new tourism, derived especially from subcultures such as manga-anime, rock festivals or art festivals, can be positioned as tourism that creates niche communities based on aesthetic reflexivity in individual consumption extended far ahead of "old" new tourism.

Is postmodern tourism liberational or repressive?

In general, Urry and especially Lash (1994), after writing *Economies of Sign and Space*, think positively about reflexive postmodernity's consumption form, even though in disorganised capitalism, the "economy of a sign and space" hides a genuine market mechanism, and individuals become increasingly subordinate to such a liquid economy. Consequently, aesthetic reflexivity will be strengthened, especially in tourism mobility, thus generating cosmopolitanism and functioning for development of regional culture and social integration. Nevertheless, Lash and Urry caution that advanced mobility might bring division to regions in a postmodern society where disorganisation is advanced. Some people will not receive the benefit of reflexive individualism. Lash and Urry (1994) also stress disparity in excessive squandering of energy resources.

On one hand, postmodernity based on aesthetically recurring nature might form a global network (cosmopolitanism). On the other hand, it might lead underclasses to shut themselves in ghettos, excluding each other because of the inability to reach cosmopolitan relations, or lead to their mutual surveillance (Lyon, 1999). Beck, Giddens and Lash (1994: 174–183) caution theorists that reflexive modernity's creative nature is not necessarily connected to reflection, leading automatically to a democratic mechanism. There is also a risk of narrow-minded pride and nationalism, of intensified movement to a reckless run of "reflexivity", and of causing "self-demolition" or "self-assault" in exhaustion of natural and cultural resources. Reflexive modernity itself has an ambivalent nature, and in the same way we can understand tourism mobility through reflexive modernity.

Conclusion: is a heterotopia of tourism possible?

Judging any form of tourism as a steppingstone of human liberation and democracy is too optimistic. As the introduction stated, tourism has progressed by commercialising objects that were not commodities prior to modernisation. *The Beach* (film) implies that travellers who seem to have rejected mass tourism remain an evolved form of mass tourists. As MacCannell mentions, a mass tourist can be a traveller or new tourist in reflexive modernity. In fact, mass tourism and new tourism flow together in the same stream, provided that tourism changes according to development of society and technology. In particular, tourism development in postmodern society is concerned with conditions of people's social identity in today's liquid society. In Japan, tourism policy has flowed along with local areas' identity politics, aiming for social integration after economic growth.

In old districts, for instance, tourism of local daily lives extends the market, and daily life's domain is colonised by tourism's identity politics. Serving as a resource, local life can transform for tourists' consumption of aesthetic experience. Whether for good or evil, tourism is newly marketing nature, culture, life resources and humanity itself, thus involving local people in the problem of "over-tourism". Contrary to this negativity, there is merit in local people noticing and discovering values of regional nature or culture by becoming objects for tourism. When I interviewed some local Yanaka people, who had become objects of tourism, they had independently noticed many things to show tourists. However, they easily distinguished the difference between the value of tourism and their everyday lives.

Urry (2002: 143) observes, "Becoming a tourist destination is part of a reflexive process by which societies and places come into the global order". This also means that "economies of signs" spread globally in consumer societies (Lash & Urry, 1994). Furthermore, for Urry (2002: 142), the touristic popularity of pre-Communist American classic cars in Cuba has attracted tourists' attention, resulting in globalised place-marketing. Additionally, I gave the examples of Hanoi and Tokyo, in which I described how a regional brand is reconstructed or re-entered into the global market.

Postmodernity and post-Fordism raise uncertainty and undecidedness to the social surface. Postmodern society makes visible human nature's fundamental anxiety. Nevertheless, some social critics view this circumstance as a chance to liberate the diversity of imperfect human nature – a task modernisation could not accomplish. One of those social critics, Gianni Vattimo (2000), observes that the experience of uncertainty, shock and physical disorder such as the "Utopia of reproductive art" realises the possibility of diversity in postmodern society. Vattimo asserts that aesthetic experiences in contemporary society provide each of us with possibilities in alternative societies. He observes that aesthetic experience is not of the order of word meaning and, in postmodernity, should consist of uncertainty and anxiety. Postmodernity thus offers humanity a chance for liberation.

As a matter of course, most aesthetic postmodern culture is commodified, a condition usually without disorder and thus another world. Nevertheless, as in Guy Debord's (1995) "society of the spectacle", the world flows more fluidly, and he mentions that it still has ambiguity, causing people to experience fluctuation and to feel physical disorder. Vattimo observes that what was brought about after the 1960s is not utopia or dystopia but heterotopia. Aesthetic experience is experience of a community. It is booted from each community's cognitive system, including that of people deprived of language but full of myth. Walter Benjamin (2008) argued that in the reproductive age, artistic reproductions do not destroy "real" values but bloom into diversity and pluralism. Vattimo's positive evaluation of Benjamin's work and postmodernity has well described the world's positive side, which modernisation's overly organised system finished.

Vattimo knows fully that this has happened during the market system's development and transformation. However, he insists that aesthetic reflexivity arises from situations of collision and disorder. As Ernesto Laclau and Chantal Mouffe (2001) point out, (radical) democracy arises from relationships generated from the impossibility of constituting them, rather than from a perfect totality. Sociology of tourism should clearly articulate the possibility of postmodern heterotopia and its limits. Lyon (1999: 100), criticising postmodernist theories, argues, "Without some alternative vision, it is hard to see how some postmodern stances will not degenerate into mere complacency or self-seeking cynicism". He thus proposes integrating postmodern and critical theories (ibid.: 100).

These results lead us again to the conclusion of tourism's ambivalence in the reflexive modernity of disorganised capitalism. As mentioned earlier, tourism that includes all domains of life and nature cannot be wholly controlled. Urry (2002: 161) calls for discussion of "how notions of chaos and complexity can help to illuminate the unexpected, far from equilibrium movements of social and physical process that currently rage across the globe". Referring to MacCannell's (2011) "second gaze" that totally de-differentiated tourism in any aspect, Urry (2002: 161) declares, "There pockets of disorder remain, of opening and gaps, memories and fantasies, movements and margins". In tourism heterotopia is an island of order in chaos. In the global order, is tourism "only at the best a contingent and temporary ordering that generates its massive and complex disordering" (ibid.: 161)?

Contemporary tourism is organising itself. Tourism's images reflexively organise the images tourists have. Next, tourists' own images organise tourism's image through (especially mobile) media by, for example, sending "Instagram-able" objects. Also, information spread by tourism researchers organises tourism's image, and thus sociologists of tourism should be both conscious and critical of their influential power. Tourism is becoming a liquid, self-organic system open to local living areas outside the traditional market. Thus, commodification and commercialisation are challenging control of a system continually changing itself to escape control.

The Beach (film) represents circulation of tourism's image. New tourism is also an image generated by mass tourism's becoming more reflexive in shifting capitalism and modernity. Therefore, many difficulties will be waiting if we desire order in tourism, especially in new tourism beyond its contingency and temporary ordering of its system. But we can certainly see ways to touch cosmopolitan human ties because the system is not closed, but open to our everyday lives in global mobility.

Notes

1 In those days, "tourism" and "leisure" were used variously, and massive investment in leisure facilities might not have been considered a tourism policy as such (Oikawa, 2017: 211).
2 Well known is that the NHK television programme *Project X* (2000) reported conflict and endogenous revitalisation of the Yufuin hot spa village.
3 Typical cases are the official character of regions named *Yuru-Kyara*.
4 The term "new tourism" was used for only two years, but words meaning the same thing have continued to be used into the present (Japan Tourism Agency, 2018).
5 Clear declaration of intention seemed required to support some model cases.
6 Because many have questioned whether these tourisms are truly consumer, bottom-up types, this issue should be argued separately.
7 There are also many examples of failure. See *Chiiki×Anime [Regions×Animation]* (Chiiki Contents Kenkyukai, 2019).
8 Here, the term "postmodernism" mainly indicates construction or art styles, distinguishing it from "postmodernity", as "postmodern" culture, or the social state.
9 See the effect of reality creation in tourism by YouTubers such as *Tokai-on-air*.
10 The "2.5-dimensional stage" which simulates the world of manga, animation and game has the same contexture.

References

Baudrillard, J. (1981) *Simulacres et simulation.* Paris: Galilée.

Baudrillard, J. (1984) *Simulations.* New York: Semiotext.

Bauman, Z. (2000) *Liquid Modernity.* Cambridge: Polity Press.

Beck, U. (1992) *Risk Society: Towards a New Modernity.* London: Sage.

Beck, U., Giddens, A., & Lash, S. (1994) *Reflexive Modernization: Politics, Tradition and aesthetics in the Modern Social Order.* Cambridge: Polity Press.

Bell, D. (1973) *The Coming of Post-Industrial Society: A Venture in Social Forecasting.* New York: Basic Books.

Benjamin, W. (2008) *The Work of Art in the Age of Its Technological Reproducibility, and Other Writings on Media,* Jenning, M.W. ed. Boston, MA: Harvard University Press.

Bishop, C. (2004) *Antagonism and Relational Aesthetics, October, 110 (Fall 2004), 51–79.* Cambridge (USA): October Magazine Ltd. and Massachusetts Institute of Technology.

Boorstin, D.J (1992) *The Image: A Guide to Pseudo-Events in America.* New York: Random House.

Boyle, D. (film) (2000) *The Beach.* 20th Century Fox.

Chiiki Contents Kenkyukai ed. (2019) *Chiiki×anime [Regions×animation].* Tokyo: seizandoshoten.

Debord, G. (1995) *The Society of the Spectacle.* New York: Zone Books.

Galbraith, J.K. (1979) *The Age of Uncertainty.* Boston, MA: Houghton Mifflin Harcourt.

Garland, A. (2011) *The Beach.* London: Penguin Books.

Giddens, A. (1990) *The Consequences of Modernity.* Cambridge: Polity Press.

Giddens, A. (1991) *Modernity and Self-Identity.* London: Polity Press.

Goffman, E. (1959) *The Presentation of Self in Everyday Life.* New York: Doubleday & Company Inc.

Hamano, T. (2017) "Shakai no Kanko: Kouki kindai niokeru shakai shisutemu no kansatsu taisho tosite" ["Tourism of society: As an object of observation in late modernity"]. *Tourism Studies Review Vol. 5-1,* 131–133. Osaka: Japan Society of Tourism Studies.

Japan Tourism Agency (2007) *Heisei 19nen Kanko Hakusho [Tourism White Paper 2007].* Tokyo: Japan Tourism Agency.

Japan Tourism Agency (2018) *Heisei 30nen Kanko Hakusho [Tourism White Paper 2018].* Tokyo: Japan Tourism Agency.

Kamata, M. (2013) *Oisemairi: Edo shomin no tabi to shinjin [Ise Pilgrimage: Travels and Religious Beliefs of Ordinary People in Edo].* Tokyo: Chuokoronshinsha.

Laclau, E. & Mouffe, C. (2001) *Hegemony and Social Strategy.* 2nd Edition. London: Verso.

Lash, S. (1990) *Sociology of Postmodernism.* London: Routledge.

Lash, S. & Urry, J. (1994) *Economies of Signs and Space.* London: Sage.

Lyon, D. (1999) *Postmodernity.* 2nd Edition. London: Open University Press.

Lyotard, Jean-François (1984) *The Postmodern Condition: A Report on Knowledge.* Trans. Bennington, G. & Brian M. Minneapolis, MN: University of Minnesota Press. [(1979) *La Condition postmoderne: Rapport sur le savoir. Paris: Éditions de Minuit.* Paris: Minuit.]

MacCannell, D. (1999) *The Tourist: A New Theory of the Leisure Class.* Berkeley, CA: University of California Press.

MacCannell, D. (2011) *The Ethics of Sightseeing.* Berkeley, CA: University of California Press.

Mori, A. (2007) *Disukaba Japan no jidai: Atarashii tabi wo souzousita shijou saidaino kyanpe-n [Age of Discover Japan: The Biggest Campaign which Created New Travelling in the History]*. Tokyo: Kotsushinbunsha.

Oikawa, Y. (2017) *Tetsudo to Kanko no kingendaishi [Modern and Contemporary History of Railway and Tourism]*. Tokyo: Kawadeshoboshinsha.

Okamoto, R. (2015) *Seichi Junrei: Sekaiisan kara anime no butai made [Pilgrimage to Sacred Places]*. Tokyo: Chuokoronshinsha.

Paolo, V. (2003) *Sienze Sociali e "Natura Umana": Facoltà di linguaggio invatiante biologico, rapprti di produzione*. Soveria Mannelli: Rubbetino Editore.

Poon, A. (1993) *Tourism Technology and Competitive Strategies*. Wallingford: CAB International.

Sadakane, H. (2015) *Chiho toshi wo Kangaeru: "Shohi shakai" no sentan kara [Thinking on Provincial City: From Tip of Consumer Society]*. Tokyo: Kadensha.

Saeki, K. (1989) *Sangyo bunmei to posutomodan [Civilization of Industry and Postmodernity]*. Tokyo: Chikuma Shobo.

Sekido, A. (2007) *Kindai tu-rizumu to onsen [Modern Tourism and Spa]*. Kyoto: Nakanishiya Publishing.

Shutz, A. (1964) *Collected Papers II, Studies in Social Theory*. The Hague: Nijhoff.

Shutz, A. (1967) *The Phenomenology of the Social World*. Evanston, IL: Northwestern University Press.

Sudo, H. (2008) *Kankoka suru Shakai [The Tourization of Society]*. Kyoto: Nakanishiya Publishing.

Sudo, H. (2017) "Kankosha no pafomansu ga gendai geijutu to deautoki: ato turizmu wo chusinni sankagata kanko niokeru 'sanka' no imi wo tou" ["Relationship between tourist performance and contemporary art: On the 'participation' of tourists in art project"]. *Tourism Studies Review Vol. 5-1*, 63–78. Osaka: Japan Society of Tourism Studies.

Sudo, H. & Endo, H. (2018) *Kanko shakaigaku 2.0: Hirogariyuku turizumu kenkyu [Sociology of Tourism: Expanding of Tourism Studies]*. Tokyo: Fukumura Publishing.

Takaoka, F. (2019) "Kanko no tsunagari no shakaigaku: Mouhitotu no taishukanko nitsuite" ["Sociology of travel connections: On alternative mass tourism"]. *Tourism Studies Review Vol. 7 No. 1*, 37–49. Osaka: Japan Society of Tourism Studies.

Teramae, S. ed. (2009) *Kanko seisakuron [Theory of Tourism Policy]*. Tokyo: Hara shobo.

Toffler, A. (1980) *The Third Wave*. New York: Bantam Books.

Urry, J. (2002) *The Tourist Gaze*. 2nd Edition. London: Sage.

Urry, J. (2014) *Offshoring*. Cambridge: Polity Press.

Vattimo, G. (2000) *La Società transparente*. Milano: Galzanti.

Yamaguchi, M. (2017) "Kanko no manazashi no sakini arumono: Koki kanko to shugouteki jiko wo meguru shiron" ["Gazing over the tourist gaze: An approach to late tourism and the collective self"]. *Tourism Studies Review Vol. 5-1*, 115–125. Osaka: Japan Society of Tourism Studies.

Yamazaki, M. (1984) *Yawarakai kojinshugi no jidai: Shohi shakai no bigaku [The Birth of Soft Individualism: The Aesthetic of Consumption]*. Tokyo: Chuokoron.

Chapter 4

Late tourism and 'boomerang' mobility in Japan

Makoto Yamaguchi

The end of tourism in Japan?

At the beginning of the 21st century, the central government of Japan announced its plan to create a 'Tourism-Oriented Nation' (2003); it enacted the Basic Law for the Promotion of the Tourism-Oriented Nation Plan (2006); and it established the Japan Tourism Agency (2008). The Japanese government relaxed visa requirements for tourist visas for citizens of neighbouring countries, including China. Along with a proliferation of LCCs (Low Cost Carriers) and a weak yen, these policy changes contributed to an increase in the number of foreign tourists visiting Japan. In 2008, Japan counted 8.35 million inbound tourists. In 2013, for the first time this number exceeded 10 million; in 2016, it reached approximately 20 million; and by 2018, it had grown to 30 million.

In the approximately two decades since 1996, by contrast, the annual number of outbound tourists from Japan to other countries has stagnated at approximately 17 million, plus or minus 10%. In 2015, the number of inbound tourists to Japan surpassed that of outbound tourists, and this gap has continued to widen each year.

The Japanese people may be known internationally as 'travel lovers', but in comparison with the peoples of other developed nations, the proportion of Japanese citizens with passports is remarkably low, having dwindled to just 23.4% in 2018. While an inbound tourism bubble is currently emerging in Japan, then, its outbound tourism remains stuck in a slump. Specifically, an 'aversion to travel abroad' has become an increasingly common issue among adults in their 20s.[1]

Has tourism in Japan changed from being an enjoyable leisure activity to a source of economic labour that relies on foreigners? It is ironic that the 'Tourism-Oriented Nation' of Japan in the 21st century seems to be rapidly facilitating *the end of tourism*.

However, we must remember that when Lash and Urry discussed 'the end of tourism', they did not declare the impossibility of tourism, but instead pointed to the emergence of two mutually contradictory tendencies (Lash & Urry 1994). The multiplication of styles of tourism, originating in the development of media and transportation, has made it increasingly difficult to distinguish the concept of 'tourism' from other activities, and it has brought about an uneven distribution of tourist trajectories among all social settings. That is to say, in contemporary society, tourism is both nowhere and everywhere. As the distinct characteristics heretofore understood to define tourism continue to dissolve, the *touristic* has come to infuse, and to exert deep influence upon, a range of social spheres.

A glance back upon early 21st-century Japan, as one mode of the so-called 'post-tourism' to succeed the experience of the 'end of tourism', enables us to make qualitative observations about some newly apparent instances of the *touristic*, despite the decline in types of tourism that have been understood quantitatively through conventional statistical surveys.

For example, in 2008, the same year in which the Japanese government established the Japan Tourism Agency, the Apple iPhone officially went on sale in Japan. Along with its rival, Android devices, the iPhone triggered an explosive proliferation of smartphones. This new communication technology catalysed many social changes and dramatically changed the profile of the *touristic* – the 'selfie' trend is a representative example. Boorstin once wrote that 'we travel not to see, but to take pictures' (Boorstin 1964: 128); now, we travel to take selfies.

It is self-evident that selfies can be taken at any time, and anywhere, within the spaces of daily life. By articulating with the experience of tourism, or of movement, the selfie has resulted in new social practices. One example is *zekkei* tourism (Figure 4.1). *Zekkei* can be translated as 'a superb view' or 'magnificent scenery'. *Zekkei* tourism has become so popular in Japan that there is now an abundance of guidebooks, TV shows, and websites about taking selfies at such locations.

Zekkei is a historical Japanese word derived from the phrase 'a landscape that takes your breath away' – or in other words, a landscape of breath-taking beauty. For example, typical *zekkei* have been considered to include such natural landscapes as valleys, coastlines, and mountains, or such cultural landmarks as Tokyo Tower and temples of Kyoto. However, in the age of smartphones and selfies, the locations regarded as *zekkei*, and the meaning of the word itself, are changing. For example, *zekkei* tourists in recent years not only take pictures of the landscapes or landmarks before their eyes, but inevitably enact the performance of capturing a selfie against a *zekkei* backdrop.

Zekkei tourism makes possible the experience of gazing not only at the world, but also at the self; the more ideal for selfies the *zekkei*, the more tourists it will attract. In other words, *zekkei* tourists experience locations and the experience of their mobility through a certain 'mediatised gaze', but upon arriving at their destination, they capture the landscape and themselves, or they desire to look at themselves more than the landscape. The landmark in their 'mediatised gaze' thus becomes a 'self-mark', and the landscape becomes a 'self-scape'.

This concept of the 'mediatised gaze' was noted by Urry in *The Tourist Gaze*; he describes it as 'a collective gaze where particular sites famous for their "mediated" nature are viewed' (Urry & Larsen 2011: 20). However, the idea of the 'mediatised gaze' does not appear in the first edition that was published in 1990 – it is mentioned only in the 11 lines of the last chapter of the second edition, published in 2002. And only in *The Tourist Gaze 3.0*, a revised edition created with J. Larsen in 2011, was the concept explained and analysed in detail as a symbolic example of 'post-tourism'.

Certainly, Japan's *zekkei* tourism catalysed by the 'mediatised gaze' is inauthentic with regard to the experience of the destination, but it may be regarded as an example of post-tourism in the sense that tourists 'play' it like a game. This reflects a type of post-tourism that T. Edensor has already observed at the Taj Mahal and other international destinations, and the case of *zekkei* tourism in Japan may not extend far beyond Urry and Larsen's discussion (Edensor 1998, 2000).

However, here we find that another crucial element has been exposed. As mentioned earlier, selfies can be taken in any of the spaces of daily life, so selfies do not demand the effort required in seeking a 'mediatised gaze' and in moving towards somewhere to attain this experience. Given that selfies do not essentially drive tourism, nor does the 'mediatised gaze' constantly stimulate tourism mobility, what drives the experience of tourism in this post-tourism era, and why do people consciously participate in tourism mobility? Underlying *zekkei* tourism in contemporary Japan, and tourism that is closely associated with selfies more generally, lies an important point that has either been overlooked, or insufficiently scrutinised, in post-tourism discourse thus far. For this reason, I would like to re-examine the discussion of post-tourism and consider a path to understanding a new form of the *touristic* appearing in the wake of the 'end of tourism'.

Figure 4.1 Zekkei tourists taking selfies at Manzamou, Okinawa, Japan.
Source: photo by the author.

Post-tourism in late modern society

The concept of 'post-tourists' was first discussed by Feifer in 1985 and was subsequently addressed by Urry (1990), Munt (1994), and Rojek (1993), among others. This term describes the characteristics of the new tourist of the postmodern era, in which society emphasises consumption over production and an enormous number of images are increasingly circulated by the media and communication technologies (Feifer 1985). The 'post-tourist' that has been emerging in the era of the 'end of tourism' has the following three characteristics when compared to 'early tourists' (Lash & Urry 1994; Munt 1994; Campbell 2005; Tesfahuney & Shough 2006; Jansson 2017, 2018a, 2018b).

Firstly, post-tourists tend to be less mobile or entirely immobile. Their experiences of tourism begin at home – particularly through TV, travel magazines, guidebooks, and other media – and do not necessarily entail physical mobility, as mobility itself is sometimes limited or eschewed (Feifer 1985). Post-tourists emphasise the symbolic consumption of images rather than the embodied production of new discoveries, such as encountering an unfamiliar Other.

Secondly, the experiences of post-tourists are inauthentic, and they are not concerned with whether the culture or products they encounter at their destinations are authentic. Rather, they prefer theme parks over historical sites; compared to tourists who seek MacCannell's 'staged authenticity', they prefer experiences that reflect the feelings and images they have already seen in the media (MacCannell 1976).

Thirdly, as a result of the previously defined characteristics, tourism mobility for the post-tourist has become game-like; they enjoy their own experiences of tourism by consciously playing the role of the tourist and relativising traditional tourism (Endo 2017; Sudo & Endo 2018).

These three elements that characterise post-tourists – *immobile, inauthentic, game-like* – have been observable at various levels of Japanese society since the 1980s, by which time post-tourists had become a topic of discussion in the West. In 1983, Tokyo Disneyland was opened and the Nintendo Family Computer video game system was launched; in 1985, the newly privatised NTT released the first practical mobile phone. During this period, early tourists who preferred traditional tourism coexisted with post-tourists who enjoyed consuming postmodern images of tourism experiences. Both types of tourists continuously increased in number well into the 1990s, when the internet became widespread, and the 2000s, when ownership of mobile phones had grown dramatically.

However, from the late 2000s into the 2010s, tourists with new characteristics began to appear in Japan. While in some respects they resembled post-tourists, their sphere of activity was clearly different. One may call them 'post-post-tourists', to distinguish this different group of tourists from post-tourists. Their most distinctive feature is their passion for the physical experience of mobility, which sometimes becomes an end in itself. For example, the smartphone game

Pokémon GO, which was released in 2016, is an 'extra-mobility-oriented' game that requires physical mobility, unlike conventional video games that players could enjoy at home. However, the authenticity of the destinations and reality of the places featured in the game's story are largely of no concern. In other words, in present-day Japan, one can find many examples of a new type of tourism in which tourists seek the experience of mobility itself rather than the destination, and the experience itself serves as the source of authenticity. Furthermore, mobility itself generates and reinforces the reality of tourism in this type (Yamaguchi 2010, 2017).

Zekkei tourism is an example of such 'post-post-tourism'. For example, tourists who visit a *zekkei* will customarily take pictures; *zekkei* tourism that is unrelated to taking pictures is rare to the point of anomaly. Many tourists who travel to a *zekkei* would take pictures of the landscape or landmark before taking selfies with the *zekkei* as a backdrop, or sometimes, they only take a selfie of themselves and then quickly leave the place without capturing the touristic destinations such as *zekkei*. This has led to a proliferation of 'selfie-oriented-*zekkei*' tourism at destinations that have become popular for being 'photogenic' or 'Insta-genic (Instagrammable)' – i.e. ideal for selfies and sharing on a social media platform. In such cases, it is clear that neither the destination nor its authenticity are important. What matters here is the existential authenticity of the experience – *how 'I' moved physically and how 'I' was moved emotionally* (Wang 1999).

In contrast to post-tourists' characterisation as immobile, certain tourists characterised by their 'extra-mobility' and 'mobility-consciousness' have become increasingly common in contemporary Japan. Scrutiny of this emerging style of tourism reveals another characteristic. To quote the discussion in Urry and Larsen's *The Tourist Gaze 3.0*, while these tourists tend to prefer the collective gaze over the romantic gaze, and to pursue the shared experience of the mediatised gaze, in practice they tend to seek individualised, private experiences. In other words, they are passionate about tourism defined by individual mobility with the collective gaze. They wish to experience the collective gaze for themselves. Unlike early tourists, who were bussed on organised mass tours, they prefer to move individually by renting a car or simply walking on their own.

While they share some characteristics with early tourists and post-tourists, it is unclear what to call these emerging tourists or 'post-post-tourists' who exhibit a clearly different mode of mobility. Considering that post-tourists emerged from the tide of postmodernity, I refer to them as 'late tourists' in this chapter as they emerge from another tide of late modernity. In the following, I compare their characteristics.

Giddens (1990, 1991, 1992), Beck, Giddens, and Lash (1994), Young (1999), Elliott (2014), and others pointed out the post-Fordism, globalisation, and individualisation that took place from the 1970s to the 1980s. They argued that these phenomena resulted in the rapid penetration of reflexivity and a 'late modernity' in which people were separated and 'disembedded' from their traditional communities and became deeply committed to a process of reflexive identity-building

(Elliott 2014, 2016). In this late modernity, reflexivity has become a central quality of late tourism as well – the most salient feature of which is that mobility itself becomes the target of reflexive development and experience. That is, the late tourist is characterised by concern not with destinations (where to go) or tourism resources (what to see) but rather with the experience of tourism mobility (how to get there), and late tourism is characterised by the centring of the authenticity of the tourist's internal experience rather than something external in the late tourists' reflexive development.

In order to discuss this more concretely, I aim to describe the characteristics of the late tourist in relation to the aforementioned three characteristics of post-tourists. First, while post-tourists tend to become immobile, late tourists are extra-mobile and mobility-conscious. Second, both late tourists and post-tourists are unconcerned with the authenticity of their destinations, but the former are highly concerned with the authenticity of their experience of mobility. In this sense, their tourism may be described not so much as inauthentic but as 'auto-authentic'. This auto-authentic character merits more detailed examination and is further discussed later. Third, both late tourists and post-tourists enjoy tourism in a game-like mobility, relativising traditional forms of tourism and centring their own experience of consciously 'playing' the tourist; however, the rules of their games differ. The auto-authentic game of mobility-conscious late tourists is more strongly reflexive than the game of post-tourists. In the late tourists' game, their own experience of mobility is constantly being monitored and checked; their reflexive mobility is not as much concerned with the consumption of images as with the construction of the self. This 'self-gaming' or 'auto-gaming' aspect is a unique characteristic that drives late tourists.

Many examples of *mobility-conscious*, *auto-authentic*, and *game-like* late tourism have thus concretely emerged in present-day Japan. Among them is *zekkei* tourism, which is closely connected to the culture of selfies. In *zekkei* tourism, the experience of mobility – how *'I' moved physically and how 'I' was moved emotionally* – assumes paramount important, and the focus of the reflexive gaze becomes nothing but oneself. Of course, this may not be limited to Japan; this type of late tourism may exist in other late modern societies all over the world. Thus, I would like to focus on the tourism mobility unique to late tourism and understand it theoretically.

Arrow and boomerang in tourism mobility

While discussions around post-tourism flourished in the 1980s, during the 'end of tourism', instances of late tourism grew remarkably salient in the late 2000s and the 2010s. For this reason, these two modes of tourism may appear to be two different generations belonging to two different time periods. However, I conceive of post-tourism and late tourism as having appeared in the same time period and as both influencing and coexisting with each other.[2]

Just as late tourism does not merely succeed post tourism, neither does late tourism simply connote a return to early tourism – that is, to the traditional tourism that preceded post-tourism. In late tourism, the meaning and function of the destination and traces of one's mobility assume new and unique characteristics. I aim to examine late tourism vis-à-vis the comparison between early tourism and post-tourism, and then to model these three modes of mobility in order to present an updated map of tourism in our present-day society.

First, over much of the long history of tourism, interest in and fascination with destinations such as sacred religious sites and sites of cultural interest had driven people to engage in tourism. The traces of early tourists' mobility may be illustrated as the shape of an 'arrow'. This 'arrow' was launched from tourists' homes or spaces of daily life towards sacred religious sites, natural landscapes, and destinations with man-made products and structures; however, the arrow's 'return' journey has seldom been discussed. Early tourism focused on *going there*, and the attraction of the destination was the greatest catalyst of tourists' mobility.

However, a postmodern society in which tourism has itself been relativised, dissolved, and brought to an end alongside other social concepts is characterised by the diversification and decrease in the value of destinations, and consequently the traditional 'arrow' model of tourism mobility has become relativised as well. Post-tourists who have been discussed in the late 20th century are less concerned with the value of the destination than with the value of tourism mobility itself as a game. In doing so, they have developed a certain mode of tourism in which the very experience of mobility – shooting the arrow – is to be enjoyed as an end in itself. This is the case for post-tourists, who are driven not by the attraction or authenticity of the destination but by the value of tourism mobility as a game – that is, the experience of 'pure arrow mobility'.

While post-tourists have reimagined tourism mobility as a game and enjoyed the pleasure of that pure experience, one group began exhibiting different tendencies. They applied reflexive awareness to tourism mobility and, in the process of enhancing the quality of the mobility experience, developed both another mode of mobility and a new type of destination. This third mode of tourism mobility may be considered 'boomerang mobility', because it is a reflexive mobility oriented towards home and oneself – a social, non-spatial destination – rather than an 'arrow' mobility towards a spatial destination away from home and oneself. Unlike the uni-directional, linear path of an arrow, 'boomerang mobility' of late tourism traces a circular path and returns home to oneself.

The reflexive experience of boomerang mobility emerged in late modern society, and the Self was rediscovered as a destination following the proliferation and refinement of this new game. This became the game of late tourism in which players move towards constructing their Selves.

The physical boomerang was derived from the arrow, and there are various types, including ones that return to the thrower and those that do not. Similarly, there are various types of boomerang mobility – not all of which necessitate a return home to the Self or whatever the start point may be. Boomerangs can also be used for sport in which throwing the boomerang high and far away, and having it return, is regarded as skilful. Similarly, boomerang mobility is gaining popularity in contemporary tourism – rather than travelling with a destination in mind, it is a mode of pure play whose goal is to obtain higher-quality reflexive experiences of boomerang mobility through which the tourist flies high and far away, yet returns in the end. This reflexive experience of boomerang mobility is the defining feature of late tourism, and the paths traced by late tourists are akin to those of boomerangs, not arrows. In Figure 4.2, I present models of the three modes of tourism mobilities that characterise early tourism, post-tourism, and late tourism.

Just as post-tourists did not exterminate early tourists, late tourists did not supplant the other two models of tourists. These three models coexist in contemporary society, and it is not uncommon for tourists of each model to co-exist in one space. Conversely, a single tourist may be an early tourist on one trip to a particular destination of traditional interest, a post-tourist who enjoys ironically playing tourist at a famous tourist spot, and a late tourist who visits a *zekkei* only to turn their back to the destination and gaze at themselves through their smartphone camera in order to take an ideal selfie shot. These three models are not mutually exclusive, and I regard them here as tools to understand the state of tourism in late modern society.

Reflexivity and the physical experience thereof have clearly influenced many aspects of tourism since long before the advent of late tourism. Tourism mobility resembling a boomerang can be found even in late 19th-century England where commercial-organised tourism companies were first organised. As such, late tourism in contemporary Japan has no monopoly on the reflexive experience of tourism and its boomerang mobility. Rather, late tourism is characterised most by

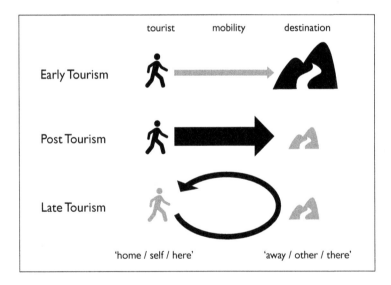

Figure 4.2 Three models of tourism mobilities.

the relativised and diminishing value of destinations, the 'game' of tourism mobility as a goal in itself, and the reflexive experience of boomerang mobility as a clear engine driving tourism. More so than any model of tourist that has preceded them, late tourists are reflexive about their own experience and mode of mobility, and they are more conscious of the quality of their physical and emotional experiences – *how 'I' moved physically and how 'I' was moved emotionally*, as opposed to the resources of the destination.

In addition to *zekkei* tourism and other forms of selfie-oriented tourism discussed earlier, many specific examples of this type of late tourism can be observed in contemporary Japanese society. For the most part, people engage in it through camera phones and other mobile devices, the Internet, and social media via social networking sites. The 2008 release of the iPhone in Japan and the subsequent proliferation of smartphones is the key to understanding the situation. The very process of capturing the ideal selfie while monitoring one's self-image on the small screen is purely a reflexive act, and this experience was enough of an attraction to further develop the tourist gaze. This reflects the mode by which unique performances of early tourism and post-tourism emerged according to the affordances of media of the day – travel guidebooks, newspapers, and other print media in the case of the former, and TV and electronic forms of mass media in the case of the latter. Of course, mobile media technology was not the sole driver of late tourism; its development is deeply intertwined with the social dynamics of late modern society, which had become individualised, liquid, and risk-aware (Beck, Giddens, & Lash 1994). The emergence and trajectory of late tourism is therefore a theme that must be investigated carefully, and observing changes in tourism following the development of late tourism is an important research task.

Conclusion

It may appear paradoxical that late tourism experiences circulated in high-tech media are more mobility-conscious than those of post-tourism and thus encourage the experience of physically moving oneself along with that media, rather than staying at or near one's home. In late tourism, a significant amount of physical mobility is not inevitable.

As we have discussed above, the key to understanding this lies in the specific and unique relationship that connects the peculiar affordances of mobile and social media with tourism mobility as a performance realised through the perception of such affordances. For example, the proliferation of camera phones made the performance of taking pictures user-friendly and ordinary. Now, with our smartphones, we can take pictures at any time and in any place. This leads to a situation in which the photogenic is everywhere and thus nowhere: as we take more pictures, the moments that previously were special and revolutionary have become increasingly relativised and disappear. What determines the value of the moment of a photograph, then, and what secures its authenticity? Rather than presuming inherent value or authenticity within the subject, value lies in the performance of taking the photograph itself and the experience of the physical mobility undertaken in doing so.

As the experience of mobility itself is centred, the performances peculiar to mobile and social media depart from experiencing the authenticity of photographic subjects – that which exists outside of the tourist – and enable tourists to extract authenticity from their own performances in a self-directed and engaged manner. In late tourism, which is characterised by the reflexive experience of boomerang mobility, in particular, authenticity is generated in the experience of mobility itself rather than by destinations or subjects. Realising this process of auto-authenticity and physically embodying that action in the performance of 'tourism' are affordances unique to mobile and social media. Authenticity in late tourism is not derived from such external things as places, objects, and cultural artefacts, nor is it staged by the host for the guest; instead, it is generated in a self-directed manner by the reflexive experience of mobility. Thus, it is the reflexive experience of boomerang mobility that functions as the source of auto-authenticity, and the return destination of boomerang mobility in late tourism is none other than the Self.

Consequently, the central destination in late tourism becomes the Self, and it is another *end of tourism* now we are observing in our society. Late tourists – or rather, we – find no value in geographical destinations other than their function as a pretext or trigger for our tourism mobility. The importance lies in the physical mobility itself, the processes of *how 'I' moved physically and how 'I' was moved emotionally*, and the construction of the Self through that boomerang mobility. The experience of mobility in late tourism is the source of the auto-authenticity of the Self that is generated therein.

However, while various iterations of late tourism have emerged in the contemporary Japanese context, one common element may be observed: they move individually and prefer to experience the collective gaze while choosing collective over romantic forms of mobility. They are passionate about tourism defined by individual mobility with the collective gaze. *Zekkei* tourism and selfie-oriented tourism not only exemplify this, but do so perfectly. Is the 'individual mobility with collective gaze' observed in late tourism a characteristic unique to contemporary Japan? Or is it a feature of tourism in late modern society that has been experienced elsewhere? To address these questions, late tourism must be examined further.

Notes

1 The slump in outbound tourism in Japan has been observed in domestic as well as international travel. For example, according to a survey by the Japan Travel Bureau Foundation, which is the oldest tourism research organisation in Japan, the number of people who had not travelled domestically or internationally in the past year because of their lack of 'interest in traveling' increased from 2% in 2008 to 10% in 2018 (Japan Travel Bureau Foundation, 2018).

2 Here, I posit that unlike post-tourism – the discussion of which began in the 1980s – late tourism exhibited a remarkable rise from the 2000s into the 2010s and that there

are increasingly numerous instances of this 'different type of tourism'. However, the relationship between the two is akin to that between postmodernism and late modernism. That is, although there is a temporal gap between the beginnings of the discussions, they should not be thought of precedentially but rather as two modes of tourism mobility that emerged in nearly the same time period from two different social consciousnesses (Beck, Giddens, & Lash 1994).

References

Beck, U., Giddens, A., & Lash, S. (1994) *Reflexive Modernization: Politics, Tradition and Aesthetics in the Modern Social Order*, London: Polity.

Boorstin, D. (1964) *The Image: A Guide to Pseudo Events in America*, New York: Harper & Row.

Campbell, N. (2005) Producing America: Redefining Post-Tourism in the Global Age, in Crouch, D., Jackson, R. & Thompson, F. (eds.) *The Media and the Tourist Imagination: Converging Cultures*, London: Routledge.

Cohen, C. (1988) 'Authenticity and Commoditisation in Tourism', *Annals of Tourism Research*, 15: 371–386.

Edensor, T. (1998) *Tourists at the Taj: Performance and Meaning at a Symbolic Site*, London: Routledge.

Edensor, T. (2000) 'Staging Tourism: Tourists as Performers', *Annals of Tourism Research*, 27 (2): 322–344.

Elliott, A. (2014) *Concepts of the Self (3rd ed.)*, Cambridge: Polity.

Elliott, A. (2016) *Identity Troubles: An Introduction*, London: Routledge.

Elliott, A. & Gay, P.D. (2009) *Identity in Question*, London: Sage.

Elliott, A. & Lemert, C. (2009) *The New Individualism: The Emotional Costs of Globalization (Rev. ed.)*, London: Routledge.

Elliott, A. & Urry, J. (2010) *Mobile Lives*, Oxford: Routledge.

Endo, H. (2017) *Tsūrizumu Mobiritīzu: Kankō To Idō No Shakai Riron [Tourism Mobilities: A Social Theory of Tourism and Mobility]*, Kyoto: Minerva Shobō.

Feifer, M. (1985) *Going Places: The Ways of the Tourist from Imperial Rome to the Present Day*, London: Macmillan.

Giddens, A. (1990) *The Consequences of Modernity*, London: Polity.

Giddens, A. (1991) *Modernity and Self-Identity: Self and Society in the Late Modern Age*, London: Polity.

Giddens, A. (1992) *The Transformation of Intimacy*, London: Polity.

Haldrup, M. & Larsen, J. (2006) 'Material Cultures of Tourism', *Leisure Studies*, 25 (3): 275–289.

Jansson, A. (2017) 'A Sense of Tourism: New Media and Dialectic of Encapsulation/Decapsulation', *Tourist Studies*, 7 (1): 5–24.

Jansson, A. (2018a) 'Rethinking Post-Tourism in the Age of Social Media', *Annals of Tourism Research*, 69: 101–110.

Jansson, A. (2018b) *Mediatization and Mobile Lives: A Critical Approach*, London: Routledge.

Japan Travel Bureau Foundation (2018) *Ryokō Nenpō 2018 [Annual Report on the Tourism Trends Survey 2018]*, Tokyo: Japan Travel Bureau Foundation.

Larsen, J. (2005) 'Families Seen Sightseeing: The Performativity of Tourist Photography', *Space and Culture*, 8: 416–436.

Larsen, J. (2008) 'Practices and Flows of Digital Photography: An Ethnographic Framework', *Mobilities*, 3: 141–160.

Larsen, J. & Urry, J. (2011) 'Gazing and Performing', *Environment & Planning D: Society & Space*, 29 (6): 1110–1125.

Larsen, J. & Sandbye, M. (eds.) (2014) *Digital Snaps: The New Face of Photography*, London: I.B. Tauris.

Lash, S. & Urry, J. (1994) *The End of Organized Capitalism*, Cambridge: Polity.

MacCannell, D. (1976) *The Tourist: A New Theory of the Leisure Class*, London: MacMillan.

Munt, I. (1994) 'The "Other" Postmodernism: Culture, Travel and the New Middle Classes', *Theory, Culture & Society*, 11 (3): 101–123.

Rojek, C. (1993) *Ways of Escape: Modern Transformations in Leisure and Travel*, London: Macmillan.

Sudo, H. & Endo, H. (2018) *Kankō Shakaigaku 2.0: Hirogariyuku Tsūrizumu Kenkyū [The Sociology of Tourism 2.0: A Study of the Broadening of Tourism]*, Tokyo: Fukumura Shuppan.

Tesfahuney, M. & Shough, K. (2006) 'The Nomos of Tourism', in Tesfahuney, M. & Shough, K. (eds.) *Privileged Mobilities: Tourism as World Ordering*, Newcastle-upon-Tyne: Cambridge Scholars Publishing.

Urry, J. (1990/2002) *The Tourist Gaze*, London: Sage.

Urry, J. (1995) *Consuming Places*, London: Routledge.

Urry, J. (2007) *Mobilities*, Cambridge: Polity.

Urry, J. & Larsen, J. (2011) *The Tourist Gaze 3.0*, London: Sage.

Wang, N. (1999) 'Rethinking Authenticity in Tourism Experience', *Annals of Tourism Research*, 26 (2): 349–370.

Yamaguchi, M. (2010) *Nippon No Kaigai Ryokō: Wakamono To Kanko Mejia No 50-Nenshi [Overseas Travel in Japan: A History of a Half-Century of Youth and Tourism Media]*, Tokyo: Chikuma Shobō.

Yamaguchi, M. (2017) 'Kankō No Saki Ni Aru Mono: Kōki Kankō To Shugōteki Jiko O Meguru Shiron' ['What Lies Beyond Tourism: An Effort to Theorize Late Tourism and the Collective Self]', *Kankōgaku Hyōron*, 5 (1): 111–125.

Young, J. (1999) *The Exclusive Society: Social Exclusion, Crime and Difference in Late Modernity*, London: SAGE.

Chapter 5

Mobility turn in rural districts in Japan

From "Kankō (tourism)" to "Kankei (relationships)"

Shingo Teraoka

Productionism in post-war Japan

Along with its surprising economic growth after WWII, Japan sustained a rapid population shift, with migration from rural to metropolitan areas. Since the 1970s, a developmental gap separating rural and urban areas has become increasingly clear. The government formulated the Third Comprehensive National Development Plan in 1977, aimed at restraining the concentration of population and industry into metropolitan areas. To support regional development, the national government planned to establish 40 settlement areas throughout Japan. The government intended to create new jobs by attracting enterprises through those settlement efforts. For agriculture, which showed difficulty in attracting young workers, the main policy was improvement of production efficiency supported by mechanization and large-scale land consolidation. Concentration of large-scale enterprises and modernization of agriculture were particularly targeted by governments.

"Critical turn" against productionism

Nevertheless, those policies were insufficient to halt the decline of rural areas of Japan. In the 1980s, criticism of productionism arose. Therefore, governments added tourism and leisure as important components of regional development policy. Governments assumed the occurrence of "hard (architectural)" development by capitalist enterprises. In 1987, the national government enacted a law called the "resort law," which prompted the construction of holiday apartments (so-called "Resort Mansions") and golf courses in the countryside. Nevertheless, matters did not progress as governments had desired. In the early 1990s, economic depression struck Japan: resort development failed. Abandoned "Resort Mansions" and ruined natural landscapes remained in many rural districts. Makoto Sato published the widely popular "Resort Archipelago," which criticized the failed local development policy (Sato, 1990).

Agricultural policy also confronted various difficulties. After the 1980s, agricultural market liberalization proceeded, which improved production efficiency through mechanization and large-scale land consolidation. The results were only a drop in the ocean: difficulties of abandoned farmland became increasingly acute.

Consequently, resistance against productionism and resort development by capitalist developers as well as a sense of crisis of farming and nature protection increased in influence among researchers, farmers, and local public servants. In some places, pioneering activities of community-based tourism have occurred. Yufuin town (Oita Prefecture) is a well-known case among them (Nakaya, 1995; Kitani, 2004). This trend prevailed among rural districts in the 1990s.

"Cultural turn": attention to rural matters and rural representation

In the 1990s, Japan was adversely affected by severe economic stagnation. The feasibility of regional development through attraction of new enterprises had been largely discredited. Aging and depopulation in rural districts worsened. Sociologist Akira Ono declared the "marginal settlements (Genkai Shuraku)" theory in 1991 (Ono, 2005). Marginal settlements refer to villages in which 50% of the population has reached or exceeded the age of 65 because of depopulation or other circumstances that make it difficult to maintain a regional community. The word "marginal," which shocked many people, was emphasized by mass media at the time.

Under such circumstances, "Green Tourism" (almost synonymous with agritourism in Japan) gained credence in Japan. In the 1990s, farmers in Ajimu town (Oita Prefecture) started a pioneering activity of Green Tourism called "Ajimu Method" (Miyata, 2010). Seiichi Miyata, the leader of the Ajimu movement, proposed the treatment of guests as "relatives and family." He hoped to continue its relation. The local government supported them positively. The national government also came to assign importance to the activity. In 1992, the Ministry of Agriculture, Forestry and Fisheries (MAFF) first used the term "Green Tourism" in its formal documents.

In fact, MAFF defined Green Tourism as "leisure activities with a stay enjoying nature, culture, agriculture, forestry, fishery and friendship with local people in rural districts" (MAFF, 1992). Soon thereafter, MAFF established laws promoting Green Tourism, and placed exchanges between urban and rural areas such as Green Tourism as aspects of basic policy for fostering job opportunities for farmers. Consequently, farm stays and agricultural experience tours prevailed. In addition, in the academic field, books introducing European Green Tourism were published (Yamazaki, Oshima, *et al.*, 1993). The Japanese translation of John Urry's "The Tourist Gaze" might well have had a certain effect on the Japanese academic field (Urry, 1990).

"Material quality and consumptional turn": from stagnation of Green Tourism to agricultural diversification

Entering the 2000s, one was able to find many books describing and recommending Green Tourism (Aoki, 2004; Aoki *et al.*, 2010). Nevertheless, Green Tourism, aside from educational tourism, had not become popular in Japan. Inoue (2011) highlighted six key features related to Japanese Green Tourism:

1   Stay days tend to be short.
2   Many go to farmer shops only.
3   Many prefer a rest with a long stay to short-time activity.
4   Many tend to use public facilities for staying.
5   Farmers tend to run farms with stays including two meals rather than a B&B.
6   For farmers, a farm stay is merely a side business.

I would like to highlight two key challenges in this context. The first is the shortage of holidays in Japanese society. Many workers have difficulty acquiring paid vacations institutionally as well as culturally. The second is that the host farmers with low mobility cannot reasonably deviate from a position of a "passive" host who merely responds to demands of guests from the city. Most Green Tourism venues required aged hosts to provide excessive hospitality, which led to burnout.

In 2008, rural sociologist Sadao Tokuno published an article with a title including the phrase "impossibility of Green Tourism" (Tokuno, 2008). He explained that it is only marginally feasible for Green Tourism to enhance the sustainability of rural districts of Japan: at most it would present a chance at intellectual stimulation.

It is ironic that city dwellers came to be able to purchase local special products on the internet in the 2000s, which promoted a consumptional view of rural areas rather than promoting understanding of the emerging predicament there. Tachikawa points out that, at this time, rural spaces were transformed from places of production into places of consumption (Tachikawa, 2005).

In actuality, informatization not only created negative effects for rural districts. Internet-supporting communication lines have crisscrossed most rural areas; mobile phones and Wi-Fi have come to be widely available. These have eased farmers' transmission of information and communication, which has allowed the diversification of farming and rural livelihood. Moreover, the possibility for non-farmers to live in rural districts has been enhanced. Tele-work has become possible also in rural districts. A book titled *Half farming, Half X. – A New Lifestyle* was published in 2003. The phrase has since come into vogue (Shiomi, 2003).

In the latter half of the 2000s, governmental support programmes for agricultural diversification started one after another. Two have been designated as "ACM-Collaboration" and "6th Industry." In 2007, governments established two policies: "The Urgent Program for Economic Revitalization of Rural Districts" and "On Measures for Local Economic Revitalization Through Collaboration Between Agriculture (Forestry, Fishery), Commerce and Manufacturers."

In 2009, rural economist Naraomi Imamura advocated the "6th Industry" concept. Agriculture, forestry, and fisheries are classified as primary industries, which are considered to produce only primary goods. However, under the 6th industry concept, farmers not only produce primary goods, they also positively participate in food processing (a secondary industry), distribution, and sales (tertiary industries) such that they accomplish diversification and gain greater profits. One from the primary industry plus two from the secondary industry plus three from the tertiary industry equals six. That conceptualization is the origin of the "6th Industry" idea. The term was transferred from academics to local administrators and farmers. Numerous related enterprises started after receiving state financing. Nevertheless, many "ACM-Collaboration" businesses, especially including tourism activities, have not been successful:

1   Discrepancies of values exist between guests who seek only a temporary pastime through Green Tourism and their hosts who regard Green Tourism as an important chance for sustainable rural development.
2   Strict requirements of authorization (such as guest transportation, meal preparation, etc.) are not explained to the host at the time of the application.
3   Lack of know-how related to practices such as troubleshooting on tours exists because they are not professional tourist agents.
4   Lack of support for sustaining collaboration. Governmental support specifically emphasizes the application stage (Sakurai and Teraoka, 2018).

ACM-Collaboration is a dynamic process that links stakeholders of different types. Their balance can change during the course of the enterprise. However, they have insufficient resilience to adapt to the changing circumstances and to maintain their collaboration.

Mobility turn: diversification of "mobility"

The age of diversification of "mobility" recognition proceeded in the 2010s. During that time, MAFF added "dual residence" as a new type of urban–rural exchange designation (MAFF, 2010).

In 2009, governments started a new programme called the "Chiiki-Okoshi Kyoryoku tai (Regional revitalization cooperators)." Local governments recruit urban people interested in rural revitalization and rural life as "Chiiki-Okoshi Kyoryoku tai." The national government provides their living and activity expenses, which are limited to three years. The sum total of "Kyoryoku tai" (as it is abbreviated) was over 5,000 people in 2018.

People of "Kyoryoku tai" are engaged in "regional cooperation activities" such as development of local specialties, regional branding, promotion, farming, tourism, and social welfare activity. This programme aims at inducing them to settle there after a period of financial support and encourages them to maintain and strengthen local vitality. According to related data, about 40% of participants are women; 70% are in their 20s or 30s. Data show that about 60% settled in the same region after financial support ceased (Ministry of Internal Affairs and Communications, 2019).

The main reason this programme is conducted among many local governments is aggravation of rural districts. Twenty years had passed since the first discussion of "Marginal Settlements (Genkai Shuraku) Theory" (Ono, 2005); a popular book titled *Rural Planning for Withdrawal* was published (Hayashi *et al.*, 2010). Publication of the "Masuda Report" played a decisive role in related social anxiety that became prominent in 2004. This report has another name: "Local Vanishing Theory (Chiho Shometsu Ron)." In 2010, one subcommittee of the advisory commission of the government published a shocking population projection that 894 local towns can be expected to disappear because of depopulation by 2040 (Masuda, 2014). Masuda is the commission head. Especially, the publication of true names of "disappearing local government" was an extreme shock to the people.

Soon after the publication of the Masuda Report, however, numerous counter-arguments were issued, especially against its projection measure (Odagiri, 2014; Yamashita, 2014). Among them, the counterargument of Hiroshi Fujiyama is known as "The Return-To-Pastoral-Life-Theory (Denen Kaiki Ron)" (Fujiyama, 2015). Fujiyama's regional development theory differs from other conventional ones in the sense that it emphasizes the high mobility of rural people.

In 2012, Fujiyama and his research team set up 227 areas in a mountainous area in Shimane Prefecture as a basic unit to promote comprehensive community development. They named it "Sato (home village)" (Fujiyama, 2015). As a result of their detailed research, which included assessments of population, traffic, purchase, social welfare, etc., of every "Sato," they found a new phenomenon: "The Return-To-Pastoral-Life (Denen Kaiki)" from city areas. More than a few people felt attracted to the idea and challenged themselves to move to inconvenient, small villages rather than to more convenient areas of rural districts. Finding this new migration trend to rural districts, Fujiyama and his team advocated a new type of coordination system for new rural districts ("I-Turner" in Japanese). A so-called "Sato No Eki Koso (Station of Small Village Plan)," building regional centres, provides all services including traffic, transportation, information, and integrated social welfare. Differently speaking, they emphasized the importance of a regional economic cyclical model.

Simultaneously, they highlighted the necessity of integrating people's flow across regional boundaries into the "Sato No Eki" system. The system provides management of diverse mobilities including tourism. High mobility and its management provide key social infrastructure for regional development of the Japanese countryside. From the same standpoint, Numao presented the current situation of rural districts as a "convection society" emphasizing traffic between urban and rural areas (Numao, 2016).

Shibasaki and Nakatsuka expanded their findings on "Chiiki Okoshi Kyoryo-kutai" to people residing in rural areas, describing key characteristics of Japanese rural districts:

> The research showed not only the stereotypical working style of migrating to rural areas and farming, but also working style travel between cities and other

areas while remaining based in rural areas, and even a working style of visiting rural areas frequently while being based in urban areas.

(Nakatsuka, 2019: 6)

From "Kankō" (tourism) to "Kankei" (relationships)

After the latter half of the 2010s, the way of life based on mobility has become more popularized by mass media. A new keyword, "Kankei Jinko (relationship population)," has taken the place of "Koryu Jinko (temporary visitors, mainly tourists)." "Kankei Jinko" is a term indicating people with diverse mobility situations between a tourist and a settler, as expressed by the phrase "more than tourism, less than settlement." One popular journal about such an alternative lifestyle, *Sotokoto*, advocated the word, and popularized it in a book titled *Building Kankei Jinko – A Local Innovation Neither Settlement Nor Exchange*, by a local journalist (Tanaka, 2017). "Kankei Jinko" is a process concept assuming increased commitment by city dwellers to the countryside: a gradual concept. Tanaka organizes it into six steps and designates it as "stages of commitment." Those steps are:

1. Local Specialty, Shopping → 2. Donating (Hometown Tax Option) → 3. Regular Visits → 4. Local Volunteering → 5. Double Residency → 6. Migration, Settlement.

(Tanaka, 2017: 59)

It is noteworthy that one need not proceed step-by-step to step 6. Rather, the relation (form of mobility) in each step is affirmed as it is. Therefore, it can be said to be a grounded (not idealistic) concept coupled with diverse mobility in the Japanese countryside. This concept breaks the dichotomy between hosts and guests, which constitutes the basic framework of conventional tourism research.

Actually, throughout the Japanese countryside, a variety of related populations (mainly young people) frequently pass back and forth between the city and countryside or settle in rural districts. In accordance with their situations, small base sites are being built in many locations. Sashide, the chief editor of the *Sotokoto* journal, calls the site a "Kankei (relationship) Information Center," parodying the "Kanko (tourist) Information Center" (Sashide, 2016). Although far more flexibility of networking exists beyond the space because of the increased use of social network services (SNS), a physical place is demanded. We can regard it as a kind of new locality in the "mobility age." Hereinafter, we take up a certain case of a small base site in the countryside.

Case study

Sakura Village Office Camp (SVOP)

A mountain village, Sakura village (pseudonym), has a population of about 1,600 organized into approximately 1,000 households. About half of the villagers are older than 65 years old: this is a "Genkai Shuraku (marginal settlement)." The village flourished because of forestry, but the workers have aged along with their experience of a persistent forestry recession. The population is decreasing by about 100 every year. Located far from a metropolitan area, attracting enterprises is improbable. Moreover, the area has no popular sightseeing spot. Therefore, Sakura village makes much of exchange and migration. A central spot is "Sakura Village Office Camp (SVOP)." In fact, SVOP is a coworking space of renovated traditional homes where everyone can visit and work, or have meetings with free Wi-Fi. A cafe is being established there as an annex where people can stop by and enjoy talking with other visitors there. More than a few people visit this village to do their work at SVOP. Sakura village has become famous these days for the migration of young people. Actually, SVOP is a symbolic place where the trend is highlighted.

The building plan of SVOP started when the village mayor and local government staff targeted "Creator" designers (architecture, fashion, IT, etc.) as well as editors and writers as young migrants to Sakura village because there was no main promising industry. The village soon realized it was necessary to create an environment for young city dwellers to visit or migrate to Sakura village without losing employment. This institution was built as a test settlement site with employment.

In planning and managing this space, young migrants are taking a central role. One member, Mr S, a designer, had lived in Osaka, but he had been to Sakura village many times since childhood because his father, an artist, owned an atelier there. After growing up, he worked in Osaka as a designer, but he became overworked and fell ill. After leaving his job and moving to his father's atelier for recuperation, he found "he could continue his work and make a living in Sakura village using the internet". He decided to continue living there without returning to Osaka. Later, one of his coworkers also migrated to Sakura village.

Before long, he and his coworkers were able to build a coworking space (SVOP) using financial aid from the local government. Soon it became popular on SNS and other media. The user fee is less than 5 US dollars per day. In 2014, its opening year, more than 1,400 people visited SVOP (including cafe guests). Eventually, three groups among them migrated to Sakura village. About 2,000 people visit SVOP every year. As of 2018, about 20 groups, collectively comprising about 30 people, have migrated to use SVOP.

Functions of SVOP

Nakatsuka (2019) cites the following four functions of SVOP:

1 Gateway for visitors
   In SVOP there is a cafe for relaxation for young migrants and villagers, with many brochures available for tourists. Many visitors stop by and ask for directions to tourist sites, or sometimes to ask for information about the traditional

culture of Sakura village. They can get concrete information and hear about episodes of migration (I-turn) too. In short, SVOP acts as an information centre for all matters related to Sakura village.

2   Symbolic space of Sakura village's efforts to promote migration from city areas
After this space was publicized by the mass media, it became popular nation-wide. Many inspectors such as local government officers and NPO staff visit this space. Most of them first know the name of Sakura village through interest in SVOP. During a migration experience tour held in Nara Prefecture, a visit to SVOP is always a required stop on the itinerary. Tour participants have dinner here, talk with young migrants here, and sometimes stay overnight.

3   Workplace
At SVOP are wide wooden tables and a Japanese-style room with a relaxed atmosphere for guests. It satisfies city dwellers' desires for fresh air and work in beautiful, natural surroundings. Furthermore, it is used for corporate training.

4   Meeting place for migrants
This is an important place for new migrants to make friends in the village. Some migrants, especially young people, sometimes feel "choked" by traditional burdensome human relationships in the old village.

> Mass media like emphasizing the rural nature of this village when they broadcast to us. However, we are not able to live along, absorbing the rural nature a full 100%. We migrants need so-called city-like space. In contrast, a good space will make young people from the city like us able to live in rural areas. SVOP is just such a place.
>
> (Mr S, interviewed on March 31, 2019)

SVOP's actual state of use

How is this co-working space used? Records reveal its actual state of use as the following. From July 1, 2015 through April 12, 2019, 232 groups have used it as a co-working space. Among them, corporations account for 52 cases; personal use accounts for 180 cases. As shown in Table 5.1, about half of them live in Nara Prefecture. About 24% of them are residents of the Kansai area, but not in Nara Pref.; say, in Osaka. Furthermore, as shown in Table 5.2, 27% of them reside outside of the Kansai area, in areas such as Tokyo.

Table 5.3 shows the visit duration; one day's use is about 63%, two days are almost 30%, and more than three days are 7%.

Table 5.4 shows the number of workers per visit: single use accounts for 55% of all cases, two workers account for 24%, three for 8%, four for 5%, and more than five workers account for 7%. There are a few cases of groups consisting of 20 people who visited and used this place.

Table 5.5 shows that, regarding correlation between the place of residence and visit duration, most people from Nara Prefecture and the Kansai area are one-day

Table 5.1 Residence of users

Place of residence	Frequency
Nara Pref.	112
Kansai area	56
Outside Kansai	64

Table 5.2 Users by type

	Frequency
Personal use	180
Corporation or group	52

Table 5.3 Length of stay

Day	Frequency
1	145
2	70
3	13
4	1
5	0
6	1
20	1

Table 5.4 Number of users per case

Number of users	Frequency
1	128
2	56
3	19
4	11
5	3
6-	15

Table 5.5 Length of stay by residence

	1 day (%)	2 day (%)	3 day (%)	4 day (%)
Nara Pref.	77	17	4	2
Kansai	68	26	6	0
Outside of Kansai	31	57	9	3

use (the former are 76%, the latter are 68%), while 57% of the visitors from areas more distant than the Kansai area are two-day use. The SVOP records show that more than several inspectors and cafe users visit there aside from coworking space users.

Catalyst of rural migration

The cases described below are migration experiences of two youths who had changed their jobs or residences with frequent use of SVOP.

Mr A, who had lived in a metropolitan area near Osaka and who had a teaching job originally, dreamed of living in a rural area. On one occasion, one of his friends gave him information about an old vacant house in Sakura village. He visited there and liked the old house and the beautiful nature of Sakura village, and decided to rent the house. However, his job was near Osaka. He was unable to leave the city area, so he used it as a second house for the time being. That is to say, he started double residency, living and working mainly in the city area and sometimes doing his work at SVOP while in Sakura village. A few years later, he found a new job within daily driving distance from his second house. He thereupon left the city and moved to Sakura village. As a villager there, he sometimes drops in to visit SVOP, communicating with people there, and organizing cultural activities such as web radio broadcasting and publishing of a local magazine.

Ms B, a book editor and writer, lived in a metropolitan area far from Nara. She had been to Sakura village at the invitation of her acquaintance on business. The acquaintance had already migrated to Sakura village. The reason she decided to leave the big city was a huge earthquake and subsequent accident at a nuclear power plant in 2011. At that time, her peaceful experience in Sakura village induced her move to Nara Prefecture. However, at first, she migrated to Nara city, which is about a one-hour drive from Sakura village. Even after moving to Nara city, she visited Sakura village once every few months and worked at SVOP. Much of her work done here is writing about rural life and related topics. After a year and a half of living in Nara city, she again moved to a small city near Sakura village. She sometimes visits SVOP and edits and writes mainly about rural life, also after moving to the small city.

In this way, the use of SVOP has had a certain effect on migration and work-style changes. As in the case of Ms B, one does not always experience single-track migration to Sakura village. It works as a catalyst for job and residence change.

Reasons for migration

Why do people migrate from city areas to the countryside? What makes their migration and work change possible? Or what impels them to take the option of migration and work change? And what kinds of living strategies do they find in the course of their migration experience?

During interviews conducted with residents, the following reasons were indicated:

1   Excessive competition among fellow traders in metropolitan areas.
2   Excessive living expenses, especially for young freelancers in metropolitan areas.
3   Tele-work is feasible in rural areas thanks to the internet.
4   Low living expenses in rural areas.
5   Increase of content production such as web-page authoring, movie-making, and research in rural areas.
6   Craft people can create their works using local materials such as wood and stones.

For them, the fact that they are writers, designers, and artisans who live in a rural area serves functions of differentiation from fellow traders in metropolitan areas such as Osaka or Tokyo. A photographer living in Sakura village says he has many requests for work related to scenic photographs of the countryside. Cafes or bakeries run by young migrants are sometimes reported by the mass media as "a cafe, bakery in beautiful nature." Writers are also requested to produce work related to topics of nature, country life, crafts, traditional culture, and rural tourism because they are living in such a situation. The forests around Sakura village are famous for high-quality wood. Artisans living there produce their works using wood obtained nearby, thereby branding themselves and their work.

Today, when mobility is highly developed, migrants have found a living strategy that balances their favourite lifestyle with enhancement of their market value by resourcing locality (such as culture and nature). At the same time, they breathe new life into rural districts while reproducing local presentations on media space.

Conclusion

In today's Japan with high mobility, do we have a real "frontier"?

One can safely say that real frontiers might include mountain villages or isolated islands. Today, even such places have highly developed freeways and internet services available everywhere. In contrast to such places, de-population of rural areas has weakened the line separating the reality of rural areas and urban life. Consequently, the "frontier" of Japan has become all the more symbolic.

Sakura village, located inland in Nara Prefecture, is located within a 30-minute drive of a shopping mall and railway station. Even from the most remote village of Nara Prefecture, one can reach a city with a big shopping mall within a two-hour drive. Furthermore, in such a village, high-speed internet is already available. Young migrants frequently visit the city for business meetings, shopping, and leisure. Of course, if they use Amazon.com, they can obtain anything they might need in a few days. Furthermore, they can do web conferences using video conferencing software. Those young migrants and people with two residences are not the last to know such a frontier is nothing but an image. They mobilize these images as resources for their work and connection making.

Nakatsuka (2019: 40) described SVOP as unique because

> they built an institution before they decided their concrete aim and plan. This is an approach by which they first set the place inducing interaction among people, material objects, money, and information etc. and entrust the place to accidental innovation.

It can be interpreted as "entrusting matters to mobility" and "entrusting matters to a relational population (Kankei Jinko)."

A person with mobility as a member of a rural community is attractive to provoke an image of new rural society. How much can a relational population truly contribute to enhancement of the sustainability of a local community? The answer is not readily forthcoming. The success or failure of many efforts on many points remains unpredictable.

Acknowledgement

This work was supported by JSPS KAKENHI Grant Number 17K02107.

References

Aoki, S. (2004) *Gurin tsurizumu jissen no syakaigaku [Sociology of Green Tourism Practice]*. Tokyo: Maruzen.

Aoki, S., Rain, B. and Koyama, Y. (2010) *Jizoku kano na gurin tsurizumu: eikoku ni manabu jissenteki nouson saisei [Sustainable Green Tourism: Practical Rural Regeneration to Learn from Britain]*. Tokyo: Maruzen.

Fujiyama, H. (2015) *Denen kaiki 1% senryaku [Retroversial 1% Strategy: Get Back Work and People Locally]*. Tokyo: Nosangyoson Bunka Kyokai.

Hayashi, N., Saito, A. *et al.* (2010) *Tettai no nouson keikaku: kaso chiiki kara hajimaru senryakuteki saihen [The Rural Planning of Withdrawal: Strategic Reorganization Starting from the Depopulated Area]*. Kyoto: Gakugei Publishing.

Inoue, K. (2011) *Gurin tsurizumu: kiseki to kadai [Green Tourism: Trajectory and Challenges]*. Tokyo: Tsukuba Publishing.

Kitani, F. (2004) *Yufuin no chiisana kiseki [A Little Miracle of Yufuin]*. Tokyo: Shincyosha.

Masuda, H. (2014) *Chiho shometsu: Tokyo ikkyoku syucyu ga maneku jinko kyugen [Disappearance of Local Districts: Rapid De-Population Caused by Overconcentration to Tokyo]*. Tokyo: Chuokoronsya.

Ministry of Agriculture, Forestry and Fisheries (1992) *Gurin turizumu cyukan hokoku [Interim Report on Green Tourism Study Group]*. Tokyo: Ministry of Agriculture, Forestry and Fisheries.

Ministry of Agriculture, Forestry and Fisheries (2010) *Syokuryo nogyo noson hakusyo [Food, Agriculture, Rural Village: White Book]*. Tokyo: Ministry of Agriculture, Forestry and Fisheries.

Ministry of Internal Affairs and Communications (2019) *Chiiki Okoshi Kyoryoku tai nit-suite [On Regional Revitalization Cooperators]*. Retrieved June 12, 2020, from www.soumu.go.jp/main_content/000689418.pdf.

Miyata, S. (2010) *Shiawase nohaku: ajimu gurin turizumu monogatari [Happy Farm Stay: Ajimu Green Tourism]*. Fukuoka: Nishi Nihon Shimbun.

Nakatsuka, M. (2019) *Kyoten zukuri karano nosanson saisei [Regeneration of Rural Areas from the Creation of Bases]*. Tokyo: Tsukuba Publishing.

Nakaya, K. (1995) *Yufuin Gentofu [My Memories of Yufuin]*. Fukuoka: Kaichosha.

Numao, N. (2016) *Kokyosuru toshi to nousanson- tairyuugata syakai ga umareru- [Cities and Rural Districts: The Birth of Convection Society]*. Tokyo: Nosangyoson Bunka Kyokai.

Odagiri, T. (2014) *Nosanson wa syometsu shinai [The Mountain Village Never Disappear]*. Tokyo: Iwanami Publishing.

Ono, A. (2005) *Sanson kankyo syakaigaku josetsu: gendai sanson no genkai syurakuka to ryuiki kyodo kanri [Introduction to Environmental Sociology of Mountain Village: Marginalization of Contemporary Mountain Villages and Collective Management of Watershed Area]*. Tokyo: Nosangyoson Bunka Kyokai.

Sakurai, S. and Teraoka, S. (2018) Feasibility and Issues of Rural Tourism Based on Inter-Industry Cooperation. Poster session, in the *6th Conference of Asian Rural Sociological Association*. Makassar, Indonesia.

Sashide, K. (2016) *Bokura wa chiho de shiawase wo mitsukeru: Sotokoto ryu rokaru saiseiron [We Find Happiness in the Local Region (Sotokoto-Style Local Regeneration Theory)]*. Tokyo: Kirakusha.

Sato, M. (1990) *Rizoto retto [Resort Archipelago]*. Tokyo: Iwanami Publishing.

Sheller, M. and Urry, J. eds. (2004) *Tourism Mobility*. Oxford: Routledge.

Shibasaki, K. and Nakatsuka, M. (2017) Nosanson ni iju shita wakamono ga egaku sei-katuzo ni kansuru ichikosatsu: chiiki okoshi kyoryokutaiin wo jire to shite [A study of the life image drawn by a young man who moved to a rural area: in the case of community revitalized cooperative members]. *Noson keikaku gakkai shi [Journal of the Rural Planning Association]* 35: 253–258.

Shiomi, N. (2003) *Han no han X toiu ikikata [The Way of Life of Half Farming and Half X]*. Tokyo: Sony Magazines.

Tachikawa, M. (2005) Posuto seisansyugi eno iko to noson ni taisuru manazashi no hen-yo. In: Nihon sonraku kenkyu gakkai ed. *Shohi sareru noson: posuto seisansyugi ka no aratana noson mondai*. [Transition to post-productionism and the transformation of "gaze" to rural areas. In: The Japan Village Research Association ed. *Consumed Rural Area: New Agricultural Problems under Post-Productionism]*, 8–41. Tokyo: Nosangyoson Bunka Kyokai.

Takahashi, H. (2016) *Toshi to chiho wo kakimazeru [Stirring Cities and Local Regions]*. Tokyo: Kobunsha.

Tanaka, T. (2017) *Kankei jinko wo tsukuru: teiju demo koryu demo nai rokaru inobesyon [Creating Related Population: Local Innovation, Neither Settlement nor Exchange]*. Tokyo: Kirakusha.

Tanaka, T. and Odagiri, S. (2017) *Yosomono to tsukuru atarashii nosanson [A new Farming and Mountain Village to Be Made with the Outsider]*. Tokyo: Tsukuba Publishing.

Teraoka, S. (2017) Ryudoka suru cyusankan chiiki to nouson kanko kenkyu no igi [The significance of rural tourism studies focusing on mobility]. *Kankogaku hyoron [Tourism Review]* 5–1: 63–76.

Tokuno, S. (2008) Nosanson shinko ni okeru toshi noson koryu, gurin tsurizumu no genkai to kanosei: seisaku to jittai no hazama de. In Nihon sonraku kenkyu gakkai ed. *Gurin tsurizumu no shintenkai: noson saisei senryaku to shite no toshi noson koryu no kadai.* [Urban–rural interaction in the progress of rural areas, limits and possibilities of green tourism: between policies and actual conditions. In The Japanese Association for Rural Studies. ed. *New Development of Green Tourism: Urban/Rural as a Rural Regeneration Strategy Challenges for Exchange.*] Tokyo: Nosangyoson Bunka Kyokai: 43–93.

Tokuno, S. (2015) Jinko gensyo jidai no chiiki syakai moderu no kouchiku wo mezashite. In Tokuno, S., Makino. A. and Matsumoto, T. eds. *Kurashi no shiten kara no Chihou saisei: chiiki to seikatsu no syakaigaku* [Toward the construction of a regional society model in the age of population decline. In Tokuno, S., Makino, A. and Matsumoto, T. eds. *Regional Revitalization from the Viewpoint of Life: Sociology of Region and Life*]. Fukuoka: Kyushu University Press: 1–38.

Urry, J. (1990) *The Tourist Gaze: Leisure and Travel in Contemporary Societies.* London: Sage.

Yamashita, K. (2014) *Chiho syometsu no wana: Masuda repo-to to jinko gensyo syakai no syotai [The Destruction of Local Extinction: "Masuda Report" and the Realities of a Declining Population Society].* Tokyo: Chikuma Publishing.

Yamazaki, M., Oshima, J. and Oyama, Y. (1993) *Gurin tsurizumu [Green Tourism].* Tokyo: Ieno hikari Kyokai.

Chapter 6

The new mobile assemblages created by *Pokémon GO*

Koji Kanda

Introduction

Following its release in July 2016, the smartphone game application *Pokémon GO* quickly gained popularity around the world. While the rapid and continuing popularity of this smartphone game is partly a product of tapping into the wildly popular fictional world of *Pokémon*, the more intriguing factor behind its success is its novel conjoining of real and fictional worlds. *Pokémon GO* players must move through the real world in order to propel their on-screen mobility. For the *Pokémon GO* player, movement through the fictional world on their screen and the real world around them become intertwined into a new synthesis of fiction and reality. In this way, *Pokémon GO* creates not only new imaginative and symbolic worlds, but also new mobilities – new forms of being in, moving through and interacting with the world.

While *Pokémon GO* certainly represents a novel technological development, its intertwining of movement though real and fictional worlds is by no means entirely new. Humans have always lived in a world full of stories, and our movements through space are always intertwined with the stories we tell about places. With the development of modern communications, however, this combining of the real and fictional has become increasingly more porous and more densely intertwined. For example, as in the case of film tourism, fictional worlds depicted on-screen have spurred many visitors to travel to the sites where these films have been staged or filmed. In the case of tourism more generally, we find tourists move imaginatively and physically to sites that have been shaped through fictional images created in various forms of media. As John Urry (1990) has pointed out, tourism has long been shaped by such seemingly postmodern features as the "melting of boundaries" and "de-differentiation." Urry has therefore called for researchers to recognize the de-differentiation of representation and reality and the movement that melts the boundaries between fiction and reality as by no means an entirely novel phenomenon.

What is novel today, however, is the way in which new forms of movement spurred by the intertwining of real and fictional worlds are materializing in unprecedented ways through a new technological assemblage; namely, the conjoining of the GPS capacities of mobile smartphones with the techniques of augmented reality (AR) that allow users to add information to the real world. An early pioneer of this technological synthesis of GPS and AR was *Sekai Camera*, software launched in 2009 that allowed users to add informative "air tags" to real-world sites displayed on smartphone screens. Not surprisingly, this new technological assemblage was quickly adopted by several tourism promotion campaigns. At an event held in Atami City in 2010, this new technology was used to enable players of a popular "romance game" to take pictures of themselves together with fictional characters from the game who appeared on their screens at specific locations. Another key step in the conjoining of GPS and AR was the release of a game called *Ingress* in 2013 by Niantic Labs, an intra-venture company of Google. *Ingress* brought GPS and AR together via the platform of Google Maps to enable players to move simultaneously through real and fictional worlds, and thereby set the stage for the appearance of *Pokémon GO*. Building on this technological conjoining of GPS and AR, *Pokémon GO* was released in 2016 through a collaboration between The Pokémon Company and Niantic Inc.[1] While the game was developed on the platform of the *Ingress* game, *Pokémon GO* added to this technological assemblage the wildly popular content of the fictional world of *Pokémon*. The result was a hugely successful product that has led millions of people to experience how this new technological assemblage is further fusing together real and fictional worlds as well as the new forms of movement that are thereby created.

This chapter examines the new forms of movement created by this highly popular and influential smartphone game application. The next section lays out the theoretical framework of the chapter, illustrating how the mobile assemblage perspective provides a lens through which to understand the complex and dynamic mobilities created by *Pokémon GO*. In the third section this perspective is employed to examine the unique features of the mobilities of *Pokémon GO* players. Finally, the fourth section questions the relation between the game and society by looking at how the game spurs issues between players and place.

The mobile assemblage perspective

Movement is a fundamental feature of *Pokémon GO* and an important topic in the literature, as scholars have increasingly turned their attention to "mobilities." This turn to mobilities began in the 1990s and occurred in tandem with several related shifts in the social sciences and humanities, including turns from structure to event, from necessity to chance, from representation and symbols to materialities, bodies and performances and, finally, from static and fixed to dynamic and fluid. Through these series of shifts – and while continuing to rethink the binary forms of thinking that fix things by delineating firm boundaries – researchers have sought to bring a relational perspective to bear on the processes generating events and to use mobilities as a lens through which to grasp the complexities of reality. In this process, the mobilities perspective has attracted increased attention as an important lens for shedding light on key features of our increasingly global and complex society.

Perhaps the key thread within the disparate discussions of mobilities is the idea that movement is shaped by a complex hybrid of people and things. What these researchers, and particularly the pioneer of mobilities studies John Urry, have continued to stress is that our unique human capabilities are dependent on our interconnections with various non-human elements of the world. For example, in the case of movement by automobile, Urry (2000, 2007) has stressed that we should not focus on car or driver but instead on the unique hybrid "car-driver" through which automobilities are performed. Urry has called attention to several other forms of movement achieved through such hybrid combinations of people and things as "train-rider," "bicycle-rider" and "landscape-spectator." From this perspective, we begin to see that the forms of movement spurred by *Pokémon Go* are also shaped by such hybridity, namely by a relational conjoining of the human player with their smartphone, or what might be written in shorthand, following Urry, as the "smartphone-player" hybrid.

However, when focusing on the new mobilities spurred by *Pokémon GO*, it is critical that we give attention to the concept of assemblage as proposed by Tim Dant. According to Dant (2005), the term hybrid refers, strictly speaking, to "entities that result from permanently combining similar types of object," a problematic point which makes it desirable to instead use the term assemblage. The reason is that, for example in the case of the automobile, "the driver-car is an assemblage that comes apart when the driver leaves the vehicle and which can be endlessly re-formed, or re assembled given the availability of the component cars and drivers." Dant adds, in addition, that "the particular drivercar may be assembled from different components with consequent variations in ways of acting, and its modal form may vary over time and place" (p. 62). This point holds true too in the case of *Pokémon GO* where the relationship between smartphone and player is not fixed but equally variable and fluid. The critical point here is that rather than examining mobilities as occurring through unchanging and generic hybrid combinations, we must instead question the types of movement that are achieved through specific and continually reconstituted and evolving assemblages.

Another critical point we must consider is the key role of software to the new mobilities spurred by *Pokémon GO*. Using the technological capacities of the smartphone, this software projects a fictional world onto the smartphone screen that propels players to move through the real world. On this point, and in the case of automobilities, Mike Featherstone (2005) emphasizes that we should not think of "car-driver" as a simple assemblage, but instead focus on the role of software in regulating the relations of the "car-driver-software" assemblage. Turning our attention back to *Pokémon GO*, the software of this game projects a fictional world that also spurs the movements of the player. Accordingly, the mobilities spurred by *Pokémon GO* should be thought of as a "smartphone-player-*Pokémon GO*" assemblage and focus should be placed on the intermediating role of software. By focusing on software, it is possible to shed light on the dissolving of boundaries between fiction and reality that accompany the progress of science and technology and the unique features of the mobilities it brings into being.

The features of the "smartphone-player-*Pokémon GO*" mobile assemblage

To understand the "smartphone-player-*Pokémon GO*" assemblage, we need to first examine the mobilities this game encourages players to perform. As noted above, the fictional world – or, in the parlance of the game, Field Map – depicted by the software of *Pokémon GO* is a dense mixture of fiction and reality in which a fictional world inhabited by Pokémon is overlain onto Google Map's abstracted traces of the physical world. In this world, an array of Pokémon appear periodically, but these Pokémon do not move from the spots where they have appeared. Similarly, other key sites in the game – including the PokéStops where key items are acquired and the Gyms where Pokémon battle – are also fixed in space. Accordingly, for the player to move their on-screen Trainer to these sites, they must first move their own bodies – in tandem with their smartphone and its GPS data – towards these locations. Additionally, player movement is also encouraged by the fact that the appearance of the Eggs from which Pokémon are hatched is correlated to the actual distances covered by the player. In this way, *Pokémon GO* spurs mobilities that combine fiction and reality.

The mobilities of the player spurred towards these sites also have several unique features. One is the requirement that the player navigate on foot through the real world around them in order to propel their on-screen Trainer. This pedestrian-restricted player must drop their line of sight to their handheld smartphone while regularly swiping and tapping the screen to control other game actions. At times, however, players must also stay stationary for significant amounts of time, for example when attempting to capture Pokémon or when putting their Pokémon into battle at Gyms. In this way, *Pokémon GO* creates rather distinctive new rhythms of movement and forms of perambulation.

What is clear from the brief discussion above of the unique mobilities encouraged by *Pokémon GO* is that the intermixed world of reality and fiction depicted by the game's software plays a critical role in the mobility of the "smartphone-player-*Pokémon GO*" assemblage. In this assemblage, the software that depicts the fictional world dominates by spurring the player and their smartphone to perform certain forms of movement. Instead of referring to this as augmented reality, it might be preferable to refer to it as an augmented fiction wherein the fictional world extends into reality.

One response to this novel mobile assemblage has been to criticize the way in which the fictional world depicted by the software of *Pokémon GO* comes to control the physical bodies of its players. An excellent example of such criticism is found in "Control," a satirical painting by a Polish artist that has been widely posted on the internet (see Gigazine, 2016a). In this work, Pikachu, the main character of the game, sits on a saddle strapped on the neck of a *Pokémon GO* player who stares down servilely at the smartphone in his hand. The reins held by Pikachu are attached to a bit in the player's mouth, an artistic depiction clearly signifying that the movement of the player is controlled by the game. As touched on above, and as creatively suggested in this caricature, *Pokémon GO*'s control of players occurs through the appearance of Pokémon, the location of PokéStops and Gyms and the regular holding of events. Such control stems too from the visual angle at which the screen is viewed as well as from various sounds and vibrations that reach the player's senses via their smartphone. In addition, since the players of this game are synchronized with GPS and their movements are caused by the game system receiving signals about where their body is, their actions are also surveilled. It can be thusly stated then that the movements of the players are indeed, in some senses, dominated by *Pokémon GO*.

However, it is not the case that players are completely controlled by the game. For example, while the previously mentioned painting shows Pikachu in the saddle and the player looking down servilely at the smartphone in his hand, it would actually be quite difficult to play the game from this completely crouched-over position. The most important reason is that the world of *Pokémon GO* depicted on the screen does not depict features of the real world that potentially threaten the safety of the player, including people, cars, bicycles and other moving objects. More basically, the world on the screen is only a vague abstraction, a simple outline of buildings and other information that is presented from above in a bird's-eye view that differs from the perspective of the player. Accordingly, to navigate safely through the real world the player must not simply stare at their screen. They must instead actively gather spatial information from the real world around them and use their other senses to perform the appropriate forms of movement through space. For this reason, when the game is first launched, a notice appears requesting players to "Remember to be alert at all times. Stay aware of your surroundings." Since *Pokémon GO* is limited in its ability to capture the dynamic nature of the real world, it is also limited in its capacity to control the movement of its players.

When we consider the above points, it becomes clear that the relationship between the components of the "smartphone-player-*Pokémon GO*" assemblage is highly dynamic. To safely play the game it is impossible for the player to simply stare at their screen. They must release their eyes from the screen to take in spatial information about their surroundings. Thus, the player must move while intermittently changing their relationship with the game. In addition, it is not the case that players move only to play the game. The game is instead often played while performing other forms of movement such as travel and commuting, during which the player happens to be moving around and gaining the distance needed to hatch Eggs. In this way, the *Pokémon GO* player is also frequently and simultaneously a tourist, a commuter or a pedestrian, making the boundaries between these other social categories increasingly ambiguous.

Another point indicative of the limited power of the game to control the player is that players have created new forms of movement meant to directly deviate from the game's control. As described above, the game attempts to mandate that players physically walk their on-screen Trainer through its fictional world. However, in order to gain the travel distance necessary to hatch Eggs, players have attempted to use other forms of travel such as trains, buses, cars and bicycles to more easily cover the necessary ground.[2] Further, looking at articles and blogs on the internet reveals that there are players who do not move themselves but instead place their smartphones on other moving objects such as automatic moving train toys. These various mobile assemblages are also examples of the new forms of mobility spurred by *Pokémon GO*. The officially designed and sold "*Pokémon GO* Plus" device has also created another mobile assemblage. This device is connected wirelessly to a smartphone and it informs players of the presence of Pokémon and PokéStops via a blinking lamp and vibration, and allows Pokémon to be captured with the push of a button. In this way, both the mobilities and the components making up the assemblage are variable and dynamic.

In addition, when considering the dynamic components of this assemblage, attention must also be paid to the relationship between players. In *Pokémon GO*, the presence of other players has a great influence on the actions of a player. Trainers are divided into three teams and which team controls which Gyms is an important factor for player actions. In addition, as the *Pokémon GO* software has been intermittently modified and updated, the importance of other players has increased with each revision. In July 2017, a new system called Raid Battle was introduced in which Trainers were asked to cooperate to battle Pokémon. Later, in June 2018, a "Friend Function" was implemented that allowed Trainers to trade Pokémon and send Gifts to other Trainers. However, players are not able to communicate by messaging with other Trainers and the actual contact between players in the game is minimal. Under such circumstances, communication between players in the real world has come to play an important role in the fictional world of the game. Furthermore, the relationship between players also continues to change. In addition to the strengthening of pre-existing relations between people who already know one another, the game has given rise to other opportunities for communication between people who did not know one another, including software outside *Pokémon GO* such as PokeMatch[3] and events such as PokemonGOkon, a term that playfully references the Japanese phenomenon of match-making get-togethers.[4]

The mobile assemblage of the "*Pokémon Go*-player-place"

Another critical point to consider is the relationship between *Pokémon GO* and place. Essentially, *Pokémon GO* is a game in which Pokémon Trainers located in the fictional world and Pokémon players located in the real world move from place to place. Since the spaces of the real and fictional worlds are superimposed upon one another through GPS, in some specific sites unique features of the fictional world depicted by *Pokémon GO* become intertwined with unique socially created features of the real world. Accordingly, from the perspective of mobility and the melting of boundaries highlighted in this chapter, the relationship between the game and place warrants significant attention. Said differently, we must not only consider the "smartphone-player-*Pokémon GO*" mobile assemblage described above, but also the dynamic relations of the "smartphone-player-*Pokémon GO*-place" mobile assemblage. This section takes up that task by examining the forms of mobility that arise from the relations of player and place.

In the fictional world of *Pokémon GO*, two "places" are of particular importance: PokéStops where items can be acquired and Gyms where battles take place. These features are located at sites in the game where *Ingress* users have requested that "portals" be installed. *Ingress* encourages users to petition for portals at places where important episodes have occurred or at places with historical or educational value or other outstanding features, but also asks users to refrain from submitting applications for places where pedestrian safety cannot be secured or where there may be interference with the operations of fire departments, police departments and hospitals, etc. (Ingress, 2019). Where a portal has been installed, its on-screen location in *Pokémon GO* is represented by an icon containing a photo of the real-world site, and some sites also have a brief written description of certain characteristics of the place. In this way, the locations of PokéStops and Gyms in the fictional world are closely intertwined with features of the actual place. Accordingly, these sites are located in heterogeneous space and are particularly unevenly distributed in urban areas.

Through this process of fixing portals in fictional space, the real-world places on which PokéStops and Gyms have been superimposed are re-valued, becoming highly attractive sites for *Pokémon GO* players. This is particularly true for places where multiple PokéStops or Gyms have been installed or at sites where rare Pokémon frequently appear. The probability of catching certain Pokémon varies from place to place and sites where large numbers of Pokémon appear are known as "*Pokémon GO* Nests," while sites where rare Pokémon appear are known as sacred sites for *Pokémon GO* players. It perhaps goes without saying that both types of sites are magnets for *Pokémon GO* players. As the boundaries between the physical reality of a site and its virtual representation become further dissolved in this manner, the lure of the fictional becomes an amenity of real places. For many *Pokémon GO* players, the meaning of places in the fictional world comes to the fore while their meaning in the real-world retreats to the background. Under such circumstances, efforts are being made to use these new place values to attract visitors. For example, private companies such as McDonald's are becoming sponsors of the game in order to have PokéStops and Gyms established in their stores, thereby using *Pokémon GO* to attract customers (see GameWith, 2019).

Potential conflict with places and their values comes, however, because of the new values and the unique mobilities of *Pokémon GO* players. With their consciousness mainly focused on the world of *Pokémon GO* on their smartphones, there is a tendency for their perception of the social meaning given to real places, the perception of others in it, as well as the affordances from the surrounding environment to become weakened. For that reason, players of the game become out of step with existing rhythms of the real world, crossing boundaries and deviating from conventional ways of being in a certain place. From various articles on the web we can see that residents and caretakers of certain places often see *Pokémon GO* players as people who are out of place. We also find frequent reports of movements and acts that are unnatural, risks of collision, recollections of crimes such as voyeurism, entrance into inappropriate sites and deviations from actions that are deemed appropriate at certain sites. As mentioned above, *Pokémon GO* players have unique mobilities – such as keeping their eyes trained downward on their smartphone screens, repeatedly tapping the screen with their fingers and repeatedly moving and stopping their bodies in response to events in the fictional world.

The result is that *Pokémon GO* players often become out-of-place visitors. Indeed, amidst the booming popularity of this game, what has drawn the greatest amount of social attention are the real-world issues created by the expansion of the game's fictional world. Such issues manifest in areas where *Pokémon GO* players tend to congregate in great numbers, including PokéStops and Gyms and especially at "*Pokémon GO* Nests" and sacred sites for *Pokémon GO*. At many of these sites, repeated calls have been made for *Pokémon GO* users to attend with greater caution to their surroundings and to observe basic social manners. In some areas, for example at the famous Izumo Shrine, playing of the game has been forbidden altogether (see JCast News, 2016). Also, in areas where problems have been repeatedly reported, PokéStops have been removed based on petitions from members of the public (see Pokémon GO, 2019).

Another important point to consider regarding so-called *Pokémon GO* Nests and sacred sites is that the location of these sites is frequently changed. An early conflict over one of these sites – a park in Tokyo's Setagaya Ward – shows their nomadic nature. Following the launch of *Pokémon GO* in Japan on July 22, 2016, players discovered that a rare Pokémon called "Mini Ryu (Dratini)" could be readily captured at a sacred site in a park in Tokyo's western Setagaya Ward (see Webmemo.biz, 2016). As players began to increasingly congregate there in growing numbers, park managers and users began to call critical attention to the growing amount of trash and litter in the park. In response, the local government posted notices regarding litter and trash in the park while also petitioning the game's distributor to somehow remedy the situation (see Livedoor News, 2016). In response to this petition, on July 30, the Mini Ryu Nest was replaced by a different and less rare Pokémon Nest (see Blog.esuteru.com, 2016), and the park subsequently returned to its former status (see Pokémon GO-soku, 2016). As can be seen from this symbolic case, sites where many players gather are not fixed in space but are instead temporary and mobile.

The features of the game highlighted above stand out prominently in tourism promotion campaigns that have attempted to use *Pokémon GO* to attract visitors. One example comes from a *Pokémon GO*-themed tourism campaign at the sand dunes of Tottori Prefecture, a well-known tourist site in the region. The governor of the prefecture developed a plan to attract *Pokémon GO* players and the "Tottori Sand Dunes Smartphone Game Free Zone Declaration" was unveiled on July 25, 2016. Since this area had previously been popular with *Ingress* users, many PokéStops and Gyms were concentrated here. In addition, since the game had been responsible for causing many issues in densely populated areas, officials believed that the vast space of the dunes would provide an ideal location to avoid such problems and maintain the safety of players and other tourists. Initially, however, the campaign failed to attract larger numbers of tourists because of the absence of any rare Pokémon Nests at the site. In response, Tottori Prefecture worked in collaboration with the Pokémon and Niantic corporations to host an event called "*Pokémon GO* Safari Zone in Tottori Sand Dune" for three days in November 2017. While this event succeeded in attracting larger numbers of tourists by providing rare Pokémon (Figure 6.1; also see ToriNet, 2017), it also created several issues. On the first day of the event more than five times the usual number of visitors came to the dunes, creating very large traffic jams and leading to widespread illegal parking. In response, on the following day, the prefectural government expanded the area of the event beyond the dunes. Subsequently, there was a series of reports to the government and police regarding such issues as increased numbers of people walking in nearby urban areas while staring at their smartphones, littering and stopping on train tracks (see Sanspo, 2017).

Figure 6.1 *Pokémon GO* players at the "*Pokémon GO* Safari Zone in Tottori Sand Dune" event.

Source: photo by the author, November 25, 2017.

The above examples illustrate the possibility as well as the difficulty of utilizing *Pokémon GO* for tourism promotion. On one hand, since *Pokémon GO* players are attracted to certain places by features found in the fictional world of the game, it is very much possible to attempt to control their movements to thereby promote tourism. However, since this requires fascinating features such as the appearance of rare Pokémon to gather large numbers of players, the campaigns are not sustainable and excessive congregation can lead to other perplexing issues.

Conclusion

This chapter has examined how new technologies and relations between real and fictional worlds in the *Pokémon GO* game have materialized in new mobilities. Using the mobile assemblage perspective, the chapter has highlighted the dissolving of boundaries and the dynamic characteristics of these mobilities. We have seen that the new mobilities created by *Pokémon GO* remain fluid and have not become fixed in any specific way. Indeed, and as noted in the chapter, it can be expected that software updates and modifications of the game will continue to reshape the mobilities of *Pokémon GO* players. Likewise, the relationship between the game and society will also continue to evolve. For example, in response to issues brought about by the game – such as the issues of overcrowding and public disturbance at the event held at the Tottori Sand Dunes discussed above – a *Pokémon GO* event held in Yokosuka City in 2018 limited the number of participants to attempt to avoid any public disturbances. While it is of course difficult to prevent all disturbances with a game that turns on pedestrians looking at their smartphone screens, efforts are being made to bring the game and its players into less conflict with their surroundings by considering the specific mobilities encouraged by *Pokémon GO*.

In the coming years, we should expect that new advances in science and technology will repeatedly transform the mobilities not only of *Pokémon GO* players but all members and facets of society. To understand our changing world, it will be imperative to observe and constantly re-examine these new mobilities.

Supplementary note

This chapter is a revised and shortened version of a paper in *Memoirs of Institute of Humanities, Human and Social Sciences, Ritsumeikan University*, 119 (2019): 119–147, and was supported by JSPS KAKENHI Grant Number 17H02251.

Notes

1 Niantic Inc. is a company established when Niantic Labs became independent from Google in 2015.
2 Many similar articles can be found on the internet. For an example pertaining to bicycles see, for example, Frame (2016). However, for such movements by car and bicycle in particular, because of the speed, type of operation and importance of cognition of

the surrounding environment, such movements have brought great risk to players and nearby people and things. For that reason, the software places a limit on speed to control the type of movement. See also Sumaho Support Line (2018).

3 For further information on PokeMatch see Gigazine (2016b).

4 For further information on PokemonGoKon see B2B Platform (2016).

References

B2B Platform. (2016) https://b2b-ch.infomart.co.jp/news/detail.page?IMNEWS4=297790 [Retrieved on July 31, 2019].

Blog.esuteru.com. (2016) http://blog.esuteru.com/archives/8645332.html [Retrieved on July 31, 2019].

Dant, T. (2005) The Driver-car. In Featherstone, M., Thrift, N., and Urry, J. (eds.), *Automobilities*, SAGE Publications Ltd, pp. 61–79.

Featherstone, M. (2005) Introduction. In Featherstone, M., Thrift, N., and Urry, J. (eds.), *Automobilities*, SAGE Publications Ltd, pp. 1–24.

Frame. (2016) https://jitensha-hoken.jp/blog/2016/08/pokemon-go [Retrieved on July 31, 2019].

GameWith. (2019) https://pokemongo.gamewith.jp/article/show/47212 [Retrieved on July 31, 2019].

Gigazine. (2016a) http://gigazine.net/news/20160809-dark-political-cartoons-pawel-kuczynski [Retrieved on July 31, 2019].

Gigazine. (2016b) http://gigazine.net/news/20160726-pokematch [Retrieved on July 31, 2019].

Ingress. (2019) https://ingress.com/support [Retrieved on July 31, 2019].

JCast News. (2016) www.j-cast.com/2016/07/22273299.html?p=all [Retrieved on July 31, 2019].

Livedoor News. (2016) http://news.livedoor.com/article/detail/11824339 [Retrieved on July 31, 2019].

Pokémon GO. (2019) www.pokemongolive.com/report-location [Retrieved on July 31, 2019].

Pokémon GO-soku. (2016) http://pokemongo-soku.com/news/post-5217 [Retrieved on July 31, 2019].

Sanspo. (2017) www.sanspo.com/geino/news/20171127/sot17112705030001-n3.html [Retrieved on July 31, 2019].

Sumaho Support Line. (2018) https://sumahosupportline.com/pokemongo-speed-limit [Retrieved on July 31, 2019].

ToriNet. (2017) www.pref.tottori.lg.jp/safarizoneintottorisanddunes [Retrieved on July 31, 2019].

Urry, J. (1990) *The Tourist Gaze: Leisure and Travel in Contemporary Societies*, SAGE Publications Ltd.

Urry, J. (2000) *Sociology beyond Societies: Mobilities for the Twenty-First Century*, Routledge.

Urry, J. (2007) *Mobilities*, Polity Press.

Webmemo.biz. (2016) http://webmemo.biz/pokemongo-setagaya-park-miniryu [Retrieved on July 31, 2019].

Chapter 7

The roots and routes of Matryoshka

Souvenirs and tourist mobility in Russia, Japan, and the world

Ryotaro Suzuki

Introduction: Russian Matryoshki in Japan

Facing the Sea of Japan, Niigata City is a Japanese trade base with Russia. A souvenir shop at Niigata Station sells Matryoshka dolls, which are a type of Russian folk craft.[1] More specifically, the shop sells Russian-imported Matryoshka dolls featuring paintings of girls wearing scarfs or Kenshin Uesugi, a 14th-century warlord and hero of Niigata. Store shelves are also lined with keychains and brooches with Matryoshka motifs and local Japanese sake and snacks. The shop clerks say that many tourists purchase these products as souvenirs of their visit to Niigata.

The typical Japanese port town of Kobe also contains shops that sell Matryoshki. The Kitano District, which once hosted Russians and other Western residents, has become an exotic tourist destination because of the rows of Western houses that line the streets. Matryoshki are available in several local shops, and many Japanese tourists purchase these as souvenirs of their visit to Kobe. Matryoshka dolls have thus become souvenir items in Niigata and Kobe because of both their Russian roots and human mobility.

This chapter examines the relationship between human mobility and the objects, discussing a case of Russian folk crafts, such as Matryoshka dolls that are sold as souvenirs in many tourist spots in Japan. Many studies have already examined tourism souvenirs. However, most have merely associated these objects with specific locations, thereby focusing on changes in the state of the objects because of their association with tourism. In contrast, this multi-sited ethnography positions souvenirs as objects that exist within the process of human mobility and tourism. Here, this process is depicted based on which souvenirs are generated and transformed within this mobility.[2]

Niigata and Kobe are not the only locations in which Matryoshki are sold in Japan. Other destinations also sell Russian folk craft as souvenirs, including Matryoshka dolls. For example, some Okinawan shops sell Matryoshki adorned with native costumes. Some dolls in Nara likewise feature depictions of the Great Buddha, while many in Kagoshima feature images of the local hero Saigō Takamori. In Chinatown of Yokohama, shops sell Matryoshka dolls featuring panda prints. These dolls became souvenirs by featuring depictions of regional symbols and heroes.

At the Naruko Hot Spring in Miyagi Prefecture, which is known as the home of Kokeshi dolls that represent the Tohoku area, many shops sell Matryoshki that feature images of Kokeshi. This wooden doll, named "Koke-shka," was created in 2010 and was based on an idea proposed by Numata Genki, a photographer and Kokeshi/Matryoshka researcher. "Koke-shka" was derived from exchanges between Russians and the Miyagi Prefecture (Numata, 2010).

Matryoshka dolls have also become souvenirs for inbound tourists visiting Japan. For example, the Nakamise Shopping Street in Asakusa, which is a famous Tokyo tourist site, contains rows of numerous souvenir shops that sell an abundance of souvenir gifts. Some of these stores sell Matryoshka dolls featuring depictions of ninjas and girls wearing traditional Japanese kimonos, but which are made in China (Figure 7.1). Interviews conducted during this research revealed that some tourists purchase these dolls as souvenirs of their visit to Japan. Similar Matryoshki are notably sold in souvenir shops at New Tokyo International Airport (Narita Airport).

Matryoshki available in Japan are made in a variety of countries and regions. Some are imported from Russia, but others come from China, and some unfinished dolls are painted in Japan after they have been imported. Needless to say,

Figure 7.1 Matryoshki depicted as ninjas and kimono-wearing girls in Asakusa with Kokeshi.

Source: photo by the author, March 10, 2019.

this does not mean that Matryoshka dolls are available at all Japanese destinations; even when sold, they may not be popular items. However, Matryoshki are typically sold as "souvenirs of the place" at many Japanese destinations. Furthermore, several Japanese stores specialize in general Russian goods. In these locations, Matryoshki are sold as interior decorations. Nevertheless, the above examples indicate that tourists purchase these dolls as souvenirs at destinations, especially those featuring regional symbols that are inscribed for that purpose.

Matryoshki found at Japanese tourist sites may initially seem strange. However, the relationship between Japanese tourist sites and Russian folk crafts began long before this century. Indeed, the wooden nested *Shichifukujin* dolls (i.e. the Seven Japanese Deities of Good Fortune) were sold during the late 19th century as souvenirs in Hakone, a hot spring tourist site on the outskirts of Tokyo. These were believed to be the roots of Matryoshka dolls. That is, Matryoshka dolls at Japanese destinations returned to their place of origin after 100 years, traversing the vast physical distance between Japan and Russia in the process.

Souvenirs on the move

Souvenirs are indispensable to the tourism industry. Several studies have been conducted in this regard, with many having considered souvenirs in terms of the movement of objects that accompanies tourism. One such study of tourist art positioned handcrafted items produced for tourists as an opening for discussing the cultural transformations caused by tourism (Graburn, 1976, 1983; Cohen, 1993). This field has recently seen a wide range of studies on souvenirs, especially those focusing on authenticity and consumer behaviour, thereby reflecting on the expansion of tourism or the development of material culture studies (Hitchcock & Teague, 2000; Timothy, 2005; Wilkins, 2011; Swonson & Timothy, 2012; Cave, Jolliffe, & Baum, 2013; Hume, 2014; Trinh, Ryan, & Cave, 2014; Torabian & Arai, 2016).

However, these studies have not sufficiently examined how souvenirs are objects created to move, or, to put it more simply, that souvenirs are "objects on the move." That is, they have not sufficiently discussed souvenirs within the entirety of such movements. When objects are perceived as immobile, objects that move as tourist souvenirs are positioned as part of an existence that transforms and deviates from its original state. Some studies have incorporated this transformational process as a reconstruction of culture and a construction or negotiation process involving ethnic identity rather than simply criticizing the movement of souvenirs. However, there is a widespread belief that tourism souvenirs are inferior to their original counterparts, or, more bluntly, they are "fake" items.

Recent social theories have primarily considered and compared these perspectives by focusing on movements, including those related to tourism; this has great implications (Sheller & Urry, 2004; Urry, 2000, 2007; Elliott & Urry, 2010). When a souvenir is perceived as something that moves as opposed to something that is fixed in one location, its meanings and values are constantly transformed by that movement because the object travels around the world through the movements of capital, technology, information, images, and even the human body (Urry, 2007). Furthermore, the movements of these objects are also components that construct contemporary social life (Elliott & Urry, 2010). In other words, according to Lury who presented an argument about the relationship between tourist mobility and objects, objects known as souvenirs are not given meaning by their relationship to a single specific location, whether that is the original location or the eventual destination. Instead, these objects acquire meaning by connecting with new objects and symbolic factors during movement, all while taking part in global consumerism (Lury, 1997, p. 83).

That being said, this perspective is by no means new. Appadurai and Miller discussed the commercialization of objects through movement that extends to a specific society while considering consumer society by critically examining material cultural study using traditional anthropology (Appadurai, 1986; Miller, 1987). However, their discussion should not be read as a text that simply connects objects in a local social and cultural context, but instead one that suggests the possibility of questioning the transformation of meanings and values that such objects bring to different social contexts in addition to the state in which the objects are distributed and utilized as they surpass their original times and places. In other words, Appadurai described a global cultural flow that expands various dimensions (Appadurai, 1996). This enables one to perceive souvenirs as nodal points of global movements and flow. Thus, Clifford's discussion of the relationship between more widespread travel and culture abundantly implies the movement of souvenir objects. He insists that residence surpasses travel and criticizes the perspective that puts "roots" ahead of "routes" in every circumstance. Rather than perceiving the practice of displacement as simply a relocation or expansion of movement, Clifford perceives displacement as the construction of diverse cultural significance (Clifford, 1997, p. 12). Expanding on these discussions, we must also consider souvenirs within a series of movement routes instead of solely conceptualizing them in contrast to their original locations, or, in other words, their roots.

As such, when Matryoshka dolls are discussed in this chapter, neither the locations of their roots nor their originals are considered as primary foci. Rather, this study traces the routes by which a wooden nesting doll, the origin of which is considered to be Hakone, Japan, became a folk craft that represents Russia until returning to Japanese tourist sites. Throughout this process, this project examined the various types of movements that have been ignored in previous souvenir studies.

The first type of movement occurs when the object that will become a tourist souvenir is brought from outside its destination and becomes localized. Tracing the historical details of tourist souvenirs reveals that a large number have been brought into a variety of areas through such movements rather than being native to the region in which they are sold. The second type of movement occurs during the production of the tourist souvenir. Souvenirs are exceptional throughout the production process, whether they are produced, distributed, or consumed at tourist sites. From the raw ingredients to the finished product, they are not typically completed in one specific region. Rather, they are more often made from raw materials and products produced in other locations before being transferred to the destinations in which they are sold. The third type of movement occurs when tourists purchase souvenirs as gifts for relatives, friends, or acquaintances. Some souvenirs continue to migrate within the purchaser's hometown once they have been given to someone else.

To include the movements listed here within a holistic view of tourist objects, souvenirs must be examined not only as items bound to specific locations but also as objects on the move. Subsequently, this chapter explores the roots and routes of Matryoshka dolls as souvenirs.

The roots and development of Matryoshki

As a folk craft, Matryoshka dolls are quite representative of Russia. Matryoshki of diverse designs are sold at Russian tourist sites, including classic dolls featuring girls wearing scarves and those designed to portray former Soviet and Russian leaders, football players, and Disney characters.

The first Russian Matryoshka dolls are said to have been created during the early 1890s by the craftsman Zvezdochkin and the painter Malyutin (Sokolova, 2011; Gorozhanina, 2012). These artists produced dolls with the support of the Mamontov family, which made a fortune in the railway business. The Mamontovs had a deep appreciation for arts and education, while the married couple Anatoly and Maria produced toys for children by establishing a "Kids' Education Workshop" factory. Anatoly's younger brother Savva built a commune in Abramtsevo, on the outskirts of Moscow, and this institution patronized the creative activities of artists. Matryoshka dolls are said to have originated from this patronage.

So, why did Zvezdochkin and Malyutin create wooden nesting dolls depicting girls as educational toys? The most likely story is that the wooden nesting *shichifukujin* dolls that were created in Hakone, Japan inspired Matryoshka dolls (Sokolova, 2011; Gorozhanina, 2012). The Mamontovs collected folk crafts from around the world, with some parts of that collection still intact. Among the contained items were the *shichifukujin* wooden nesting dolls produced in Japan, which are known as *Fukuruma*. The nested *shichifukujin* was an object from which the seven deities successively emerged from *Fukurokuju* (the god of happiness, wealth, and longevity). The dolls were produced in the *Kokeshi* area of Hakone and Tohoku, Japan during the 19th century.

The traditional drawings featured on Matryoshka dolls depict women wearing scarves as designed by Malyutin. However, the idea of drawing on wooden nesting dolls is considered to be based on the *Fukuruma*; that is, the Hakone *Shichifukujin* dolls. Parts of the Mamontov collection are stored in the Sergievsky Posad Toy Museum (Figure 7.2). Here, the *Fukuruma*, which were the inspiration for creating Matryoshka dolls, is indeed present; curators agree that Matryoshki most likely originated in Hakone.

Some Russian-based television programmes have also presented the roots of Matryoshki based on this story. Matryoshki bestowed to Hakone by the television

Figure 7.2 Fukuruma Exhibition at the Sergievsky Posad Toy Museum.

Source: photo by the author, August 30, 2013.

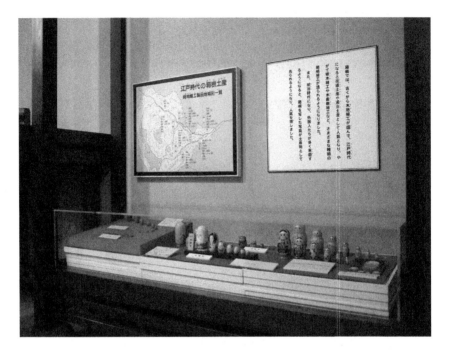

Figure 7.3 Exhibition at the Hakone Museum of History and Folklore.

Source: photo by the author, February 12, 2015.

research crew who visited Hakone during one such production are presented at the Hakone Museum of History and Folklore alongside *Shichifukujin* dolls (Figure 7.3). This story was introduced into Japan during the 1970s, and records from that time indicate that travellers to the region heard similar stories in Moscow or had seen the *Fukuruma* at the Sergievsky Posad Toy Museum (Ogawa, 1979; Ominami, 1982).

This raises some important questions. Why was the first *Shichifukujin* nesting doll created in Hakone? How did it then travel across the seas before ending up in the Mamontov collection? The answers can be found in a study by Iwasaki that details the history of Hakone's wooden crafts (Iwasaki, 1988). Hakone has been a prominent producer of wooden products since the 15th century. From the 17th century onward, these wooden products were sold as souvenirs to travellers on the road connecting Tokyo (formerly Edo) and Kyoto, and nesting *Shichifukujin* dolls were among these souvenirs.

Why were wooden products from Hakone carried to Russia? A Hakone summer residency of the Orthodox Church in Japan was built in Hakone in 1880, and this provides us with a clue. Hakone was developed during the late 19th century as a summer resort for Western visitors to Japan. The Orthodox Church in Japan, which descended from the Russian Orthodox Church, constructed a summer residence in Hakone, where many Russians visited. While the facility was constructed in 1880, the first Matryoshka dolls can be dated to the early 1890s. Thus, the timing coincides. As such, the idea that nesting *Shichifukujin* dolls were brought to Russia by Russians who visited Hakone and gifted the dolls to the Mamontovs is by no means implausible.

Matryoshki created in Russia during the 19th century eventually achieved international fame as a prominent form of Russian folk craft. The direct impetus for this representation was the Paris Exposition, which was held in 1900. Matryoshki exhibited there won the bronze medal in the educational toy section, instantly garnering worldwide fame. Thereafter, a large volume of orders from France and Germany were sent to Russia. Wooden products, such as monasterial religious objects and pilgrimage souvenirs, were already being created in Sergievsky Posad at that time. As it was close to the Mamontovs' artist commune Abramtsevo, the city also began to mass-produce the dolls (Gorozhanina, 2012).

Matryoshki became a widespread and indispensable toy for girls living in the USSR until the 1970s. Production areas thus emerged across Russia (primarily in western Russia), with a unique format being established in each region. Nevertheless, some have argued that Matryoshka dolls were also produced in Germany and other European countries at an earlier time. This particularly includes the post-World War II Eastern European region (Gorozhanina, 2012). However, the popularity of Matryoshka dolls began to decline during the 1970s because of the circulation of cheap plastic toys.

However, the circumstances surrounding Matryoshka dolls greatly changed during the 1990s. Western tourists began visiting Russia after the USSR collapsed at the end of the Cold War. Matryoshki sales thus increased because of their popularity as tourist souvenirs. There were also many interactions among the so-called Eastern Bloc countries during the Cold War. Matryoshka dolls were therefore taken abroad as souvenirs in this context. However, there was a limited overall number of these dolls. On the other hand, the number of tourists to Russia continuously increased beginning in the mid-1990s, thereby increasing the demand for souvenir Matryoshka dolls. Doll designs also evolved to include leaders and athletes, as mentioned previously. What was once a simple doll for girls began to acquire a new status as a tourist souvenir.

Matryoshki are presently sold as souvenirs around the world, primarily in former Eastern Bloc countries and socialist nations. For example, Matryoshka dolls were distributed primarily in the northern region of Vietnam during the population interactions that took place during the Cold War, while Matryoshka dolls featuring traditional Vietnamese lacquer and ceramic arts are presently sold in Vietnam. Low-cost Matryoshka dolls are also mass-produced in China. These are distributed throughout the entire Southeast Asian region, including Vietnam. In addition, Matryoshka dolls manufactured in India and China are available as souvenirs in Malaysia. This reflects the multi-ethnic makeup of the nation. Furthermore, Matryoshka dolls in Japan can be seen as part of this trend.[3]

It is crucial to reiterate that the transformation of Matryoshka dolls into tourist souvenirs during the 1990s was not the result of commoditization by tourism to Russian folk craft and traditional culture; the dolls were originally consumer products, entering the commercial sphere because of international tourism. These Matryoshka dolls and the *Shichifukujin* dolls that served as their roots thus became commercial products. They were then turned into iconic representations of the Russian nation at the World Exposition, a product trade fair in modern consumer society.

Travelling Matryoshki: nesting doll routes

It is important to note again the historical context of the birth of the Matryoshka doll, a representative Russian folk craft that spread throughout the world. At first, the wooden crafts were developed in Hakone, Japan, and they were popular among 17th-century travellers. Then the nesting *Shichifukujin* dolls of the 19th century were taken abroad by Russian visitors. *Shichifukujin* dolls were eventually added to the Mamontov collection of international toys, thus inspiring the first Matryoshka dolls.

Matryoshka dolls exhibited at the Paris Exposition were mass-produced. This was necessary because the dolls had achieved worldwide recognition. In the Soviet era, these dolls were not only circulated as domestic toys for girls but also popular souvenirs in Eastern Bloc countries, including Vietnam. Furthermore, a wide variety of Matryoshka dolls were sold as souvenirs to tourists visiting Russia from Western Europe after the end of the Cold War, while some Matryoshka dolls were produced in China and sold as souvenirs in Southeast Asia. At Japanese destinations, regionally designed Matryoshki became souvenirs for foreign tourists, and some Matryoshki represented Japan's connection with Russia.

As "wooden nesting dolls," it is possible to trace the history of Matryoshki to Hakone, Japan. However, the roots of Matryoshka dolls as items of Russian folk craft featuring the traditional drawings of girls are strictly limited to those created by Zvezdochkin and Malyutin. To quote Gorozhanina,

> It is possible that the Japanese Machine-tooled figurine *Shichifukujin* influenced the concept of the first Matryoshka, but its realization was carried out on the basis of the traditional folk craft and was the result of the collective work of professional painters, handicraftsman and organizers of the craft industry.
>
> (Gorozhanina, 2012, p. 7)

However, examination of the subject based on this line of thinking means that the same could be said of Matryoshki in Japan and throughout the rest of the world. These dolls acquire significance specific to the area in which they are made through a link formed by local craft workers and traditions. Koke-shka, which are made in the same region of Japan that produces Kokeshi, is a prime example of this phenomenon. Where did the craftsmanship necessary for creating the nesting dolls originate? Even if the *Shichifukujin* dolls themselves originated in Hakone, the art of creating nesting dolls did not originate in Japan. Rather, many think that it migrated from China during the Heian era (794–1185). China, from which many mass-produced items are distributed to places such as Asakusa, Vietnam, and Malaysia, is thus the ultimate origin of the first Matryoshka. There are also instances in which Matryoshka dolls have become souvenirs because of the historical routes of people and objects. This can be seen among Matryoshki found on the routes in Niigata, Kobe, Vietnam, and others that persist.

If we consider souvenirs as objects on the move, it becomes irrelevant to trace them from their "roots" to their "routes." That is, the significance of authentic Matryoshki becomes irrelevant. Wooden nesting dolls are circulated throughout the world in a series of movements created by people and objects, including those related to tourism. From the modern era onward, they are thus connected with the pre-existing craftsmanship, images, and symbols of various tourist destinations. It is crucial to consider the history of wooden nesting dolls according to various eras and regions. In other words, their cultural biography (Kopytoff, 1986) begins with the development of Japanese roads during the 17th century, continues into the formation of modern nation-states during the 19th century, extends beyond the fall of the Russian empire and the World Exposition during the early 20th century, and finally persists through the end of the Cold War.

Conclusion

This chapter examined various passageways that have not been sufficiently examined in previous tourism souvenir studies through an investigation of the Russian Matryoshka doll folk craft. Throughout the chapter, we attempted to trace the series of linked movements and routes travelled by the people, objects, and craftsmanship related to souvenirs rather than pursuing the roots of such items. Thus, we did not simply discuss Matryoshki by focusing on changes resulting from tourism or by contrasting the traditional authentic state of the objects with their existence as commercial products that travel with tourists. Travelling Matryoshki are produced through craftsmanship and resources. They move from the production area to the sales areas to become tourist souvenirs. After waiting at shops for encounters with tourists who will purchase them, these souvenir products then move to their homes. Souvenirs of this type may also experience further movement as gifts, as can be seen through the *Shichifukujin* dolls that were added to the Mamontov collection after travelling from Hakone. The flow of people, objects, information, and images along these movement routes that had not been considered in previous studies can also be supported by several coincidental connections.

Rather than viewing a souvenir as an object bound to a specific place or solely connected to a specific mode of movement (e.g. tourism), considering such items through the context of the different modes of transportation that construct this phenomenon reveals all the types of Matryoshka dolls discussed in this chapter; they indeed exist as functions of these movements. Souvenirs can be perceived as items created by mobility instead of resulting from changes made to an extant object in a fixed location through external factors, such as tourism. Just as souvenirs mark the memory of the tourist's travel experience at the tourist site, these souvenirs also contain the memories of the paths through which the objects themselves moved.

During such movements, nesting dolls travel with tourists, thereby becoming linked with new symbols, images, and craftsmanship at their eventual destinations. In this sense, nesting dolls fit the logic of tourist mobility just like the souvenirs, such as t-shirts, keychains, and refrigerator magnets depicting characteristic symbols or inscriptions relevant to the destination, which clatter at tourist sites around the world. If there is no significance in questioning the roots of a keychain, then what is the significance of questioning the roots of a nesting doll? Rather, the souvenirs at tourist sites exist at the nodal point of the flows of people, objects, and images that surround tourists and souvenirs. It is difficult to pinpoint the beginnings and ends of this process, as many objects are caught in the movements on the routes created by such flows. Furthermore, the meaning of souvenirs is constantly reconstructed because of their travel. The series of linked movements that souvenirs experience is a process by which authenticity and locality fluctuate. For this reason, one limitation in a discussion of the authenticity and locality of an object makes it necessary to extrapolate its segments. Paradoxically, this suggests that souvenirs can become nodal points in a flow because they are replaceable objects on the move.

Souvenir shops are places in which a wide variety of objects are constructed in a format that fits the movement mode of tourism. They are accumulated after moving through a complex and wide distribution network. The expansive tourist mobility of people incites the widespread demand for souvenirs that accompany such movements. This demand gathers various objects that were produced in faraway areas. During this process, souvenirs are given the form of commercial products by being inscribed with images and objects symbolic of the destination. Souvenir studies must thus examine souvenirs as they are related to a network of movement that includes a wide range of people and objects as opposed to viewing them as objects that only accompany the movements of tourists.

Notes

1 The Japanese word that generally corresponds to the English term "souvenir" is "*omiyage.*" However, there is a difference. While the main connotation of souvenir is merely that of a travel memento, *omiyage* implies strong overtones of gifts that are handed out to family, acquaintances, and friends after travelling. In other words, they are "souvenirs as gifts." Previous anthropological studies have examined *omiyage* in relation to the custom of gift-giving in Japan (Graburn, 1983; Hendry, 1993; Oedewald, 2009).
2 This chapter is based on a study I have been conducting since 2007. I also considered research areas outside of Japan, including Vietnamese locations such as Hanoi, Ho Chi

Minh City, Da Nang, and Nha Trang and other locations such as Moscow, Kuala Lumpur, Hong Kong, and Macao. Japanese research areas included Asakusa, Hakone, Okinawa, Naruko Hot Springs, Nara, Kobe, Niigata, and others. Research was conducted at these sites by combining different approaches, including interviews with sellers, retailers, wholesalers, tourists, tour guides, museum employees, and other related parties as well as observations of production/sales processes and comprehensive research on souvenir shops.

3 For more information about Matryoshka dolls in Southeast Asia (including Vietnam), see Suzuki (2016, 2017).

References

Appadurai, A. (1986). Introduction: Commodities and the Politics of Value. In A. Appadurai (ed.), *The Social Life of Things: Commodities in Cultural Perspective* (pp. 3–63). Cambridge: Cambridge University Press.

Appadurai, A. (1996). *Modernity at Large: Cultural Dimensions of Globalization.* Minneapolis, MN: University of Minnesota Press.

Cave, J., Jolliffe, L. & Baum, T. (eds.). (2013). *Tourism and Souvenirs: Global Perspectives from the Margins.* Bristol: Channel View.

Clifford, J. (1997). *Routes: Travel and Translation in the Late Twentieth Century.* Cambridge, MA: Harvard University Press.

Cohen, E. (1993). Introduction: Investigating Tourist Arts. *Annals of Tourism Research.* 20(3): 1–7.

Elliott, A. & Urry, J. (2010). *Mobile Lives.* London: Routledge.

Gordon, B. (1986). The Souvenir: Messenger of Extraordinary. *Journal of Popular Culture.* 20(3): 135–146.

Gorozhanina, S. (2012). *Russian Matryoshka.* Moscow: Interbook Business.

Graburn, N. (ed.). (1976). *Ethnic and Tourist Arts: Cultural Expressions from the Fourth World.* Berkeley, CA: University of California Press.

Graburn, N. (1983). *To Pray, Pay, and Play: The Cultural Structure of Japanese Domestic Tourism.* Paris: CIRET.

Graburn, N. (1984). The Evolution of Tourist Art. *Annals of Tourism Research.* 11: 393–419.

Hendry, J. (1993). *Wrapping Culture: Politeness, Presentation, and Power in Japan and Other Societies.* New York: Oxford University Press.

Hitchcock, M. & Teague, K. (eds.). (2000). *Souvenirs: The Material Culture of Tourism.* Farnham: Ashgate.

Hobson, J. & Christensen, M. (2001). Cultural and Structural Issues Affecting Japanese Tourist Shopping Behavior. *Asia Pacific Journal of Tourism Research.* 6(1): 37–45.

Hume, D. (2014). *Tourism Art and Souvenirs: The Material Culture of Tourism.* London: Routledge.

Iwasaki, S. (1988). *Hakonezaiku Monogatari (History of Handicrafts in Hakone).* Yokohama: Kanagawashinbunsha. [in Japanese].

Kopytoff, I. (1986). The Cultural Biography of Things: Commoditization as Process. In A. Appadurai (ed.), *The Social Life of Things: Commodities in Cultural Perspective* (pp. 64–94). Cambridge: Cambridge University Press.

Lury, C. (1997). The Objects of Travel. In C. Rojek & J. Urry (eds.), *Touring Culture* (pp. 75–95). London: Routledge.

Miller, D. (1987). *Material Culture and Mass Consumption*. New York: Blackwell.

Numata, G. (2010). *Matryoshka Daidukan (Encyclopaedia of Matryoshka)*. Tokyo: Futamishobo. [in Japanese].

Oedewald, M. (2009). Meanings of Tradition in Contemporary Japanese Domestic Tourism. In S. Guichard-Anguis & O. Moon (eds.), *Japanese Tourism and Travel Culture* (pp. 105–128). London: Routledge.

Ogawa, M. (1979). Onnanoko ni natta fukurokuju (Fukurokuju Became a Girl) In K. Kato (ed.), *Hermitage Museum* (pp. 85–90). Tokyo: Kodansha [in Japanese].

Ominami, K. (1982). Matryoshka no ru-tsu ha Hakone shichi fukujn (Roots of Matryoshka Is Hakone shichi fukujin). *USSR Today*. 620: 70–71 [in Japanese].

Sheller, M. & Urry, J. (eds.). (2004). *Tourism Mobilities: Places to Play, Places in Play*. Oxford: Routledge.

Sokolova, N. (2011). Eastern Roots of the Most Famous Russian Toy. *Russian Geographical Society News*, 2011–3–242 (https://web.archive.org/web/20140301205606/http://int.rgo.ru/news/eastern-roots-of-the-most-famous-russian-toy, last accessed: 5/10/2018).

Suzuki, R. (2016). Matryoshka in Vietnam: Migration and Tourist Souvenirs. *Rikkyo University Bulletin of Studies in Tourism*. 18: 123–132 [in Japanese].

Suzuki, R. (2017). Traveling Matryoshka: Routes and Roots of Omiyage on the Move. *Tourism Studies Review*. 6(2): 153–168 [in Japanese].

Swonson, K. & Timothy, D. (2012). Souvenirs: Icons of Meaning, Commercialization and Commoditization. *Tourism Management*. 33: 489–499.

Timothy, D. (2005). *Shopping Tourism, Retailing and Leisure*. Bristol: Channel View.

Torabian, P. & Arai, S. (2016). Tourist Perceptions of Souvenir Authenticity: An Exploration of Selective Tourist Blogs. *Current Issues in Tourism*. 19(7), 697–712.

Trinh, T., Ryan, C. & Cave, J. (2014). Souvenir Sellers and Perceptions of Authenticity: The Retailers of Hội An, Vietnam. *Tourism Management*. 45: 275–283.

Urry, J. (2000). *Sociology Beyond Societies*. London: Routledge.

Urry, J. (2007). *Mobilities*. Cambridge: Polity Press.

Wilkins, H. (2011). Souvenirs: What and Why We Buy. *Journal of Travel Research*. 50(3): 239–247.

Chapter 8

"Transference of traditions" in tourism

Local identities as images reflected in infinity mirrors

Hideki Endo

Introduction

There are many cases of local communities inventing new traditions or customs, as well as events, through their relationship with tourism. Tourism research has identified many examples of the transformation or invention of local traditions. However, a closer examination reveals curious cases that cannot be explained by theoretical concepts like the "transformation of traditions" or "invention of traditions." These cases are examples of a phenomenon that I call the "transference of traditions." In this chapter, I would like to consider this phenomenon.

First, I will explore the transformation and invention of traditions in the context of tourism, arguing that traditions are not objective phenomena but, rather, social constructs that reflect people's desires and interests. Next, I discuss the transference of tradition with reference to a specific case study: the Yosakoi Festival. Then, I highlight the issue that I believe the transference of tradition raises and argue that local identities have become fluidized.

Transformation and invention of traditions in tourism

E. Hobsbawm defined the invention of tradition as follows: "Inventing traditions, it is assumed here, is essentially a process of formalization and ritualization, characterized by references to the past, if only by imposing repetition" (Hobsbawm and Ranger, 1983). Hobsbawm discussed the invention of tradition in the context of nation building. However, the invention of traditions is also frequently observed in the tourism phenomenon.

Kecak, for instance, is a traditional Balinese dance performed for tourists. However, as is well known, Walter Spies, a Russian-born German who was a painter and musician during the 1930s, helped invent *kecak* as a tourist-oriented art form. Originally, *kecak* did not include narrative elements; it simply involved intense chanting and dancing to a simple rhythm. The dance subsequently became linked with the Ramayana epic poem and evolved into a tourist spectacle (Yamashita, 1996, 1999). The *hula* is another example; Yamanaka argues that this highly admired Hawaiian dance is an invented tradition reflecting the popular image of Hawaii (Yamanaka, 1992).

Another example is Kyoto's Daimonji bonfire (*Daimonji Gozan Okuribi*). This event is a summer tradition in Japan. However, the modern-day Daimonji bonfire becomes one that has been invented and transformed via its relationship with tourism. There are various bonfire events involving the lighting of cere-monial bonfires, including the Daimonji bonfire on Mount Higashiyama Nyoigatake, the Hidari Daimonji bonfire on Mount Okita behind the Kinkakuji pavilion (Mount Daimonji), the Myoho bonfires on Mount Matsugasaki Nishiyama (Mount Mantoro) and Mount Higashiyama (Mount Daikokuten), the Funagata bonfire on Mount Nishigamofune, and the Toriigata bonfire on Mount Saga Mandala. These ceremonial bonfires (*okuribi*, literally "send-off bonfires") originally had religious connotations; they signified a time when the spirits of the dead, having visited the land of the living for the Bon season, would return again to the netherworld. Nowadays, however, these events are accompanied by modern features such as "Daimonji concerts" and "Daimonji sales campaigns" in department stores. Thus, the ceremonial bonfires have been reinvented and redefined as tourist events, and their form is continually in flux (Wazaki, 1999).

Nara City's annual Tokae lantern festival is another example, as it is an invented and transformed tradition. The Tokae lantern festival is held annually in Nara City from early to mid-August. It is characterized as a "light and darkness event" in which the streets on summer nights are illuminated by candlelight.

The lantern festival began in 1999. The Young Entrepreneurs' Group of the Nara Chamber of Commerce and Industry, Young Entrepreneurs' Group of the Nara Economic Association spearheaded a plan to end the Nara Festival, which had run for 10 years, and invent a new Nara event to replace it. The second Tokae lantern festival was held in 2000, and the voluntary organization Nara Tokae Association was established to ensure that the Tokae lantern festival would become a permanent event in the local community. In 2001, the Ministry of the Environment selected it as one of the 100 best beautiful landscapes, and in 2003, the Ministry of Land, Infrastructure, Transport and Tourism awarded it the Minister's Community-building Organization Prize. In 2019, the 21st Nara Tokae Festival was held from August 5 to 14.

Many local volunteers take part in this event, including local residents and students of universities located in Nara. The number of volunteers (called "day supporters") alone stands at about 300 each year. Since so many local residents participate in the event, it has come to be represented by people as a classic summer tradition in Nara (Endo, 2005).

The Yuwaku Bonbori Festival in the Yuwaku Onsen district of Kanazawa City, Ishikawa Prefecture may become another example of an invented tradition. This festival was invented based on a fictional festival depicted in the anime series *Hanasaku Iroha* (broadcast from April to November 2011). Recently, tour-ists and local residents have started representing the event as a tradition. H. Endo identifies this case as an interesting example of how popular culture (anime) can foster the invention of traditions (Endo, 2014).

As the above cases illustrate, in the context of tourism, traditions are invented and transformed, and during this process, they begin to be represented by people as traditions. Therefore, whether or not a traditional event historically existed in the area is not an important issue.[1] What is important is that people start to represent such events as long-established local traditions (Endo, 2003; Bruner, 2005). S. Adachi explored this issue, focusing on the case of the Gujo Odori dance festival in Hachiman-cho, Gujo-gun, Gifu Prefecture. The key issue, according to Adachi, was how this local dance festival was constructed around the shared narrative that "it is a local tradition dating back to ancient times" (Adachi, 2010). R. Handler and J. Linnekin argued that traditions are not necessarily objective phenomena; rather, they are social constructs that are determined by people's various interpretations, meanings, desires, and interests (Handler and Linnekin, 1984).

However, there are tourism cases today that cannot be adequately explained by theoretical concepts like the transformation or invention of traditions. Rather, we must move the discourse forward. To this end, I propose the theoretical concept of the transference of traditions.

Case study: the Yosakoi Festival

What is the transference of traditions? I will illustrate this concept by referring to the Yosakoi Festival.

The Yosakoi Festival is a Tosa Province carnival held over a four-day period from August 9 to 12 (August 9 is "Yosakoi eve," August 10 and 11 are the main carnival days, and August 12 is the concluding day of the festival, culminating with a national dance competition). The carnival takes place in the streets and in performance venues in Kochi City; it features dazzlingly ornamented floats and dancers carrying wooden clappers (*naruko*). The festival was initiated in August 1954 by the Kochi Chamber of Commerce and Industry with the intention of promoting trade in the shopping district. In this sense, it is another invented tradition now represented by locals as a traditional event of Kochi Prefecture (Figures 8.1 and 8.2).

Only 750 people and 21 organizations took part in the first festival in 1954. Subsequently, the festival grew in scale. At the 30th festival, more than 10,000 dancers took part. As the scale of the festival grew, it increasingly took on the appearance of a major tourism event of Kochi Prefecture; music, hairstyles, costumes, and choreography became more extravagant, incorporating elements of samba and rock. This phenomenon illustrates how traditions are adapted for tourism purposes (Tsuboi and Hasegawa, 2002).

However, an analysis of the Yosakoi Festival reveals an issue that cannot be fully accounted for by theoretical concepts (e.g. invention or transformation of traditions). The Yosakoi Festival is an example of the transference of tradition in that a tradition was transferred from the area where it historically existed to different areas.

Figure 8.1 Yosakoi Festival.
Source: photo by the author, 08.11.2005.

Figure 8.2 A dance performance at Yosakoi Festival.
Source: photo by the author, 08.12.2006.

For instance, the Yosakoi Festival has been transferred to Sapporo, Hokkaido, where it exists as the Yosakoi Soran Festival. The Yosakoi Soran Festival emerged as a blend of Kochi's Yosakoi Festival and Hokkaido's Soran Bushi (a sea shanty). It was initially started by university students in Hokkaido. One of the students was impressed by the Yosakoi Festival in Kochi and persuaded her friends to create a similar festival in the local community.

The first Yosakoi Soran Festival was held in June 1992. Ten teams and 1,000 individuals took part; additionally, there were 200,000 spectators. At the 28th festival in 2019, there were 279 teams and 28,000 individuals participating, and approximately 2,111,000 spectators. The festival is held every June; it is a well-established early summer event of Sapporo and Hokkaido. As such, it has come to be represented by local people as a tradition.[2]

The Yosakoi Festival has also been transferred to Nara, where it is known as the Basara Festival (Figure 8.3). Held in late August, the Basara Festival is intended as a rallying call to inspire a bustling, vibrant, and energetic 21st-century Nara. The festival began in 1999, and it was held for the 21st time in 2019. Using Kochi's Yosakoi Festival as a motif, various teams perform creative and unique costumed dances.

As a new summer festival of Nara, the event has drawn the interest of not only locals but also many people who visit Nara in the summer, and it is often featured

Figure 8.3 Basara Festival.
Source: photo by the author, 08.27.2005.

in the local media. The festival is organized by the Basara Festival Implementation Committee, a body of young entrepreneurs from the shopping district near Kintetsu Nara Station and local supporters. This body manages all aspects of the festival, including the production of posters and brochures, as well as the design of the *naruko* and templates for costumes and choreography. For example, it has selected "odoru-nara, sora!" as a Basara Festival dancing song.[3]

Thus, the transference of tradition occurs when an event represented as a local community's tradition is transferred to another local community and redefined in the new community's context. The Yosakoi Soran Festival and the Basara Festival are nothing other than traditions that have been transferred to and redefined in Hokkaido and Nara, respectively. Kochi Prefecture's Yosakoi Festival has been transferred to various places as far north as Hokkaido and as far south as Okinawa. Almost every region of Japan now has its own Yosakoi Festival.

Local identities as images reflected in infinity mirrors: with reference to the ideas of Freud and Lacan

In the cases of both the Yosakoi Soran Festival and the Basara Festival, an event "represented" as a long-established local tradition was transferred to another local community and redefined in the new local community's context. As such, authenticity is not an issue here. What, then, is the issue posed by the transference of traditions?

The issue concerns local identities. In the transference of traditions, something that was originally invented and represented as a cultural tradition of a local community is presented as the tradition of another local community. One could expect local events to be invented and represented according to local contexts, but this is not so in the case of the Yosakoi Soran Festival and Basara Festival; both of these events assume the form of the Yosakoi Festival, which is a representation of Kochi's local identity. In other words, the desires and interests that are projected onto a traditional event of one local community mirror the desires and interests projected onto a traditional event of another local community. I believe that this issue is central to the transference of traditions.

Transference is a concept developed by psychoanalysts such as Sigmund Freud and Jacques Lacan. The concept describes the synchronization of one's thoughts and feelings with those of another. In his discussion of the case of a paranoid patient, whom he named Aimée, Lacan reported that in the course of psychotherapy, his emotions and desires synchronized with those of Aimée's; in fact, he developed a desire to be Aimée's son, and Aimée – conversely – developed a desire to be his mother.

K. Shingu, who employed Freud and Lacan's theories and advanced psychoanalysis in Japan, discussed one of his cases in which a similar phenomenon occurred. During the course of therapy, Shingu's desire to study in Britain synchronized with his client's desire to study in France. As a result, Shingu ended up studying in France, and his client switched her major to British culture (Shingu, 1995). The transference of the client's affection and resentment towards her father onto the person conducting the psychoanalysis was a manifestation of the synchronization of thoughts and feelings.

To paraphrase from Lacan's famous thesis, "the desire of man is the desire of the other" (*le désir de l'homme est le désir de l'autre*), though it may seem that our thoughts, intentions, and desires originate from within, they actually originate from others. Insofar as we are mutually bound with others through the medium of language, we absorb the thoughts, intentions, and desires of others and they become our own.

Arguably, a similar phenomenon occurs with local identities. The thoughts and intentions projected onto traditional events of Hokkaido and Nara synchronized with the thoughts and intentions projected onto a traditional event in another local community, Kochi, such that this other community's traditional event came to be identified with Hokkaido and Nara.

The thoughts and intentions we project onto local traditional events may appear to originate from within us, but this is not the case. They are constructed by other people and other local communities in an infinity-mirror effect (Figure 8.4). One of the dancing teams participating in the 2006 Yosakoi Festival provided a striking illustration of this phenomenon. This team from Kagawa Prefecture performed the Yosakoi dance in Kochi Prefecture, incorporating elements from the Awa Dance of Tokushima Prefecture (Figure 8.5).

There are, of course, cases in which a traditional event that was transferred to another local community influenced or transformed the style of the event in the source area. For example, Hokkaido's Yosakoi Soran Festival has influenced the

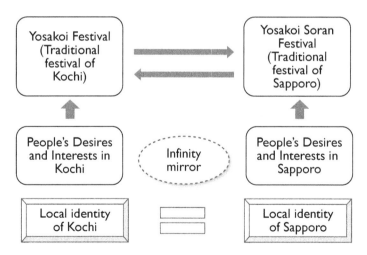

Figure 8.4 Infinity mirror of local identity.

Source: by the author.

Figure 8.5 The team from Kagawa Prefecture performing the Yosakoi dance in Kochi Prefecture, incorporating elements from the Awa Dance of Tokushima Prefecture.

Source: photo by the author, 08.12.2006.

style of Kochi's Yosakoi Festival. When discussing transference of traditions, the importance is not identification of the original version of the tradition or the means of transmission or imitation of that version; the important issue is how local identities are constructed as reflected images within, as it were, an infinity mirror.[4]

The fluidization of local identities: tourism is expanding non-originality

In the context of modern tourism, there are many cases in which local identity appears as a reflected image in an infinity mirror. To use Nara Tokae as an example again, this event in which the ancient capital of Nara is illuminated with candlelight can be observed as well in Kyoto, which also promotes itself as an ancient capital and holds a similar event, Kyoto Hanatouro.[5] The main difference between the two events is that electric candles are used in Kyoto Hanatouro festivities. Given that many local residents of each community have come to regard their event as a tradition dating back to ancient times, it may be considered an invented tradition. However, we could also consider it as the transference of tradition. Both events showcase the ancient city aspect of Nara and Kyoto, respectively, as if the identities of each place are being reflected in an infinity mirror (Figures 8.6 and 8.7).

Figure 8.6 Nara Tokae.
Source: photo by the author, 08.13.2004.

Figure 8.7 Kyoto Hanatouro.
Source: photo by the author, 03.16.2014.

Kobe also has a similar event; the Kobe Luminarie has been held at the end of each year since 1995. The event involves walking through an illuminated arcade from Kobe Chinatown (*Nankin-machi*, "Nanjing town") to the "old foreign settlement" (*Kyoryuchi*). The illumination creates a romantic atmosphere, and the event has become an essential representation of Kobe's identity (Figure 8.8). The Kobe Luminarie concept was transferred to Tokyo's Marunouchi district in 1999 with the initiation of the Tokyo Millenario. The event continues to be held albeit under a new name – Tokyo Michiterasu. As in Kobe, it has become an essential representation of Marunouchi's identity.[6]

Thus, there are many tourism cases in which local identities are constructed as reflected images in an infinity mirror.[7] Local identities are being stripped of their endemic contexts and are drifting about as deracinated entities.

A local community's tourism enterprises are always linked to the thoughts, intentions, and desires of tourists (the other) who come to the community from another community. As such, the local community must synchronize its thoughts, intentions, and desires with this other and construct its local identity accordingly. Therefore, in the context of tourism, local identities are increasingly fluid, and non-originality is expanding.

Figure 8.8 Kobe Luminarie.
Source: photo by the author, 12.15.2007.

In this chapter, I argued that in tourism, traditions are invented and transferred, which leads to the construction of local identities as reflected images in an infinity mirror.

However, our response to this phenomenon should not simply be to rebuke or ignore it. We need to challenge our assumption that the identities we discover within us – identities that have their origins within us – are inherent entities. We must then search for a new way to make local communities thrive in today's fluid-ized mobile world.

It may be wise to learn from the post-modern approach – in other words, to accept the images in the infinity mirror with all their diffused reflections and utilize them deftly and flexibly for our own identities.

Notes

1 Regarding authenticity in tourism, Endo (2003) outlines the discourses on this topic that have developed in fields such as tourism sociology and tourism anthropology.
2 Yosakoi Soran Festival official website, www.yosakoi-soran.jp, accessed on August 18, 2016.
3 Basara Festival website, www.basaramatsuri.com, accessed on August 18, 2016.

4 This is why I avoided using terms like "transmission of tradition" or "imitation of tradition" and instead used the psychoanalytical term "transference." I intend for "transference of traditions" to convey the nuance that local identities only exist as "reflected images" and that they are constantly in flux.
5 Kyoto Hanatouro official website, www.hanatouro.jp, accessed on August 18, 2016.
6 Tokyo Michiterasu official website, www.tokyo-michiterasu.jp, accessed on August 18, 2016.
7 Here, another issue arises – namely, the issue of "hegemony" over traditions/events. In cases of transference of tradition, hegemonic conflicts are beginning to emerge over which local community's event is the "original" version. In the case of the Yosakoi Festival, Hokkaido's Yosakoi Soran Festival became even more of a major event than Kochi's Yosakoi Festival. In response, Kochi Prefecture started holding a Yosakoi National Championship in an attempt to assert its version of the festival as the original version. A similar hegemonic struggle, albeit modest in scale, has emerged between Nara and Kyoto over which version – Nara Tokae or Kyoto Hanatouro – is the original. As I mentioned previously, the transference of traditions phenomenon is far removed from arguments about authenticity in tourism, and it renders somewhat meaningless the distinction between the original and a copy. Nevertheless, it paradoxically gives rise to hegemonic struggles over the original version. When it comes to tourism-based community development, hegemony over the original version may be closely connected to the issue of local identities.

References

Adachi, S. (2010). *Gujo Hachiman: Dentō o ikiru – chiiki shakai no katari to riariti (Gujo Hachiman: Living through Traditions: Narrative and Reality in Local Communities)*. Tokyo: Shin-yo-sha.
Bruner, E.M. (1989). Tourism, Creativity, and Authenticity. *Studies in Symbolic Interaction*, 10, pp. 109–114.
Bruner, E.M. (2005). *Culture on Tour: Ethnographies of Travel*. Chicago, IL: University of Chicago.
Elliott, A., & Urry, J. (2010). *Mobile Lives*. Oxford: Routledge.
Endo, H. (2003). Kankō no ōsentishiti o meguru shakaigaku riron no tenkai (The Development of Sociological Theories on Authenticity in Tourism). In Yamajo, T., Horino, M. (eds.), *Gendai kankō e no apurōchi (Approaches to Modern Tourism)*. Tokyo: Hakutoshobo, pp. 197–210.
Endo, H. (2005). Chiiki no katachi – chiiki shakaigaku kara no shiten (The Shape of Local Communities: From the Perspective of Sociology of Local Community). In Nara Prefectural University, *Chiiki sōzō e no shōtai (An invitation to Regional Creation)*. Kyoto: Koyoshobo, pp. 13–20.
Endo, H. (2014). Dentō no sōzō (The Invention of Tradition). In Ohashi, S., Hashimoto, K., Endo, H., Kanda, K. (eds.), *Kankōgaku gaidobukku (Tourism Studies Guidebook)*. Kyoto: Nakanishiya Shuppan, pp. 114–119.
Fukuhara, T. (2005). *Lacan – Kyōzō dankai (Lacan: Mirror Stage)*. Tokyo: Kodansha.
Handler, R., & Linnekin, J. (1984). Tradition, Genuine or Spurious. *Journal of American Folklore*, 97, pp. 273–290.
Hobsbawm, E., & Ranger, T. (1983). *The Invention of Tradition*. Cambridge: Cambridge University Press.
MacCannell, D. (1976). *The Tourist: A New Theory of the Leisure Class*. New York: Schocken Books.

Nakayama, G. (2015). *Furoito Nyūmon (Introduction to Freud)*. Tokyo: Chikuma Shobo.

Shingu, K. (1995). *Lacan no seishin bunseki (Lacan's Psychoanalysis)*. Tokyo: Kodansha.

Shingu, K., & Tsuiki, K. (eds.) (2005). *Furoito = Lacan (Freud and Lacan)*. Tokyo: Kodansha.

Sudo, H., & Endo, H. (2005). *Kankō shakaigaku – Tsūrizumu kenkyū no bōkenteki kokoromi (Sociology of Tourism: The Adventures of Tourism Studies)*. Tokyo: Akashi Shoten.

Tsuboi, Y., & Hasegawa, G. (2002). *YOSAKOI sōran matsuri – machizukuri NPO no keieigaku (Yosakoi Soran Festival: Management of Community-Building NPOs)*. Tokyo: Iwanami Shoten.

Yamanaka, H. (1992). *Imeiji no "rakuen" – Kankō hawai no bunkashi ("Paradise" as an Image: The Cultural History of Hawaiian Tourism)*. Tokyo: Chikumashobo.

Yamashita, S. (1996). "Rakuen" no sōzō – Bari ni okeru kankō to dentō no saikōchiku (The Invention of "Paradise": The Reconstruction of Tourism and Tradition in Bali). In Yamashita, S. (ed.), *Kankō jinruigaku (Anthropology of Tourism)*, Tokyo: Shin-yo-sha, pp. 104–112.

Yamashita, S. (1999). *Bari: Kankō jinruigaku no resson (Bali: Lessons from the Anthropology of Tourism)*. Tokyo: University of Tokyo Press.

Wazaki, H. (1999). Toshi seikatsu no naka no dentō to gendai – minzoku no henbō to sōzō (Tradition and Today in Urban Life: Transformation and Invention of Folk Customs). In Fujita, H., Yoshihara, N. (eds.), *Toshi shakaigaku (Urban Sociology)*. Tokyo: Yuhikaku, pp. 177–192.

Chapter 9

Marathon mobilities

A western tourist perspective on Japanese marathons

Jonas Larsen

Introduction

Running is a basic form of human mobility. Yet running has been strikingly over-looked by the mobilities paradigm that has focused on how machines mobilise people over great distances and at much speed, in cars, trains, boats and planes. This is largely to do with the fact that this paradigm was in dialogue with transport scholars, on the one hand, and technology scholars, on the other. Coupled with an interest in everyday life, the mobilities paradigm became preoccupied with mundane commuting, machine complexes and spatially extensive movements – including tourism mobilities (Hannam, Butler & Paris, 2014; Sheller & Urry, 2004) – across the planet (Sheller & Urry, 2006; Urry, 2012). The irony is that the mobilities paradigm in that process immobilised the human body and movement on foot or bicycle. Or so it was until recently. There are now many publications about cycling (e.g. Spinney, 2006), running (Latham, 2015) and running events (Cidell, 2014; Edensor & Larsen, 2018). This chapter contributes to the (tourism) mobilities literature by giving an embodied tourist perspective on the Tokyo Marathon and the Kyoto Marathon. I explore why *westerners* travel to and experience these faraway events and cities.

First, I approach marathon running as a specific form of corporeal mobility and account for how marathons involve and generate long-distance travel, conspicuous consumption, disrupted mobilities and corporeally active bodies. Second, this is followed by a short history of marathon running in Japan and the globalisation of marathons. Third, drawing on my own running, observations and interviews, I write two vignettes about the races that are inspired by non-representational calls for animating ethnographies of live sporting events (Andrews, 2017; Vannini, 2015).

Tourism (running) mobilities

The 'mobilities paradigm' (Sheller & Urry, 2006) explores how recently networked modern cities, mobile lives and events (such as marathons) are constructed and experienced through mobilities of things, technologies, information and, not least, mobile people. It is argued that tourist travel is central to much social life and that routinised practices often inform and fuel tourism mobilities. This paradigm does not reduce mobility to functional transport (as transport studies) but analyses the politics, social relations, sensuous experiences, skilled dispositions and habitual routines of moving through and between places. The mobilities paradigm has a particular focus on how technologies, infrastructures and environments facilitate or foreclose the movement of (certain) people. The attention is on the transport of bodies (and other entities) and how cars afford flexible commuting and planes long-haul travel. Such machines ensure 'sedentary comfort' (Bissell, 2008) that liberates bodies from physical work and inclement weather (Larsen, 2018). This is also the case with 'event mobilities', as in Urry (2012) where the focus is upon the travel to *watch* particular events. As Cidell argues: 'This conceptualization treats "event mobilities" as "events" as separate from "mobilities," where travel is required to get to a *static* event' (2014, p. 575) where people are seated spectators. This argues that corporeal, physical movement – walking, cycling and running – on the ground and in the air has somewhat fallen through the cracks of this paradigm. Ironically, at least until recently, there were few accounts of active self-propelling bodies that struggle with hilly terrains, inclement weather, high pulse and tired legs (but see Larsen, 2018; Spinney, 2006).

This focus on transported bodies and spectatorship also explains the disregard of sport despite the fact that much sport – just think of cycling and running – is movement per se. Indeed, there has been almost no dialogue between mobilities and sport scholars. In her article on event running, Cidell illustrates – perhaps inadvertently – why the mobilities paradigms have snubbed running: 'Running is a particularly unusual form of mobility because it is one of the few where mobility is done for its own sake' (Cidell, 2014, p. 576). Running, we learn, is odd because in terms of transport, it has no purpose. Yet Cidell argues that running events are interesting for mobilities scholars: (1) they attract many out-of-town and international runners; (2) corporeal mobility – running – is the event and they engage people as mobile bodies; (3) they are 'transgressive' as they temporarily displace cars (and other vehicles), circumvent traffic rules and make roads fully available for runners to move so 'that they can through space in a way that can only be done at that time' (Cidell, 2014, p. 576).

Sport scholars have also noticed the lack of sport in the mobilities paradigm:

> However, many of us who locate ourselves and our work within the disciplinary boundaries of physical education, health studies, sport studies, kinesiology, and related fields have found the active human body – and particularly as it exists in various sporting contexts – to be conspicuously absent from early deliberations on mobility.
>
> (Newman & Falcous, 2012, p. 39)

Newman and Falcous's research (2012) focuses on the power relations of the mobilities of professional sport in a neo-liberal globalised economy. Thorpe is another sport scholar who is inspired by the mobilities paradigm (2012). She demonstrates the elitist nature of serious snowboarding, as it requires sufficient economic (as well as social and cultural) capital to travel to desired places and events (see Rickly's (2016) study of rock climbers in north America): 'Approaching the sport from a position of privilege, many snowboarders also travel extensively – locally, nationally, internationally and virtually – in pursuit of new terrain, fresh snow and social interactions and cultural connections' (Thorpe, 2012, p. 318). Thorpe is also committed to apprehending snow-boarding as a specific form of corporeal mobility that entails certain embodied and emplaced skills in order to ride a board successfully. Somewhat similarly, sport sociologists Hockey and Allen-Collinson (2015) have developed a multi-sensuous phenomenological focus on how runners listen to their bodies, perform physically and sense the environment, and how their movement and sensuous experiences are affected by terrains, topographies and weather-worlds.

The literature discussed above allows me to analyse how the Tokyo Marathon and the Kyoto Marathon are events that are more or less (dis)connected from international flows of people, ideas and other events, as discussed next. But it also enables me to discuss the sensuous sensations of marathon running, from seeing landmarks and hearing sounds to experiencing internal somatic sensations such as pain (nocioception), muscles and organs (proprioception) and body temperature (thermoception).

Marathon running in Japan

Marathons as serious, small-scale events for elite runners have been around for a long time around the world. The first city marathon was Boston Marathon, which has taken place every year since 1897, the year after the first successful Olympic Marathon in Athens in 1896. Yet 'the earliest distance races in Japan, the United States and elsewhere drew relatively few entries and were often dominated by unusually well-conditioned laborers, deliverymen and, in the Japanese case, rickshaw drivers' (Havens, 2015, p. 12). The mass marathon for ordinary people first took off in the mid-1970s with the 'jogging movement' and the jogging-friendly New York Marathon. After an indifferent start where a few hundred participants did repeated loops in Hyde Park, New York Marathon's popularity began in 1976 when the course was redesigned to run the five boroughs' fully closed-off streets and boulevards that were lined with cheering locals and music (Bryant, 2010, p. 9).

The 'jogging marathon boom' blossomed late in Japan despite the fact that many people – so-called 'citizen runners' – ran for fitness. For instance, the Tokyo International Marathon (1980–2006) was a competitive event for male elite runners. 'Citizen runners' were not welcome. For many years, serious 'citizen runners' had to travel abroad to participate in general-participation marathons. In *Marathon Japan*, Havens claims that Honolulu Marathons have always been popular with Japanese 'citizen runners' and that two thirds of the 20,000 contestants were Japanese (2015, p. 144). With so many potential participants, it is not surprising that the number of Japanese marathons doubled from the mid-1990s to the mid-2000s (Havens, 2015, p. 4). In 2007, the Tokyo International Marathon changed name to the Tokyo Marathon and, more importantly, the organising committee – the governor and metropolitan government – now incorporated 'citizen runners' and the event became designed with their needs and aspirations in mind as much as those of elite runners. This event was planned in a top-down fashion to cater for a growing running population. This had a positive bottom-up contagious effect. As Havens writes:

> When Tokyo held its first general-participation marathon in 2007, the impact on people's outlook on running was huge. The generous seven-hour limit allowed many duffers to take part; the 1.78 million spectators watching them live and many millions more on television realized 'I too can run', leading to a new wave of both experienced and inexperienced for the 2008 and subsequent iterations of this performative event.
>
> (2015, p. 5)

Since the designation 'international' was omitted, the organising committee initially had a local race in mind. The first Kyoto Marathon took place in 2012 to support the reconstruction of the 2011 Great East Japan Earthquake and the race is still free of charge for runners from earthquake-affected regions.

Marathon running is today hugely popular in Japan: the world-famous Japanese fiction writer Murakami (2009) has published a best-selling biographical book about marathon running; marathons get much media coverage; they attract many local spectators and huge sponsor deals; and many are over-subscribed and use lotteries to manage entries (Havens, 2015, p. 141). For instance, for the 2019 event, 331,211 runners applied for the 35,000-capacity Tokyo Marathon and more than 300,000 runners – including me – received this heart-breaking laconic e-mail:

> Thank you for registering to the Tokyo Marathon 2019.
> We regret to inform you that you were not selected for the Tokyo Marathon 2019 entries.
> We look forward to your application for our future events.

However, I had luck with securing a start number for the slightly less competitive 16,000-capacity Kyoto Marathon (that takes place a week before Tokyo) that received 65,948 entries that year. These figures reflect the magnitude of the Japanese 'marathon boom'; Japan almost matches the US when it comes to hosting mega marathons. While Japanese marathons are dominated by domestic runners, they are increasingly becoming international tourism events. For instance, the Kyoto Marathon course takes full advantage of the city's world-famous sights and it is promoted as ideal for sightseeing. The organisers write:

Running the course while enjoying the attractions that only Kyoto can offer! … Located along the course are the seven UNESCO World Cultural Heritage sites of Tenryu-ji Temple, Ninna-ji Temple, Ryoan-ji Temple, Kinkaku-ji Temple, Kamigamo-jinja Shrine, Shimogamo-jinja Shrine, and Ginkaku-ji Temple, as well as many other tourist attractions including Umenomiya-taisha Shrine, Matsunoo-taisha Shrine, Seiryo-ji Temple, Daikaku-ji Temple, Hirano-jinja Shrine, Wara-tenjin Shrine, Daitoku-ji Temple, Imamiya-jinja Shrine, and Heian-jingu Shrine … Runners follow a course along the Katsura River with a view of Togetsukyo Bridge in Arashiyama, and then pass through the picturesque Sagano area and Hirosawa-no-ike Pond. The course then leads to Kinukake-no-michi Road, which has been famous for its scenic beauty for over 1,000 years, passes through the Kyoto Botanical Gardens, extends along the Kamo River, a symbol of Kyoto, and then takes the runners on a trip through history in the verdant Kyoto Gyoen National Garden (Kyoto Imperial Place). Yet another major thrill of the Kyoto Marathon is the view of the five mountains that are the focus of the Gozan no Okuribi festival.

(www.kyoto-marathon.com/en/info/course.php)

The Tokyo Marathon, in particular, now embraces international runners. It has become the marque marathon that has put Japan on the 'global marathon map'. It joined the World Marathon Majors (www.worldmarathonmajors.com) as the sixth city in 2012. The Majors started in 2006 and now comprise some of the greatest marathons hosted by world-famous and much-visited cities: Boston Marathon, New York Marathon and Chicago Marathon in the US, London Marathon and Berlin Marathon in Europe and Tokyo Marathon in Asia. The Majors is a championship-style competition where top athletes score points for their finishing place in each race and compete for high prize money. But it is also designed to appeal to non-competitive runners – so-called 'everyday champions' that become victorious not through competition with others, but by *finishing* all six marathons, irrespective of their time or placing. The effort of travelling to and finishing all six marathons is what matters in this competition. In summer 2019, there were more than 6,000 'six-star finishers' from 88 countries. Reflecting that three of the races take place in the United States, Americans top the list with 1,138 finishers, followed by runners from the UK (607), Italy (378), Germany (359), China (340), Spain (251), Canada (243) and Japan (220). This event generates much air travel and attracts mobile people that live 'high-carbon lives' (Elliott & Urry, 2010). Each finisher needs to make between three and five long-haul intercontinental flights in addition to shorter domestic and continual journeys. When we further take into account that these races are expensive to enter and that runners (and their families) need accommodation, we realise that few can afford a six-star finishing medal. Indeed, studies show that marathon runners are high earners (Bryant, 2010) and this is certainly the case amongst six-star finishers.

The next section presents the first vignette. It is autoethnographic (see Larsen, 2014) and connects with the above literature by discussing how the weather affects corporeal movement and body temperature (Allen-Collinson *et al.*, 2018) and to what degree tourist gazing (Urry & Larsen, 2011) is in fact possible on an otherwise picturesque marathon course. I begin with the Expo's fascinating local character.

Ethnographic vignette 1: Kyoto Marathon

After spending a couple of hours at the international registration desk, it was clear that this event attracts extremely few westerners and that the international runners come from neighbouring Asian countries. The Expo-booths have a particular Japanese flavour and all the western running brands, events and sponsors are conspicuously absent. I marvel at products, gadgets, 'shows' and foods that appear so familiar to a seasoned marathon runner and yet so different. Japanese is foreign to me but it sounds fantastic and I constantly gawk at posters with graphically stunning Japanese letters and gaudy multihued prints. There is more to entertain the western 'tourist gaze' such as the plastic menu display (so typical in Japan) of croissants, red bean buns, rice crackers, oranges, strawberries and tomatoes that runners will be served during the race or the food stalls that serve Japanese specialties. I devour a mammoth grilled octopus stick and do not yearn for the usual generic marathon-Expo pasta dish.

Upon leaving the Expo, a cold wind and snowflakes touch my skin. While observing amazed Thai runners photographing the snow, it strikes me that I have never run a winter marathon before and that some extra layers of clothing are needed tomorrow.

While I'm not stressed about how I will perform tomorrow as the race plan is not to race fast but just to saunter and enjoy the course, the usual pre-race nerves once again ruin my night. I'm worried about getting to the starting area. The college porter said that it was impossible to book a taxi and his late-night instructions about public transport only caused more stress and insomnia.

BEEP BEEP My alarm goes off at 5.30.

My sleepy eyes peep out of the window and I sigh with relief that there is no snow on the ground or movement in the trees. After a strong coffee, energy drinks, a light sugar-rich breakfast and a visit to the loo, I walk heavy-eyed into a nippy and idle Sunday morning. No wonder marathons are Sunday morning events, when the city's other mobilities rhythms are unusually dormant. Luckily, a vacant taxi appears. I hand the suit-wearing taxi driver with white gloves my note with the address: 'Nishikyogoku Athletic Park'. Marathon, right? He nods. We drive through the drowsy streets in silence.

I arrive at the starting area two hours before the race starts. Although it is freezing, we need to undress early as our bags must be delivered to the trucks that will drive them to the finishing area an hour before the start. In return, we are given a thin wind-resisting plastic poncho to protect our exposed racing bodies. This is not enough to keep our bodies sufficiently warm and we soon become aware of the sense of thermoception (the sense by which humans perceive temperatures). Despite wearing an extra old jumper, I am freezing cold. I am stuck in a long, slow-moving queue for the toilet, where my shivering body observes many other bodies that quiver and hug themselves. As an experienced marathon runner, my sensuous knowledge tells me that it is better to wear light clothing and freeze a little at the beginning, because our bodies will quickly heat up once the race starts, and over-heating, not freezing, is the real concern. Today, at this moment, I would like be one of those inexperienced runners who wear excessive clothing.

The freezing sensations only get worse in the windy open football stadium where the start line is. The sun is still subdued by the grey sky and there is no hiding from the wind. But minutes before the start, the sun finally breaks through and its warm rays reheat our bodies and lift our mood, and I dispose of my poncho when the starting gun goes off.

My body temperature and the ambient temperature are still low, and combined with my moderate pace, my body, it feels, refuses to 'warm up' and my bone-frozen body overshadows other sensations during the first three or four kilometres. At one point, in panic, I grab a discarded poncho from a bin and throw it around me, and it does not take long before my body heats up and runs smoothly, and my attention drifts away from the bad weather and what Leder calls my 'dys-appearing body'. This testifies to Leder's (1990) claim that a well-functioning body disappears and becomes absent. This in turn affords time and energy to indulge the senses in the sensations around me: the breath-taking scenery of snow-clad mountains on the horizon and the vibrant atmosphere and spectacles that enliven the streets for this day: enthusiastic high-fiving locals, bands, boisterous university cheer groups, Geshai artists and martial arts practitioners.

While most marathons are topographically flat, the Kyoto Marathon becomes hilly around the 8-km mark. Although my body is functioning well, it briefly 'appears' when we face another incline and heavy breathing resonates between us. But at this point the extra work is not ruining my appreciation of the astonish-ing shrines, temples and cheering monks that we pass by over the next 7–8 kilometres. I'm flowing, absorbed in this sublime place rather than being burdened by the task at hand. Running on closed-off streets means that we can submit ourselves to gazing at the surroundings rather than being attentive to cars and weaving around pedestrians.

When we pass the half-marathon mark, the course becomes flat and less spec-tacular. I also begin to feel the distance in my joints and muscles, which is a worrying sign so early in the race. Perhaps I was too overexcited on those hills; did they make me go too fast and not listen to my body? Yet the nice detour through the cherry trees blossoming in Kyoto Botanical Gardens and along the enchanting Kamo River provides enough distraction to keep my tourist gaze occupied. However, my pace is slowly dropping and my body is reappearing, feeling low on energy and with heavy legs, and I find it increasingly difficult to get excited by surroundings in the modern part of the city. While this part of the course is perhaps less intriguing to the 'tourist gaze', the point is rather that a troubled body is self-obsessed and oblivious to the wider environment unless it affects one's pace.

At the 40-km sign, I walk for the first time ever in a marathon, being so tired, in pain and without the willpower to 'dig in' (Hockey & Allen-Collinson, 2015). Marathon runners are in a constant dialogue with their 'embodied mind' and, if one is not very highly motivated, it becomes nearly impossible to resist the benevolent voices that urge one to stop, to put an end to the misery. This illustrates two fundamental facts about running and mobile bodies: firstly, they are not as resolute as machines, and proper fuelling does not prevent them from running out of steam; secondly, corporeal movement is a mental as much as a physiological act, as one needs to be ready to 'dig in' (Hockey & Allen-Collinson, 2015), to endure fatigue-induced pain and ignore the burning desire to stop.

Whereas this is a vignette reported from my moving body, the next one about the Tokyo Marathon is more traditional and draws upon 18 pre-race interviews with westerners outside the Expo area and three extensive post-race home interviews, with three Danish runners who had recently become six-star finishers at the Tokyo Marathon. Indeed, the theme of this next vignette is very much the significance of the Majors series in luring people to Tokyo.

Vignette 2: Tokyo Marathon

A week after the Tokyo Marathon, I stroll through the gigantic Tokyo Marathon Expo. While there is a Japanese flavour to it, the atmosphere is also international, even touristy, because of the many international products, western runners and people with trolleys. Many are busy writing their name and messages on walls, buying souvenirs and posing and photographing friends in front of camera-friendly showcases, printed walls and simulated Tokyo Marathon finish lines. This is clearly a Facebook-and-Instagram trophy moment. Nowhere is this 'tourist attitude' more prevalent than at the World Major Marathon booth that swarms with especially western runners waiting for their turn to be photographed as a proud soon-to-be six-star finisher or to take pictures of the glass-framed cabinets with the individual medals for each of six marathons and the whopping six-star medal. I learn that a record number of 600 runners will become six-star finishers on Sunday and all this activity suggests that many more are on the same mission. The prospect of collecting yet another prestigious medal and acquiring, or getting one step closer to, that conspicuous holy grail of international marathon running clearly entices many to come to Japan for this particular event.

The degree to which the World Major Marathon series competition overshadows the Tokyo Marathon becomes fully evident during my 20 short interviews with western runners *outside* the Expo area and three protracted home interviews with Danish runners. Virtually all of them had completed one or more Majors elsewhere and they declared quite frankly that they would probably not have run the Tokyo Marathon (at least this year) had it not been a Majors event.

'Why have you come all the way to Tokyo to run a marathon?' I ask an English guy in his mid-40s.

> Because I want to complete all of the six major marathons. I have done London and New York, so this is the next one and I have the other three ones later in the year. I got entry for all of them.
>
> (Personal communication)

Later I asked a Swiss middle-aged couple about their 'marathon biography' and their motivation for doing the Tokyo Marathon:

> I have run 13 marathons, including Berlin five times. Then I was doing New York and then we decided to do the six Major Marathons and Tokyo was the next where we could get the starting number. In the autumn, we are in Chicago.
>
> (Personal communication)

Afterwards I happened to interview two travel guides from the Danish marathon travel company *Marathon Rejser*. They informed me that their package tours to the Tokyo Marathon (and the other Majors) are sold out years in advance despite the substantial fee (at least €2,700) and that people participate because it is a Major.

We may say that the interviewees visit Tokyo because of this event and this event appeals to them because it is part of a bigger network of prestigious events. While Tokyo is not the main attractor, I am not suggesting that it, and Japan more generally, plays no role in attracting runners. My interviewees stress that it is wonderful that the Tokyo Marathon gives them the opportunity to experience this exotic place and that the six-star finisher project is alluring because it allows them to have an excuse for (re)visiting must-see cities and to combine their love of running with tourist travel. While all my interviewees' main concern was the race itself and how their body would cope with this gruelling distance on the day, many – especially those who did not plan on going all-out for a new PB ('personal best') – said that they hoped to experience something of Tokyo's famous street life and landmarks. Take Ove as an example. A couple of months after he became a six-star finisher in Tokyo, I asked him how he experienced the Tokyo Marathon:

> The race was great even before it started. I knew I would be a six-star finisher. So the whole race should be something I would enjoy – ALL THE WAY. I know that a marathon gets hard at some point, but you can enjoy it anyway … In New York, I had a lovely, amazing race where I high-fived all the time and had time and energy to gaze because my objective was not an all-out race. I aimed for 3.15 but I ended up in 3.20, but it didn't matter. Going into the Tokyo race, I swore I'd keep an eye on all those cameras so I could remember to cheer, give high-fives and wave. And to watch the cheering and entertaining

audience. I had promised myself to keep an eye on that because time didn't matter today. So, I did. I must say that Tokyo is the perfect race for this because the atmosphere is crazy and so many are dressed up.

(Personal communication)

The tourist gaze is always multi-sensuous (Urry & Larsen, 2011) and the sonic element is important to marathon runners as the longed-for atmosphere is not just visual, but equally important, audible, produced through clapping, loud music, vocal support and so on. Many of the interviewees anticipate or remember the multi-sensuous atmosphere of the race more vividly than the actual sights and neighbourhoods that they passed by. Like Ove, they look forward to or have experiences of impressions that are related to their movement and the spectators that they see and hear: those crazy dressed-up ones, those that yell their name (printed on their start number) or those with whom they high-five. These vague impressions and interactions, more than those of specific landmarks, stick in the memory of these western runners. This is in part because Tokyo is somewhat unknown to most of the runners and they struggle – unlike in New York and London – with differentiating between the various neighbourhoods. Another finding – that resonates with my own experience at Kyoto Marathon – is that the interviewees know from previous races that the 'tourist gaze' (Urry & Larsen, 2011) escapes them if their mind is fully on running fast and beating their best time. This wears out their body and produces a 'tunnel vision' with an exclusive eye for running. As one PB-chasing runner says:

If London and Berlin are anything to go by, then I will barely remember anything about the landmarks. I have done London three times and I can barely tell you what it is like in the second part of the run, except the part when you come to the Houses of Parliament and Big Ben. That's all I can remember and I have run it three times, so probably not. It's a shame. I will run 26 miles tomorrow and not remember much else than the result.

(Personal communication)

However, others discovered – similarly to my experience in Kyoto – that a well-paced marathon runner who is not time-obsessed can enjoy a mobile embodied gaze that opens up to the world around him or her. As Klaus said, when I asked him how much he saw of Tokyo during the race:

You try as much as possible. It depends on your mindset for that particular race. If you go out and run all out, then you put your head down between your legs. But if your attitude is that you would like to get some fun out of it and experience the city, it is clear that you see much more of it. It was that attitude that I ran with in Tokyo, it was not a 'personal best' attempt. And I saw much of the city and had fun.

(Personal communication)

This extensive form of marathon running is evidently also a mode of tourism. Some say, half-jokingly, that marathon running is an excuse for travelling and seeing great cities. This is plausible because most of my interviewees travel with their non-running partner or family members, and they want much more than just seeing the marathon. All the interviewees are excited and grateful about being in Tokyo and most of them stay extra nights to do some sightseeing, while others embark on longer trips to other cities. For instance, Klaus, who was supported by his non-running brother and parents, were at the race because they were about to head off on a two-week journey to other parts of Japan. The Swiss couple who were drawn to the Tokyo Marathon because it was a Majors competition had never contemplated holidaying in Japan, and yet they were now very excited about being here and the prospect of touring Japan. Many find it wrong and superficial to travel that long just to run and not immerse oneself further in the city. For instance, more than half of those who travelled with *Marathon Rejser* had signed up for the full package that involved a classic seven-day sightseeing tour around Japan.

I finish the last interview of the day and I ache for a gentle 6-km run back to my flat. I'm used to running more or less everywhere in Copenhagen, and as Cidell states: 'One of the advantages of running as a form of exercise or a hobby is the ubiquity of its availability' as it can be 'done ... anywhere and at any time' (2014, p. 577). I was about to learn that this is not the case in Tokyo (and many other cities), where crammed pavements dominated by rhythms of walking make it virtually impossible and indeed 'transgressive' to run. I soon give up and jump on the tube. Later in the evening, when googling 'running in Tokyo', I learn that running is an early-morning activity and that it takes place in parks, along canals and, not least, around a 5-km loop around the Imperial Palace, not on pavements (Havens, 2015, p. 8).

The day after the marathon I run the Imperial Palace loop. While it affords a nice unhindered running flow and the panorama is riveting, I commiserate with the local runners who must be really bored with endlessly circling around in this restricted loop to the sound of speeding cars. How different it was yesterday when runners were the celebrated kings of the streets and they could use the entire city. No wonder Japanese marathons are so extraordinary and festive when their everyday running cultures are so ordinary and restricted.

Conclusion

I end with some general observations. While the mobilities paradigm is interested in mobility per se, it has overlooked mobilities of sporting bodies immersed in the weather-world and the terrains and topographies of places. I have addressed this deficiency by giving a preliminary account of what I have termed 'marathon (tourism) mobilities' in relation to an ethnographic study of why and how western runners do the Kyoto Marathon and the Tokyo Marathon. I have argued that 'marathon *tourism* mobilities' involve tourist travel to exciting cities. As discussed by Latham and McCormack (2010), extraordinary marathons are not staged in unknown, nondescript places but in world-famous, well-connected global cities that are already 'overrun' by tourists. The Majors are, to a large extent, popular because they take place in famed and tourism-friendly cities, whereas other marathons struggle because the hosting city sells few tickets. Yet the case of the Kyoto Marathon illustrates that the extraordinariness of Kyoto and the tourist-gaze-friendly course is not enough to attract western runners. The paramount reason is that this race is not a Major. If it were exceptionally fast, it would appeal to PB-chasing runners, but as we have seen, this is not the case because of the many inclines.

Indeed, the research in Tokyo demonstrated the globally networked nature of elite marathon events. It was overwhelmingly the case that westerners 'ran Tokyo' as part of a larger quest to become six-star finishers. The six-star finishers' medal is a form of conspicuous consumption (Veblen, 2005) where (mainly western) middle-aged and upper-middle-class people demonstrate 'event travel careers' (Getz & McConnell, 2011), wealth and cosmopolitanism as much as athletic ability (indeed, the average six-star finisher is no faster than the average marathon runner).

I have also argued that accounts of marathon (tourism) mobilities must discuss the embodied and physical sensations of running this mythical distance in a highly affective environment, with closed-off streets exclusively reserved for runners and brimming with affective sensations: spectacular landmarks, massive support and a festive atmosphere. In the first vignette, inspired by non-representational ethnography, I paid particular attention to the corporeal sensations of running long distances while always being immersed, or emplaced, in different weather-worlds and terrains. I have tried to demonstrate that sensations of running and gazing-while-running are highly contingent as they are affected by and depend upon always shifting configurations of bodily energy and rhythm, running strategies, weather conditions, material environments, sights and affective atmospheres.

References

Allen-Collinson, J., Jennings, G., Vaittinen, A., & Owton, H. (2018). Weather-wise? Sporting embodiment, weather work and weather learning in running and triathlon. *International Review for the Sociology of Sport*, *54*(7), 777–792.

Andrews, G. J. (2017). From post-game to play-by-play: Animating sports movement-space. *Progress in Human Geography*, *41*(6), 766–794.

Belson, K. (2012). Tokyo will be added as the sixth major marathon. *New York Times*, www.nytimes.com/2012/11/02/sports/tokyo-will-be-added-as-sixth-major-marathon. html?_r=0 (accessed 22 June 2019).

Birtchnell, T., & Caletrío, J. (Eds.). (2013). *Elite Mobilities*. London: Routledge.

Bissell, D. (2008). Comfortable bodies: Sedentary affects. *Environment and Planning A*, *40*(7), 1697–1712.

Bryant, J. (2010). *The London Marathon*. London: Random House.

Cidell, J. (2014). Running road races as transgressive event mobilities. *Social and Cultural Geography*, 15, 571–583.

Cook, S., Shaw, J., & Simpson, P. (2016). Jography: Exploring meanings, experiences and spatialities of recreational road-running. *Mobilities*, *11*(5), 744–769.

Edensor, T., & Larsen, J. (2018). Rhythmanalysing marathon running: 'A drama of rhythms'. *Environment and Planning A: Economy and Space*, *50*(3), 730–746.

Elliott, A., & Urry, J. (2010). *Mobile Lives*. London: Routledge.

Getz, D., & McConnell, A. (2011). Serious sport tourism and event travel careers. *Journal of Sport Management*, 25(4), 326–338.

Hannam, K., Butler, G., & Paris, C. M. (2014). Developments and key issues in tourism mobilities. *Annals of Tourism Research*, *44*, 171–185.

Havens, T. R. (2015). *Marathon Japan: Distance Racing and Civic Culture*. Honolulu, HI: Iniversity of Hawai'i Press.

Hockey, J., & Allen-Collinson, J. (2015). 'Digging in'. In *Endurance Running: A Socio-Cultural Examination*, edited by W. Bridel, P. Markula and J. Denison (pp. 227–242). London: Routledge.

Hockey, J., & Collinson, J. A. (2007). Grasping the phenomenology of sporting bodies. *International Review for the Sociology of Sport*, *42*(2), 115–131.

Larsen, J. (2001). Tourism mobilities and the travel glance: Experiences of being on the move. *Scandinavian Journal of Hospitality and Tourism*, *1*(2), 80–98.

Larsen, J. (2014). (Auto) ethnography and cycling. *International Journal of Social Research Methodology*, *17*(1), 59–71.

Larsen, J. (2018). Commuting, exercise and sport: An ethnography of long-distance bike commuting. *Social & Cultural Geography*, 19(1), 39–58.

Larsen, J., & Urry, J. (2014). Gazing and performing. *Environment and Planning D: Society and Space*, *29*(6), 1110–1125.

Latham, A. (2015). The history of a habit: Jogging as a palliative to sedentariness in 1960s America. *Cultural Geographies*, *22*(1), 103–126.

Latham, A., & McCormack, D. P. (2010). 'Globalizations big and small'. In *Urban Assemblages: How Actor-Network Theory Changes Urban Studies*, edited by I. Farías and T. Bender (pp. 53–72). London: Routledge.

Latham, A., & McCormack, D. P. (2017). 'Affective cities'. In *Routledge Handbook of Physical Cultural Studies*, edited by M. L. Silk, D. L. Andrews and H. Thorpe (pp. 53–72). London: Taylor & Francis.

Leder, D. (1990). *The Absent Body*. Chicago, IL: University of Chicago Press.

Murakami, H. (2009). *What I Talk About When I Talk About Running*. London: Vintage Books.

Newman, J., & Falcous, M. (2012). Moorings and movements: The paradox of sporting mobilities. *Sites*, 9(1), 38–58.

Rickly, J. M. (2016). Lifestyle mobilities: A politics of lifestyle rock climbing. *Mobilities*, *11*(2), 243–263.

Sheller, M., & Urry, J. (2004). *Tourism Mobilities: Places to Play, Places in Play*. London: Routledge.

Sheller, M., & Urry, J. (2006). The new mobilities paradigm. *Environment and Planning A*, *38*(2), 207–226.

Shipway, R., & Jones, I. (2007). Running away from home: Understanding visitor experiences and behaviour at sport tourism events. *International Journal of Tourism Research*, *9*(5), 373–383.

Spinney, J. (2006). A place of sense: A kinaesthetic ethnography of cyclists on Mont Ventoux. *Environment and Planning D: Society and Space, 24*(5), 709–732.

Thorpe, H. (2012). Transnational mobilities in snowboarding culture: Travel, tourism and lifestyle migration. *Mobilities, 7*(2), 317–345.

Urry, J. (2012). *Sociology beyond Societies: Mobilities for the Twenty-First Century.* London: Routledge.

Urry, J., & Larsen, J. (2011). *The Tourist Gaze 3.0.* London: Sage.

Vannini, P. (2015). Non-representational ethnography: New ways of animating lifeworlds. *Cultural Geographies, 22*(2), 317–327.

Veblen, T. (2005). *Conspicuous Consumption* (Vol. 38). London: Penguin.

Chapter 10

Performative nationalism in Japan's inbound tourism television programmes

YOU, Sekai! (The world), and the tourism nation

Adam Doering and Tsz Hei Kong

Introduction

Over the past decade international inbound tourism has garnered unprecedented attention by the Japanese national government and is now recognised as a major pillar of the economic growth strategy and a critical industry for facilitating rural and regional revitalisation (Prime Minister of Japan & His Cabinet, 2016). More than just an economic policy, international inbound tourism has been described by the Ministry of Land, Infrastructure and Transport (MLIT) (2003) as an attempt to establish itself as *kanko rikkoku*, translated as 'tourism nation', 'tourism state' (Yamashita, 2008), 'tourism-oriented nation-building' (Ishimori, 2009), or 'tourism-oriented developed nation' (MLIT, 2016), depending on the author or report. Positioned as *kanko rikkoku*, inbound tourism to Japan is as much about national cultural revitalisation and political stability in the face of increasing diversity as it is an economic strategy (Ishimori, 2009; MLIT, 2012, 2016). Research has shown how the intensification of cross-border mobilities has renewed and even amplified the complexities and contradictions of national identity in a rapidly globalising Japan (Burgess, 2004, 2010; Graburn, Ertl, & Tierney, 2008; Iwabuchi, 2015). However, these studies focus on the construction of national identity in the context of transnational migrant mobilities (Burgess, 2010) and the global export of Japan's media and popular culture (Iwabuchi, 2015). Investigations into how cohesive national cultural identities are maintained and/or transgressed in an era of rapidly increasing international inbound tourism are limited.

The chapter begins to examine how inbound tourism offers a familiar yet new context for understanding the complexities and contradictions of national identity and nationalism in the context of Japan's tourism nation-building efforts. We do this by examining the performative Japanese/non-Japanese social relations that enact and reinforce well-established national cultural boundaries within the context of Japan's inbound tourism television programmes. More specifically, we analyse the performative role of inbound tourism media representation and discourse in (re)organising emergent cultural diversity, and the ways inbound tourism functions to (re)demarcate rather than break down nationalistic ideologies within the Japanese context. Our discussion focuses on two inbound tourism television programmes, *YOU wa nani shi ni Nippon he*? [Why did you come to Japan?] and *Sekai! Nippon Ikitai Hito Ōendan* [Who wants to come to Japan?].[1] We argue the emergence of such Japan-praising inbound television programmes constitutes a familiar mode of performative nationalism that is reinventing itself as Japan moves towards becoming a tourism nation.

We begin by contextualising the rise of inbound tourism in Japan and the national government policies that have supported the tourism nation programme. Next, we discuss the literature relating to the historical construction and performativity of Japanese national identity. Our analysis then draws attention to three performative elements of Japan's inbound television programmes: the representation of 'The good tourist' as a marker of Otherness and cultural distance, 'Rediscovering Japaneseness' as a self-orientalising discourse which reaffirms essentialised cultural boundaries, and a discussion concerning the 'other Others' whose stories and experiences are undermined as a result of the normative tourism performance involving authentically Japanese hosts and culture appreciating Western guests. As part of our analyses we examine how these representations are negotiated, understood, contested, confirmed, and problematised by the audience through online communities dedicated to the show. Through a close reading of inbound television programmes we investigate how particular categories of 'foreign tourist' and 'Japanese host' are implicated in repetitive performative acts that reinforce binaries between Self–Other, Host–Guest, West–East, and national–transnational. Critical analysis of these tensions is needed if we are to better understand how the concept of a tourism nation functions at this particular historical moment. Alongside others, we argue this kind of cultural critique is a necessary first step towards encouraging a more inclusive and diverse Japan (Burgess, 2015; Iwabuchi, 2015; Yonekura, 2015).

Making a tourism nation: Japan's inbound tourism policy between 2003 and 2016

For much of the twentieth century tourism was not a national priority for the Japanese government (Funck, 2017; Ishimori, 2009; Nagai, Doering, & Yashima, 2018; Ota, 2016). Post-World War II nation-building focused primarily on manufacturing industries and foreign trade, but with the collapse of the economic bubble in the 1980s the government was forced to rethink these priorities. A weakening economy and declining population – combined with the increasing mobilities of goods, services, media, and people on a global scale – meant that manufacturing and foreign exports alone could not sustain Japan's economic standing (Henderson, 2017; Ota, 2016). Against this background, international inbound tourism emerged as a major pillar of the economic growth strategy (Prime Minister of Japan & His Cabinet, 2016).

The launch of the Visit Japan Campaign (*Yokoso! Japan*) in 2003 marked the beginning of a national branding strategy to encourage inbound tourism, initially aiming to attract 10 million international tourists annually by 2010 (Prime Minister of Japan & His Cabinet, 2016). According to the Japan National Tourism Organisation (JNTO, 2019), inbound arrivals surpassed the 10 million target in 2013 and since then have grown exponentially. In 2018, a record high of 31 million international tourists visited Japan, marking a six-fold increase in international inbound tourists since the launch of the Visit Japan Campaign (VJC) (JNTO, 2019). The national government now plans to attract 40 million international tourists by 2020 and 60 million by 2030 (JTA, 2018). These figures indicate the Japanese government's mission to establish itself as a tourism nation has partially been achieved.

International arrival statistics tell only half the story. A close reading of Japan's governmental policy between 2003 and 2016 reveals that inbound tourism is as much about national cultural revitalisation as it is economic.[2] When the national government first launched the VJC in 2003 the then-Prime Minister Junichiro Koizumi declared his intention to establish Japan as *kanko rikkoku*, a tourism nation. For Koizumi, attracting inbound tourists also meant 'encouraging each region to rediscover and enhance its charms', thereby revitalising 'the beauty of Japan' and establishing itself as a culture-creating nation (MLIT, 2003, p. 37). This early stage of inbound tourism policy development repeats the familiar rhetoric of the *Discover Japan* (1970s) and *Exotic Japan* (1980s) domestic tourism campaigns that endeavoured to take advantage of Japan's national nostalgia for rural and regional heritage (Creighton, 1997; McMorran, 2008; Robertson, 1997), but this time designed for the international inbound market.

In 2007, the *Tourism Nation Promotion Basic Law* (Basic Law) came into law, further emphasising a regional focus and making the claim that international tourism was 'capable of inspiring pride and love in its residents' (JTA, 2018). The Basic Law also identified for the first time 'the importance of having global points of view' as one of its guiding principles for realising a tourism nation (JTA, 2018). The Basic Law was implemented in 2012 when the *Tourism Nation Promotion Basic Plan* (Basic Plan) was approved by the Cabinet (MLIT, 2012). Policy discourse began to shift away from focusing only on fostering regional pride to a discussion of how regional communities could, would, and should engage with increasing numbers of inbound tourism. The plan outlines four fundamental principles for realising a tourism nation, including economic justifications such as tourism-supported disaster recovery and tourism-derived economic development, but also principle number three, the 'Enhancement of mutual international understanding' (MLIT, 2012). Principle three identifies the importance of cross-cultural exchange with the aim to 'cultivate Japanese cultural groundings that will be accepted in the world, [and] encourage people from overseas to have a better understanding of Japan' (MLIT, 2012, p. 4). To achieve this aim, the plan further stipulates, 'All people in Japan should participate in tourism, mak[ing] tourism attractive by having hearty communications with travellers' (MLIT, 2012, p. 4). International communication and cultural exchange are employed here for the purposes of representing and circulating certain tourism-inspired visions of Japanese cultural identity to the world. According to the Basic Plan, it is up to the local regions to enact this specific version of Japanese culture via person-to-person communication and cultural exchange.

With the target of 20 million inbound tourists achieved earlier than expected, a new approach was needed to reflect the increasing number of tourists in Japan. In March 2016, the 'New Tourism Strategy to Invigorate the Japanese Economy' (New Tourism Strategy) was introduced which set out three new visions for becoming 'a developed country in tourism' (MLIT, 2016). This policy marked another discursive shift that acknowledged the increasing role of *the tourist* in promoting Japan's regions and cultural tourism resources. The New Tourism Strategy aims to maximise the attractiveness of tourism resources by 'drastically shift[ing] from prioritizing conservation of cultural properties to utilizing them by promoting understanding *from the tourist's point of view*' (MLIT, 2016, p. 181, emphasis added). It is at this moment that the New Tourism Strategy takes an interesting performative turn.

By performative, we are referring to the fact that the New Tourism Strategy is not only about creating a proper representation of a Japanese culture for visitors to gaze upon, but rather that the Japanese cultural resources are to be understood and enacted through the reiterative practices of international tourists themselves. The concept of performativity will be discussed in more detail later on. For now, it is important to highlight the fact that the New Tourism Strategy is about enacting a Japanese national culture and identity *through* the meanings and practices of international tourists themselves. Faced with the very real and embodied difficulties of maintaining national identities through overt exclusion of others in an increasingly globalised Japanese society, the performativity of Japan's national culture becomes expressed through sophisticated forms of *inclusion* (Burgess, 2004). Burgess (2004) gives examples of how other related concepts like *kokusaika* (internationalisation) and *tabunka* (multiculturalism) function to maintain the idea of a unique and cohesive Japanese national identity rather than diversify it. The New Tourism Strategy therefore represents a discursive shift in tourism nation-building policy away from (re)presenting Japan to the Other towards a performative Japanese cultural nationalism enacted *through* inclusion of the Other.

Performative nationalism in Japan: a brief history

The idea that Japanese national identity is performed in relation with the Other, or more precisely performed *through* the Other, has a long and complicated history. Although Japan's national consciousness has been built over centuries, the National Reforms brought about by the Meiji restoration in 1887 and its subsequent opposition ushered in a new era of cultural nationalism intent on (re)discovering and preserving the ideology of Japanese cultural uniqueness. This reimaging of Japan's national identity in the late 1800s was constructed in direct contrast to its new found Other, the West (Iwabuchi, 1994, 2015). During the century following the Meiji Restoration, Japanese national identity has been as much about how the West perceives Japan as how the Japanese self-identify (Iwabuchi, 1994).

Ruth Benedict's (1946/2005) seminal text *The Chrysanthemum and the Sword* is important text in this regard, as it helped to solidify a new field of study on Japanese cultural nationalism. Benedict set out to discover what precisely made 'the Japanese' so culturally unique. This helped establish a field of study referred to as *Nihonjinron*, meaning the dedicated study of the unique national characteristics of Japanese people and culture (Burgess, 2010; Ryang, 2004). The impact of Benedict's text and *Nihnjinron* remains today. First, it encouraged a Western orientalist discourse that constructs and sustains an essentialist ideology of Japaneseness (Burgess, 2010; Fukuda, 2018; Iwabuchi, 1994). Clearly demarcating a cultural boundary between Japan and its Western Other, the lingering importance of this work lies in the ongoing and persuasive endorsement of Japanese exceptionalism (Iwabuchi, 1994). Second, the Western orientalising gaze of Japanese otherness was embraced rather than rejected in Japanese nationalist discourse and practice. As Iwabuchi (1994, p. 51) argues, 'Japan's own construction of "Japaneseness" has successfully utilized the difference from the West'. In order to maintain any semblance of a cohesive Japanese national cultural identity since the Meiji era, the existence of a non-Japanese other, a role frequently played by the West, is required.

The reproduction of *Nihonjinron* discourse continues today, but arguably in subtler ways. As noted earlier, maintaining cultural distinctiveness and preserving national cultural boundaries in a globalising Japan are achieved today more by inclusion of otherness than exclusion (Burgess, 2004, 2010). Research concerning the production of Japanese cultural nationalism has shifted from analyses of top-down management and control towards investigations of banal nationalism (Hambleton, 2011; Iwabuchi, 2015; Perkins, 2010), cultural nationalism (Fukuda, 2018; Yoshino, 1992), and soft power diplomacy (Burgess, 2015). Two key points of this literature on Japanese cultural nationalism are important for our analysis. Firstly, this current trend describes how Japanese national cultural identity is maintained and performed in many different facets of everyday life. Japanese food (Hiroko, 2008), popular culture (Iwabuchi, 2015), and leisure (Leheny, 2003) are the important sites of analysing how cultural nationalism manifests in everyday life. Secondly, the significance of everyday nationalism is that essentialised and homogenic national identities are reaffirmed and even strengthened within in response to an increasing engagement with processes of globalisation.

The everyday becomes the productive space of regenerating a national cultural identity when faced with a rapidly diversifying landscape. Everyday events, objects, and social practices once taken for granted take on new significance and a deepened symbolic meaning of Japaneseness within the context of a global Japan (Fukuda, 2018; Hambleton, 2011; Iwabuchi, 2015; Perkins, 2010; Yoshino, 1992). This creates excess meaning for mundane cultural practices that are the result of increased interaction with otherness. Like the Self defined through the Other, national identity is also developed through transnational engagement (Iwabuchi, 2015). As Iwabuchi (2015, p. 3) describes it, 'cross-cultural connections are more often administered in ways to strengthen a national thinking and feeling ... such re-nationalising gravity is resilient and flexible enough to overpower such radical possibilities in Japan'. This raises important questions about how particular performances of Japanese national identities are enacted and reproduced within Japan's tourism nation-building project.

The performance turn of tourism studies is also useful for us here, as we examine how emergent inbound tourism television programmes in Japan not only reconstruct an 'authentic Japan' for tourists to gaze upon, but moreover stage tourism spaces, places, social relations, and identities in a way that privileges particular host/guest performances over others (Edensor, 2002; Franklin & Crang, 2001; Baerenholdt, Haldrup, Larsen, & Urry, 2004). Looking through a performative lens, we see that the 'nation' is not 'natural', especially a tourism nation. Edensor (2002) notes that tourism's staging of the nation encapsulates both entertainment and educational features of national culture, which in this chapter functions to inscribe and instruct a domestic viewership on how to relate to tourists, which kinds of tourists to relate with, and how that relationship should unfold. Such cultural imperatives inscribe performative expectations on both host and guest, prescribing 'the right way' of social relations within Japan's tourism-oriented nation. This in turn celebrates and privileges certain subjectivities who perform 'properly' while silencing those who do not. In what follows, we analyse the ways in which Japan's inbound tourism television programmes are implicated in specific performances of Japanese nationalism.

YOU and *Sekai!* Unpacking Japan's inbound tourism television programmes

The past decade has seen a rise in a variety of nationalistic television programmes praising Japanese culture and society as seen through the eyes of foreigners (Fukuda, 2018; Hambleton, 2011). The two shows under analysis in this chapter, *YOU wa nani shi ni Nippon he?* and *Sekai! Nippon Ikitai Hito Ōendan*, fit within this broader trend of 'Japan-praising' television programming. The two programmes started broadcasting in 2013 and 2016 respectively, coinciding with the inbound tourism increases in Japan and governmental policies promoting the concept of tourism nation-building. Both shows are designed to follow the journeys of foreign visitors around Japan, highlighting the inbound tourists' passion for Japan to Japanese audiences. Paralleling the national tourism policy objective to encourage person-to-person exposure, communication, and exchange through tourism, the programmes also aim for *mitchaku shuzai*, translated as 'close-contact reporting' with foreign visitors. In familiar *nihonjinron* style the programmes are designed to demonstrate to a domestic audience what makes Japanese national culture exceptional and unique in the world as perceived through the views of foreign visitors.

YOU wa nani shi ni Nippon he? first premiered as a pilot show in June and October 2012. The English name of the television programme is officially translated as 'Why did you come to Japan?' (TV Tokyo, 2019c). *YOU* is produced by TV Tokyo and hosted by the comedy duo Osamu Shitara and Yuki Himura. Starting in January 2013, *YOU* was promoted to a weekly broadcast with a late-night Wednesday time slot. After three months, it was re-scheduled to the primetime slot. In this inbound tourism television programme, the production team rotates between international airports to locate 'a treasure trove of funny and interesting foreigners' (TV Tokyo, 2019a). Throughout the programme the foreigner travellers are casually referred as 'You'. Foreigners who accept the interview are invited to participate in the television programme by allowing the production team to film their travel experience in Japan. A typical show consists of interviews with between nine and thirteen international visitors. Taking one episode aired on 30 July 2018 as an example, the show had a total of nine scenes, with nine out of eleven people interviewed comprising Western males. Most interviews last for two to three minutes, while the two featured interviews, numbers six and seven, lasted around fifteen minutes each. These interviews epitomise the performative nationalism the inbound tourists enact during the show; one German female student doing research on the modern *Oiran Kimono* practices and a Swiss male living in Japan with a Japanese wife whose family has operated a traditional tea house for sixteen generations. These two interviews are discussed in more detail later on.

The second inbound television programme examined is *Sekai! Nippon Ikitai Hito Ōendan. Sekai!*, meaning 'The world', which is broadcast every Wednesday night and usually follows *YOU. Sekai!* differs from *YOU* in that instead of waiting for foreigners to interview at airports in Japan, the production team travels abroad to recruit foreigners who are fans of Japanese culture. Most of the foreign visitors are learning what is considered to be traditional Japanese culture; in our sample, activities like making soy sauce, studying haiku, cooking traditional food, and learning traditional building techniques (e.g. *shikui* wall plaster and *fusuma* traditional sliding doors). However, the nationalist narrative built around the show as explained by the foreigners themselves is that they cannot achieve the skill level of their chosen Japanese art outside Japan. Therefore, their dream is to travel to Japan and advance their skills. In the setting of the show, the production team will arrange for the foreigner to travel to Japan. A tailor-made tour is provided to the foreign travellers and they are able to learn skills and communicate with the masters who are exceptional practitioners of their arts. In the conclusion there is always a scene where both the foreigner and Japanese master have dinner together and frequently end in displays of emotion reaffirming how exceptional and emotive the experience has been.

Methods and data collection

The data collection and thematic analysis of the two programmes comprised two phases. First, the main narratives of the two programmes were developed by viewing and drawing out the main themes of the featured interviews in eight episodes of *Sekai!* between September 2018 and February 2019. The data for *YOU* was collected over a ten-month period between May 2018 and February 2019. Our analysis of *YOU* was done over the same timeframe as Yonekura's (2015) study between May and August 2014. We were interested in seeing how or if the storyline adjusted over the five-year period between the studies. Where required, additional participant information was gathered from the official website of TV Tokyo (TV Tokyo, 2019a). Detailed demographic information of the featured inbound visitors, such as place of origin, race, nationality, and interest in Japan, was recorded for further analysis.

The performances of the nation on television programmes are not static; they are shared, disseminated, reproduced, and renegotiated in a variety of ways. In the second phase of analysis we investigated how such performances of national identity are disseminated and shared, how they are shaped to permit particular performances in everyday life, and how contesting performances orient around such attempts of normalising national identities through inbound tourism. In order to explore audience responses to the two programmes and to provide supporting evidence for the discourse analysis in the previous phase, a netnography was used (Kozinets, 2002). In tourism studies, netnography has been associated with the study of travel motivation (e.g. Li, Wang, Xu, & Mao, 2017) and travel experiences (Chandralal, Rindfleish, & Valenzuela, 2015; Zhang & Hitchcock, 2017). Fukuda (2017) also employs the use of online audience responses to examine the resurgence of cultural nationalism in Japanese mainstream media. Here we are also inspired by a netnography method to examine the dissemination and responses the performative nationalism as it plays out in the two inbound television programmes and online.

According to Kozinets (2002), the first step of netnography is to identify appropriate online communities. The selected online communities should be relevant to the research focus, with high traffic of postings, containing interactive material, and rich in data. Relevant online communities of interest were located using the name of the two television programmes and the Japanese term *kansou* (impression, commentary, review) as keywords in Google. The discussion board of *Yahoo! Japan* returned as the top result for both programmes.[3] The total number of comments obtained from the two discussion boards are 509 and 250 for *YOU* and *Sekai!* respectively. Ameba (www.ameba.jp), a popular Japanese blogging and social networking website, was also identified as an important source of information. The titles of both television programmes were independently used as keywords and a search was performed for impressions of the show inside Ameba.

Seventeen independent blogs were identified as being active online communities. The two authors discussed the collected data from the television shows and blogs, and inductively identified key themes that emerged from the data.

The performative 'good tourist': welcoming Western cultural tourism

YOU – the abbreviated name of the full title of *YOU wa nani shi ni Nippon he* – clearly sets the stage for the ways particular performances of national identity are organised and enacted in the show. *YOU* are not us. As the English version of the TV Tokyo website describes on its programme overview, '"YOU" is a friendly nickname of foreigners we use at our show' (TV Tokyo, 2019a). No such explanation of the term 'YOU' is given on the Japanese website. Given the show is produced by a Japanese production team and created for a domestic audience, 'You' embodies the foreigner while the subject 'I' becomes a taken-for-granted domestic Japanese audience.

The entire performance of the inbound tourism programming relies on first establishing a clear cultural distance between an explicitly constructed 'you' and implied 'I'. As we have seen, the clear and explicit ways boundaries are constructed between ethnic Japanese and non-Japanese have been a long-standing feature of Japanese national identity construction (Burgess, 2010; Fukuda, 2018; Iwabuchi, 1994, 2015). Following this historical trajectory, inbound tourist performativity encouraged by these programmes and the national government's mission to develop a Japanese national identity from the 'tourist's point of view' (MLIT, 2016) intersect. Through the title we already see how these inbound tourism programmes encourage a clear demarcation of non-Japanese and Japanese. This in turn encourages the production of distinct kinds of roles and activities by the Japanese hosts and Western guests, which sustains a host of performative norms.

Demarcating a clear distinction between 'you' and 'I' is a necessary first step in staging the cross-cultural or international exchange of the inbound tourism programmes. The normative choreography of inbound tourism is that the 'good tourist' – the welcomed ones who enact acceptable and predictable national narratives – are those who celebrate the uniqueness and distinctiveness of Japanese culture. Foreign visitors invited to Japan in *Sekai!* and the featured interviews in *YOU* are people who are either self-proclaimed fans of Japanese culture, or whose life in Japan is heavily invested in some way in Japanese cultural practices. Referring back to the episode on 30 July 2018 as an example, in the featured interviews, numbers six and seven, the cultural practices are related to traditional Japanese culture practices, namely learning about Kimono and making tea. The primary motivation for foreign visitors to Japan is narrated as an immersive cultural experience. Although modern Japanese pop culture and sport culture also receive coverage in *YOU*, the point is the staging of the inbound tourism programmes is almost entirely based on the celebration of a unique and difficult-to-master Japanese culture.

Inbound tourist practices in the shows help organise a national discourse for the domestic audience whereby the 'good tourist' is expected to celebrate the uniqueness, distinctiveness, and exceptionalism of Japanese culture. The inbound tourist who enacts this normative role is generally welcomed in the commentary of the shows. For example, one audience member of *Sekai!* wrote of his surprise at the fact foreign visitors are interested in Japanese culture, writing, 'I am surprised that there are foreigners who are interested in Japanese culture. Many of them are not only interested in Japanese culture but they actually learned a lot about it' (*Sekai!*, No. 111, 2017, 15 June). Similarly, an audience member of *YOU* commented on an inbound tourist from Sweden who loves Japanese tea, exclaiming, '(That the tourist) devoted himself in Japanese tea and was extremely enthusiastic about it … he went to a Japanese tea education center in Shizuoka Prefecture and learnt and worked there without pay. I feel happy about that' (*YOU*, No. 261, 2016, 16 May). Such comments reinforce a sense of national pride being performed via inbound tourism through the cultural appreciation by the foreign visitors.

The reality of inbound tourism to Japan suggests this focus on western appreciation of culture is potentially over-stated. Research indicates that visitors to Japan are not as overtly invested in deep cultural experiences as the inbound programmes suggest (JTA, 2018). For instance, a recent JTA (2018) survey identified eating Japanese food and shopping as the two most common motivations for tourists in Japan, accounting for 70.5% and 54.4% respectively. Only 20.6% of international visitors surveyed identified experiencing Japanese culture and learning its history as their primary motivation. Moreover, Ahn and McKercher (2015) argue that tourists who travel greater physical distances are more motivated by cultural experiences, such as visiting heritage sites, as opposed to short-haul tourists who tend towards theme parks and shopping. In the case of Japan's inbound television programmes, the majority of westerner visitors are long-haul travellers compared to their counterparts coming from Asian countries, which may help explain why they receive a disproportionate amount of attention. Inbound tourists from the 'West' are key features in the performance of Japanese cultural nationalism by sustaining the idea of Japan as a unique cultural entity that has remained essentially untouched through time. The stage of the tourism nation is set against this co-constitutive relationship of Japan and the West; as Iwabuchi (1994, p. 63) describes this, 'Both need each other to define themselves'. The Western tourist needs a culturally distinctive Japan to perform the good tourist, while the domestic audience relies on the West to realise its own cultural uniqueness.

Japan's national identity is being carefully organised and managed by disproportionately and repeatedly averting the viewers' attention to the impassioned cultural tourist. In this way, inbound tourism programmes help shore up the idea of a cohesive, essentially unchanged, and homogenous society (Befu, 2001). Recent studies have shown how the increase of non-Japanese within Japanese media appeals to the nationalistic sentiments of a domestic audience, reinforcing an imagined homogenous Japanese self-identity in an increasingly transnational

Japan (see Creighton, 1997; Hambleton, 2011, Suzuki, 2015; Yonekura, 2015). In similar ways the performative 'good tourist' – enacted through the idealised Western cultural tourists – establishes new norms of conduct designed to appeal to and instruct a domestic audience on how to engage with increasing inbound tourism mobilities. The performativity of the good tourist also inscribes particular knowledge of which kinds of guests are welcomed, the particular cultural practices to be engaged in, and how these social relations should unfold.

It's not about 'You': rediscovering Japaneseness through the Other

The previous section showed how the production of otherness and establishment of a you–I binary is enacted through the Western tourist's emphasis on the uniqueness and value of Japanese culture. In this section we turn our attention to how the staging of inbound tourism in this way creates a performative space in which 'Japaneseness' is rediscovered through the inclusion of foreign visitors. Previous studies indicate that the inclusion of foreigners in Japan-praising television programming serves as a medium in which ideas of Japanese national identity and nationalism are being reinforced (Fukuda, 2018; Hambleton, 2011). The inbound tourist in the shows plays an interesting and paradoxical role in that by positioning Japan as essentially unique and culturally distant from their own culture, they imply they will never be able to fully understand or appreciate it (Fukuda, 2018; Hambleton, 2011). This not only simplifies the complexities of such cultural mobilities and the spaces between us and them, but also normalises essentialised notions of Japaneseness, of who truly belongs to the nation and who does not.

The 'rediscovering of Japaneseness' narrative begins with the inbound tourists acknowledging the unique value of Japanese culture, followed by a recognition of their own limited ability to fully know and appreciate their chosen Japanese cultural practices. The inbound tourists of the two shows under analysis repeatedly expressed an inability to master Japanese cultural practices. *Sekai!*, for instance, shows us how the nationalist ideology that only ethnic Japanese can truly know and understand the culture of Japan is delivered to the domestic audience *through* inbound tourists themselves. Taking the show broadcast on 26 November 2016 as an example, we see the performative features of the 'mastery' narrative at work. This episode introduces us to a couple who run a local Japanese restaurant and serve Japanese food in a small Mexico town. The following excerpt introduces us to the owners of the restaurant and demonstrates the common-sense way the mastery narrative sets the stage for the rest of the show.

NARRATOR: There are currently fifteen kinds of Japanese food on the menu, but …
VISITOR: Frankly speaking, the Japanese food being served in our restaurant is not perfect. We feel sorry for customers who eat our food and believe it is real Japanese food.
COMMENTATOR: That's honest.

NARRATOR: There are around fifteen customers per day; after deducting rent and payroll for two part-time staff, there is almost no money left. Going to Japan is almost an impossible dream for them. So we will invite them to come to Japan.[4]

Similarly, in another episode on 17 December 2018, the foreign visitor started his interview by expressing a concern that his technique for making Japanese-style sliding doors was not authentic. The subtitles in Japanese were written as 'not the correct way' and the foreign visitor said he 'wants to learn the real technique'. In these short introductions, it is the foreign visitors themselves, not the Japanese narrator or commentator, who recognise that what they are doing is 'not perfect' (*kanpeki dewaarimasen*) and 'not the real or authentic thing' (*honmono dewaari-masen*). This sets the stage for the programme's main narrative where the foreign visitors travel to Japan in search of the authentic masters of their respective cultural practices.

The visitors' desire and struggle to achieve a culturally authentic skill is a plot designed to appeal to a domestic audience's nationalistic sentiment that ultimately Japanese culture belongs solely to the Japanese, instilling the belief that only Japanese properly understand Japanese culture (Fukuda, 2018). Although seemingly harmless, this ongoing and repetitive discourse about who can truly 'know' or appreciate Japanese culture contributes to what Fukuda (2018, p. 232) describes as 'the cultural nationalistic tenet that ... Japanese culture belongs solely to the Japanese'. As we now explore, this makes possible the contemporary rediscovery of the uniqueness and value of 'Japaneseness' in an emergent tourism nation.

Another performative feature of the inbound tourism television programmes starts to emerge, namely that they open a space for the domestic audience to rediscover the virtues of Japanese culture, thereby renewing a sense of national identity in an increasingly diversifying tourism nation. Audience responses to the shows offer evidence for the fact that the inbound tourism television programmes are creating a space for the Japanese audience to be reflexive on what makes Japan unique within the context of a supposed tourism nation. For example, one Japanese audience response to *Sekai!* commented, 'I enjoy this show because I am impressed by Japanese culture and how wonderful the Japanese people are ... I especially like the part that introduces the features of Japanese culture that the Japanese themselves do not understand' (*Sekai!*, No. 123, 2017, 28 July). Echoing a similar sentiment, one viewer of *YOU* expressed how excited he is by the show and how he is able to 'rediscover' (*saihakken*) the uniqueness and value of Japanese food through inbound tourists:

I am very delighted that (foreigners) are deeply moved by Japan! We take Japanese food for granted. Regarding the food we are eating every day, I feel it is really great! The programme allows me to *rediscover* Japanese food.
(*YOU*, No. 378, 2017, 25 September, emphasis added)

Otherness emerges through the inclusion of these selective inbound tourists, which in turn instrumentalises foreign bodies in a way that reinforces essentialised national and cultural boundaries. Appreciation of one's own culture is the foundation of the shows; this is what sells. One viewer of *Sekai!* writes that although there are several stylistic concerns with the programming, the fundamental premise of the show – offering a space to rediscover Japanese culture – keeps him tuned in:

> Whether or not the cast of the show is appropriate or not is certainly debatable, but the more essential aspect of the show is that by watching the programme I am able to reaffirm my appreciation for Japanese traditions and other exceptional things in Japan.
>
> *(Sekai!*, No. 45, 2016, 5 October)

Although the show's protagonists are the foreigners travelling in Japan, the audience responses describe how such inbound tourism programming enables a rediscovery of the uniqueness and value of Japanese culture *through* the inbound tourist's own perspective. This supports Hambleton's (2011) findings that the primary purpose is to use the positive value judgements of Japanese culture made by foreign visitors to encourage the rediscovery of Japanese cultural uniqueness by a new generation of the Japanese public.

In *YOU* and *Sekai!* attention circulates around the performative features of Japaneseness rather than understanding the inbound tourist experience or the experience of difference within Japan. By doing so, certain versions of national culture and identity are reified. In these shows we see how Western inbound tourism is creating a space for a conservative public to reinvent tradition and rediscover Japan in a rapidly emerging tourism nation. Importantly, however, this is not the end of the story as performativity of the inbound tourist also comprises those who do not belong, whose stories are undermined by this dominant framing of national identity.

The other Others: on the performative suppression of difference

The presence and absence of certain races play significant roles in constructing who is welcomed within Japan's emerging tourism nation. In his book *National Identity, Popular Culture and Everyday Life*, Edensor (2002, p. 70) argues that in performing national identity certain 'enactions are carried out that re-inscribe who belongs to place, and crucially, who does not'. This claim builds on the theory of performativity that demonstrates how the power of a performative act is in the way certain groups are excluded because of certain normative framings of the social world (Butler, 1993). The performativity of any act is not only that it promotes a certain hegemonic vision of the world, but that in doing so it actively silences alternative worlds and worldviews. The performative act *is* its silences.

Asian tourists comprise a significantly larger section of the international inbound tourism market than visitors from European, Australasian, or North American countries (JTA, 2018). However, there is a clear Western bias in Japan's inbound television programming (Yonekura, 2015). In 2014, Yonekura (2015) compared the nationality of foreigners appearing in *YOU* with actual international visitor arrivals between May and August 2014. Yonekura (2015) found a clear Western nationality bias in the show, with Asian tourists representing 66% of all international arrivals in 2014, but accounting for only 19% of inbound tourists on the show. He points out two reasons for this bias. Firstly, the clear visual differences in hair and skin colour makes it easier for the domestic audience to discern who is host and guest. Secondly, he argues Western tourists are more interested in sightseeing than their Asian counterparts, and suggests this is more interesting for the target audience. Because, as Butler (1993, p. 2) suggests, 'Performativity must be understood not as a singular or deliberate "act," but, rather, as the reiterative and citational practice', we examined whether or not this Western bias changed over the past four-year period and to what extent these performative aspects of national identity are constituted over time.

Figure 10.1 compares the nationality of inbound tourists receiving interviews in *YOU* with the actual inbound tourism data from JTA (2018) between May and August 2018, four years after Yonekura's (2015) initial study. To date, a similar kind of bias remains, and is even slightly more prevalent in the 2018 season of *YOU*. Asian travellers now account for over 80% of actual international inbound tourist arrivals (JTA, 2018), but now only represent 8% of those interviewed in the show in that time period. We observe once again the Western bias of *YOU*, where white skin colour and an assumed cultural distance of the visitor establishes an

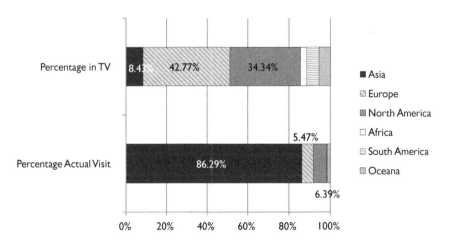

Figure 10.1 Comparison between foreigners in *YOU* and actual international tourist arrivals in Japan (May to August 2018).

Source: adopted from Yonekura (2015, p. 198).

oversimplified way for a domestic audience to distinguish who is the guest. Moreover, the hosts in both shows also present the audience with an essentialised understanding of who comprises a Japanese host: those who were born and live in Japan, and apparently are only able to speak in Japanese. The homogeneity of Japanese national identity is legitimised and constructed around the familiar nationalist trope of an ethnically homogenous and mono-lingual Japan (Befu, 2001; Buntilov, 2016).

The stereotypical image of Western cultural tourists and the seeming immobility of the Japanese host, however, are not reflective of current multiple modes of transnational mobilities shaping contemporary Japan (see Willis & Murphy-Shigematsu, 2008). *YOU* consistently and constantly repeats the same Western bias over and over again, which is necessary for a national cultural norm to be reinscribed (Edensor, 2002; Perkins, 2010). The performance of national identity presented in *YOU* simplifies and organises the diverse reality of inbound tourism, minimising difference and consolidating a narrative of a homogenous and exceptional national identity.

With the tourism nation staged in this way, the audience responses to the shows draw on this set of stereotypes and perform them in a way that reinforces long-standing normative ideas about foreignness and Japaneseness. The performance of such social norms plays an important role in the management and containment of difference as Japan's national and cultural borders become increasingly mobilized (Iwabuchi, 2015). Commentary on the shows related to white Western guests, or the 'typical' foreigner, is overall positive, and as examined earlier, inspires an appreciation of Japanese culture by the domestic audience. When it comes to under-represented Asian tourists, the commentary can become quite dramatic. For example, a 23 March 2015 episode of *YOU* featured a surprise wedding between a German man and a Korean woman. The staff of *YOU* agreed to help the German man arrange for the surprise wedding. This episode was unique for the fact that it did not focus on cultural tourists. The responses to this episode are harsh, with one audience of *YOU* stating:

> It is interesting to see the perspectives of foreigners [*ikoguhitotachi*] who are having fun in Japan. It's unfortunate, but I don't want to watch the show anymore. I don't want to see any Koreans in this programme. Ahh, now I realise that maybe I liked the show because [until that episode] there were no Koreans. Why would people who are anti-Japanese have a wedding ceremony in Japan? Why did they find it necessary to show us that? I really can't understand that.
> (*YOU*, No. 186, 2015, 23 March)

Another comment in the same thread reinforced this idea: 'Why did the television programme film the wedding ceremony of a Korean? Of course, I did not watch it. I don't want to watch this programme anymore. Why would I want to watch a Korean wedding ceremony in Japan?' (*YOU*, No. 186, 2015, 24 March). Of course, the historical, cultural, and political proximity between these two nations complicates the tourism situation in Japan. In contrast to the overly positive connotations associated with the Western cultural tourists visiting Japan, Korean tourists are too closely associated with negative emotions and are bound up in complex social relationships that limit their ability to participate in the hegemonic performance of the 'good tourist'.

YOU and *Sekai!* serve as performative conventions, with the Japanese audience, who are also 'actors' in the performance of the shows, helping to reinscribe who belongs within the tourism nation narrative, and most importantly, who does not. Those who do not fit neatly into these normative conventions, in this case Korean representations in the show, do not belong to the official space of performance. These reiterative performances normalise certain guest–host relations over others, solidifying stereotypical understandings of foreignness and Japaneseness that privilege specific racial demographics over others, thereby normalising exclusion. This has the performative effect of sustaining essentialised identities for both inbound tourists and the Japanese.

Conclusion

This chapter examined how international inbound tourism offers a familiar and yet new context for analysing the reproduction of Japanese national identity, and the ways these are performatively sustained and reinforced in the context of Japan's tourism nation building. Ultimately, the idea of building a tourism nation is riddled with contradiction. On the one hand, national governmental tourism policy claims that inviting large numbers of foreign visitors within its own borders will not only contribute to economic recovery, but also promote the enhancement of mutual international understanding. Such policy-making suggests a deconstructive role of inbound tourism, claiming that 'This may change the Japanese society, which is said to be introverted' (MLIT, 2012, p. 4). In other words, international inbound tourism is said to contain the possibility of encouraging a more diverse, international, and multicultural Japan.

On the other hand, the tourism nation policy explicitly employs inbound tourism as a means to (re)construct a unified national cultural identity in response to the diversifying socio-cultural Japanese landscape that engaging with international tourism invites. Drawing on the example of Japan's inbound tourism television programming, we illustrated how essentialised ideologies of 'Japaneseness' and 'foreignness' are reproduced through systems of tourism performances. Despite both programmes following the journeys of foreign visitors to Japan, the staging here aims to create a space for the domestic audience to be reflexive on the uniqueness and value of specific aspects of 'Japanese culture' within the context of an emerging tourism nation. However, as we have detailed, Japan's tourism nation building is constructed on a specific tourism system that accentuates essentialised notions of white Western Otherness that reinforce the idea of a unique yet closed-off Japanese national identity. The performative relations between host and guest, based on biological factors, mono-linguistic ideals, and (in)ability to master traditional Japanese culture, all help solidify normative ideas of national and cultural boundedness that become difficult to breach (Perkins, 2010). It could be argued then that the world of tourism being broadcast in Japan does much less to promote cross-cultural understanding and exchange than it does to reinforce the pervasive and ubiquitous hegemony of homogeneity that Befu (2001) argues has characterised Japan's national cultural discourse and identity for nearly a century.

As others have pointed out in different contexts, Japan's attempts to engage on a global stage are commonly accompanied by renewal of national symbolism, the containment of cultural diversity, and the reinforcement of national cultural borders (Hambleton, 2011; Iwabuchi, 1994, 2015; Perkins, 2010). The tourism nation described in this chapter presents another site with which normative national identities and structures of difference are being reinforced. That said, we must be careful not to assume the universality of the inbound tourism performativity presented here. The diffusion and reception of Japan's normative system of inbound tourism performativity are without a doubt being contested and reworked in a multiplicity of ways. Although it is absolutely necessary to examine the processes of performative nationalism through time, it is equally critical to draw attention to the ways in which groups, categories, practices, activities, social networks, and tourist sites, which do not fit easily into the normative modes of performative nationalism, carve out alternative spaces of belonging in Japan. Greater attention to the embodied elements of this performative tourism system is necessary. Doing so might aid in the creation of tangible spaces of difference and more radical conceptions of otherness *through* international inbound tourism, which we argue is necessary to develop a more inclusive and diverse Japan.

Notes

1 Henceforth, we will refer to the shows using the abbreviated names '*YOU*' (TV Tokyo, 2019c) and '*Sekai!*' (TV Tokyo, 2019b). The English translations of the shows are as indicated on the programmes' websites.
2 As McMorran (2008) points out, however, the use of culture and 'heritage' is frequently seen simply in economic terms by tourism actors on the ground. However, even if the focus is economic, sociocultural changes are unavoidable.
3 Comments were last collected from the discussion board for Sekai! on 6 August 2019 from https://tv.yahoo.co.jp/review/312422 and the discussion board for YOU was last accessed on the same date from https://tv.yahoo.co.jp/review/36963.
4 The original dialogue was presented in Japanese. Translations were done independently by each of the authors and the accuracy of these translations was then confirmed with a native Japanese-language speaker. A similar process was conducted with all translations of the text unless otherwise stated.

References

Ahn, M. J., & McKercher, B. (2015). The effect of cultural distance on tourism: A study of international visitors to Hong Kong. *Asia Pacific Journal of Tourism Research, 20*(1), 94–113.

Bærenholdt, J. O., Haldrup, M., Larsen, J., & Urry, J. (2004). *Performing tourist places.* London: Ashgate.

Befu, H. (2001). *Hegemony of homogeneity: An anthropological analysis of "Nihonjinron."* Melbourne, Australia: Trans Pacific Press.

Benedict, R. (2005). *The chrysanthemum and the sword: Patterns of Japanese culture.* Boston, MA: Houghton Mifflin Harcourt.

Buntilov, G. (2016). Common narratives in discourses on national identity in Russia and Japan. *Asian Philosophy, 26*(1), 1–19.

Burgess, C. (2004). Maintaining identities: Discourses of homogeneity in a rapidly globalizing Japan. *Electronic Journal of Contemporary Japanese Studies.* Retrieved from www.japanesestudies.org.uk/articles/Burgess.html.

Burgess, C. (2010). The 'illusion' of homogeneous Japan and national character: Discourse as a tool to transcend the 'myth' vs. 'reality' binary. *The Asia-Pacific Journal, 8*(9), 1–23.

Burgess, C. (2015). National identity and the transition from internationalization to globalization: 'Cool Japan' or 'Closed Japan'? In I. Nakane, E. Otsuji, & W. Armour (Eds.), *Languages and identities in a transitional Japan* (pp. 15–36). London: Routledge.

Butler, J. (1993). *Bodies that matter: On the discursive limits of 'sex'.* London: Routledge.

Chandralal, L., Rindfleish, J., & Valenzuela, F. (2015). An application of travel blog narratives to explore memorable tourism experiences. *Asia Pacific Journal of Tourism Research, 20*(6), 680–693. https://doi.org/10.1080/10941665.2014.925944.

Creighton, M. (1997). Consuming rural Japan: The marketing of tradition and nostalgia in the Japanese travel industry. *Ethnology, 36*(3), 239–254.

Edensor, T. (2002). *National identity, popular culture and everyday life.* London: Bloomsbury Publishing.

Franklin, A., & Crang, M. (2001). The trouble with tourism and travel theory? *Tourist Studies, 1*(1), 5–22.

Fukuda, C. (2017). Gaijin performing gaijin ('A foreigner performing a foreigner'): Co-construction of foreigner stereotypes in a Japanese talk show as a multimodal phenomenon. *Journal of Pragmatics, 109*, 12–28.

Fukuda, C. (2018). The resurgence of cultural nationalism in Japanese mass media: A television representation of domesticated enka in Africa. *Japanese Studies, 38*(2), 229–252.

Funck, C. (2017). Tourism in Japan. In C. M. Hall & S. J. Page (Eds.), *The Routledge handbook of tourism in Asia* (pp. 361–371). New York: Routledge.

Graburn, N., Ertl, J., & Tierney, R. (Eds.). (2008). *Multiculturalism in the new Japan: Crossing the boundaries within.* Oxford: Berghahn.

Hambleton, A. (2011). Reinforcing identities? Non-Japanese residents, television and cultural nationalism in Japan. *Contemporary Japan, 23*(1), 27–47.

Henderson, J. C. (2017). Destination development: Trends in Japan's inbound tourism. *International Journal of Tourism Research, 19*(1), 89–98.

Hiroko, T. (2008). Delicious food in a beautiful country: Nationhood and nationalism in discourses on food in contemporary Japan. *Studies in Ethnicity and Nationalism, 8*(1), 5–30.

Ishimori, S. (2009). Tourism big bang and making Japan a tourism-oriented nation. *Japan Spotlight* (July/August 2009 Issue), 20–21.

Iwabuchi, K. (1994). Complicit exoticism: Japan and its other. *Continuum, 8*(2), 49–82.

Iwabuchi, K. (2015). *Resilient borders and cultural diversity: Internationalism, brand nationalism, and multiculturalism in Japan.* Lanham, MD: Lexington Books.

Japan National Tourism Organization. (2019). *Hounichigaikyakusuu (2003nen-2018nen)* [Visitors arrivals to Japan (2003–2018)]. Retrieved 6 August 2019, from www.jnto. go.jp/jpn/statistics/since2003_visitor_arrivals.pdf.

Japan Tourism Agency. (2018). *Hounichigaikokujin no shouhidouko 2018 nen nenjihou-gokusho* [Consumption trend of foreign visitors in Japan Annual report 2018]. Retrieved 26 July 2019, from www.mlit.go.jp/common/001285944.pdf.

Kozinets, R. V. (2002). The field behind the screen: Using netnography for marketing research in online communities. *Journal of Marketing Research*, *39*, 61–72.

Leheny, D. (2003). *The rules of play: National identity and the shaping of Japanese leisure*. Ithaca, NY: Cornell University Press.

Li, M., Wang, D., Xu, W., & Mao, Z. (2017). Motivation for family vacations with young children: Anecdotes from the internet. *Journal of Travel and Tourism Marketing*, *34*(8), 1047–1057. https://doi.org/10.1080/10548408.2016.1276007.

McMorran, C. (2008). Understanding the 'heritage' in heritage tourism: Ideological tool or economic tool for a Japanese hot springs resort? *Tourism Geographies*, *10*(3), 334–354.

Ministry of Land, Infrastructure and Transport. (2003). *White paper on land, infrastructure and transport in Japan*. Retrieved 15 June 2019, from www.mlit.go.jp/english/white-paper/mlit03/p2c2.pdf.

Ministry of Land, Infrastructure and Transport. (2012). *Tourism nation promotion basic plan*. Retrieved 22 June 2019, from www.mlit.go.jp/common/000234920.pdf.

Ministry of Land, Infrastructure and Transport. (2016). *White paper on land, infrastructure, transport and tourism in Japan 2016*. Retrieved 19 June 2019, from www.mlit. go.jp/common/001216008.pdf.

Nagai, H., Doering, A., & Yashima, Y. (2018). The emergence of the DMO concept in Japan: Confusion, contestation and acceptance. *Journal of Destination Marketing and Management*, *9*, 377–380.

Ota, M. (2016). Challenges for tourism-oriented country. *System, Control and Information*, *60*(4), 134–140.

Perkins, C. (2010). The banality of boundaries: Performance of the nation in a Japanese television comedy. *Television and New Media*, *11*(5), 386–403.

Prime Minister of Japan & His Cabinet. (2016). Meeting of the council for the development of a tourism vision to support the future of Japan. Retrieved 29 July 2018, from http://japan.kantei.go.jp/97_abe/actions/201603/30article1.html.

Robertson, J. (1997). Empire of nostalgia: Rethinking internationalization in Japan today. *Theory, Culture & Society*, *14*(4), 97–122.

Ryang, S. (2004). *Japan and national anthropology: A critique*. London: Routledge.

Sekai!, No. 45 (2016, 5 October). Sekai! nippon ikitai hito oendan [Who wants to come to Japan] [Discussion Board Comments]. Retrieved 6 August 2019, from https://tv.yahoo. co.jp/review/detail/312422/?rid=14756067906241.f751.30931&o=2&s=44.

Sekai!, No. 111 (2017, 15 June). Sekai! nippon ikitai hito oendan [Who wants to come to Japan] [Discussion Board Comments]. Retrieved 6 August 2019, from https://tv.yahoo. co.jp/review/detail/312422/?rid=14975277257032.5d3c.23230&o=2&s=110.

Sekai!, No. 123 (2017, 28 July). Sekai! nippon ikitai hito oendan [Who wants to come to Japan] [Discussion Board Comments]. Retrieved 6 August 2019, from https://tv.yahoo. co.jp/review/detail/312422/?rid=15011849082151.c285.02828&o=2&s=122.

Suzuki, S. (2015). Nationalism lite? The commodification of non-Japanese speech in Japanese media. *Japanese Language and Literature*, *49*(2), 509–529.

TV Tokyo. (2019a). Program overview: Why did you come to Japan? Retrieved 31 July 2019, from www.tv-tokyo.co.jp/youhananishini_eg/intro.

TV Tokyo. (2019b). Sekai nippon ikitai hito oendan [Who wants to come to Japan?]. Retrieved 20 May 2019, from www.tv-tokyo.co.jp/nipponikitaihito.

TV Tokyo. (2019c). You wa nani shini Nippon he? [Why did you come to Japan?]. Retrieved 20 May 2019, from www.tv-tokyo.co.jp/youhananishini.

Willis, D. B., & Murphy-Shigematsu, S. (Eds.). (2008). *Transcultural Japan: At the borderlands of race, gender and identity.* New York: Routledge.

Yamashita, S. (2008). Transnational migration in East Asia: Japan in a comparative focus. In Shinji Yamashita, M. Minami, D. W. Haines, & J. S. Eades (Eds.), *Senri Ethnological Reports 77* (pp. 3–13). Osaka, Japan: National Museum of Ethnology.

Yonekura, R. (2015). Representation of foreign visitors to Japan and foreign residents in Japan by terrestrial commercial broadcasters: Focusing on variety shows of terrestrial commercial broadcasters in Japan. *Journalism & Media, 8,* 189–205.

Yoshino, K. (1992). *Cultural nationalism in contemporary Japan: A sociological enquiry.* London: Routledge.

YOU, No. 186 (2015, 23 March). You wa nani shi ni Nippon he? [Why did you come to Japan?] [Discussion Board Comments]. Retrieved 6 August 2019, from https://tv.yahoo. co.jp/review/detail/36963/?rid=14271173346146.ffde.26505&o=2&s=186.

YOU, No. 187 (2015, 24 March). You wa nani shi ni Nippon he? [Why did you come to Japan?] [Discussion Board Comments]. Retrieved 6 August 2019, from https://tv.yahoo. co.jp/review/detail/36963/?rid=14271815321494.93de.26932&o=2&s=187.

YOU, No. 261 (2016, 16 May). You wa nani shi ni Nippon he? [Why did you come to Japan?] [Discussion Board Comments]. Retrieved 6 August 2019, from https://tv.yahoo. co.jp/review/detail/36963/?rid=14633996441388.1fc0.06655&o=2&s=261.

YOU, No. 378 (2017, 25 September). You wa nani shi ni Nippon he? [Why did you come to Japan?] [Discussion Board Comments]. Retrieved 6 August 2019, from https://tv.yahoo. co.jp/review/detail/36963/?rid=15063358193756.7669.08606&o=2&s=378.

Zhang, Y., & Hitchcock, M. J. (2017). The Chinese female tourist gaze: A netnography of young women's blogs on Macao. *Current Issues in Tourism, 20*(3), 315–330.

Chapter 11

Shibuya Crossing as a non-tourist site

Performative participation and re-staging

Fumiaki Takaoka

Introduction: a strange tourist site

Shibuya Crossing in Tokyo is a strange tourist site. At rush hour, some 3,000 people expertly cross this intersection while avoiding colliding into one another. One of the world's most famous intersections, many foreign tourists visit it every day, walking excitedly and capturing the chaotic scene with their cameras. According to a survey by TripAdvisor, Shibuya Crossing is one of the most popular tourist attractions in Tokyo, along with Shinjuku Gyoen National Garden, Meiji Jingu Shrine, Tokyo National Museum, and Senso-ji Temple. Lonely Planet calls 'the busiest intersection in the world' a 'must-visit recommendation', while the Michelin Guide praises 'the staggering sight'. Tourists from around the world have uploaded several videos of Shibuya Crossing on YouTube.

Shibuya Crossing, opposite Shibuya Station, which is one of Tokyo's iconic terminal stations, is by no means a typical tourist destination. It has no cultural heritage in the form of a temple, shrine, or castle, and does not display any valuable works of art or materials such as those found in museums. There are no traditional Japanese lifestyles depicted or local festivals held there for tourists to see. It is no more than an intersection. A sight that is mundane for people living in Tokyo reflects as something found 'nowhere in the world' in the eyes of the foreigners (Asahi Shimbun, 5 March 2016). Why do such a huge number of foreign tourists visit this simple intersection? In what way do tourists perform there, what do they experience, and what do they create?

In this chapter, I will analyse the strange tourist site of Shibuya Crossing from the perspective of the sociology of tourism. In doing so, I would like to focus on the participatory practice of tourists. At Shibuya Crossing, tourists participate in two senses of the word – they do not merely gaze at the scene of pedestrians and vehicles crossing the intersection as spectators; they cross the intersection themselves. They pause to take pictures or videos, which they share with others through social networking sites and blogs. They do not just gaze passively; they use their bodies to participate aggressively. In this chapter, we will call this practice 'participation in a programme'.

The value of Shibuya Crossing as a tourist destination is supported by such tourist performances. If no tourists came here, it would just be ordinary streets, traffic lights, pedestrians, vehicles, and buildings. There would be no producers or mediators or caretakers. The tourist gaze and tourist participation are what give this intersection the quality of 'found nowhere in the world'. The tourist desire itself composes this strange tourist site in a performative way. We call this practice 'participation in the programming'.

Today, tourists are not merely consumptive participants in readymade programmes. More and more of them engage in the production of tourism. Participation by tourists performatively re-constructs Shibuya Crossing as a tourist site. Research on tourist practices at Shibuya Crossing may clarify the performative aspects of contemporary tourism.

Shibuya as a staged city

For a long time, Shibuya Crossing was not a tourist site. It began brimming with foreign tourists from 2000 onwards. Shibuya was originally a shopping district where Japanese youngsters, with an interest in youth culture such as fashion and music, would gather. In a Lonely Planet edition published in 2003, Shibuya was described as being 'not exactly rich in sights'. In this section, I will give an overview of the history of Shibuya town.

Sociologist Syunya Yoshimi (1987) applied Erving Goffman's dramaturgical perspective to urban studies to sociologically analyse Tokyo. According to Yoshimi, the city centre of modern Tokyo moved from Asakusa to Ginza in the 1920s, to Shinjuku in the 1960s, and to Shibuya in the 1970s. From the 1970s to the 1980s, Shibuya came together with Harajuku, Aoyama, and Roppongi, proudly flourishing as the capital city of consumption society.

From the 1970s, Japan entered the post-industrial age and started emphasising culture and art instead of industry. The Japanese economy was at the height of its bubble, and the keywords of the age moved from production to consumption, and labour to leisure. The semiology and social analysis of Roland Barthes and Jean Baudrillard gained popularity, and people used terms and concepts such as fashion, image, mode, code, sign, and representation to talk about society, culture, and eras. In the cities, cutting-edge culture blossomed, and excellent urban studies and urban critiques were published that interpreted the city as a text, and these were read by a variety of audiences, not just specialists.

The railway company Tokyu had already opened a department store and cultural complex at the terminal station of Shibuya, but in the 1970s, it also opened shopping stores that targeted the young generation, such as TOKYU HANDS (1978) and Shibuya 109 (1979). Shibuya was a colony of Tokyu, but in 1968, another railway company, Seibu, opened a department store there, following it up with PARCO Part1 in 1973, PARCO Part2 in 1975, and PARCO Part3 in 1981. In 1987, LOFT was opened, expanding the range of shopping stores that targeted the young generation in this area. Around the same time, Seibu founded Mujirushi Ryohin (MUJI) as a private brand inspired by Baudrillard's *La société de consummation, ses mythes, ses structures*, and increased store locations with Shibuya at the centre. In the 1980s, Seibu taught people a new way of life – consumption of cultures – and Shibuya became a symbolic town of consumption society.

Not only did Shibuya gain a large number of department stores, but with the opening of famous record shops, such as Manhattan Records, Tower Records, HMV, and WAVE, Udagawa town in Shibuya became the biggest record shop town in the world. Musicians active in Shibuya's disco clubs created a new style of music called Shibuya-kei (Shibuya style), which became a cultural trend that exemplified the 1980s. At movie theatres like Eurospace and Cinema Rise, artistic and creative cinema was shown every week. The brand new, cutting-edge fashion style of the young people visiting Shibuya was called Shibu-kaji (Shibuya casual) and became an object of adoration for young people all over Japan.

Seibu's urban development of Shibuya closely resembled the space strategy of Tokyo Disneyland, which opened in 1983. The streets were given Western-like and attractive names, such as Kouen-Douri (Park Avenue) and Supein-Zaka (Spanish Slope), and Shibuya town became like a theme park, full of chic, European, and modern signs and images. Yoshimi's analysis considered a feature of Seibu's strategy to be 'stageness'. Shopping stores run by Seibu and Tokyu were scattered all over the town of Shibuya, so customers had to walk from store to store. However, beyond being just customers walking around town, they were performers embodying the Shibuya style, and they themselves were objects of the gaze. Customers were positioned as the latest consumers, and 'making Shibuya a huge stage' was Seibu's fundamental marketing strategy.

Many record shops, movie theatres, bookstores, art galleries, and cafés in the staged city of Shibuya were set up by Seibu and Tokyu, and these provided youngsters with the latest goods and cultural content. Town magazines acted as 'scripts which tell young people where to go, what to do'. For young people, performing in Shibuya, the staged city, with town magazines in hand, was the vogue of that period.

The death and life of great Shibuya

Today, Shibuya is no longer the capital city of consumption society or the Holy Land of popular cultures. From the 1990s, large-scale development has taken place in Tokyo districts one after the other, such as Ebisu (1994), Daiba (1996), and Roppongi (2003); Shibuya's position as a consumption city has gradually fallen. In this section, I will focus on the changes, starting from the decline of Shibuya as a staged city to the birth of 'nowhere in the world'.

In 2016, the idol girl group Keyakizaka46, boasting tremendous popularity among teenagers, released a new song titled 'The Day PARCO Disappeared from Shibuya'. The song's motif is the death of Shibuya. PARCO was a symbolic shopping store of Shibuya, but later on, it also opened outlets in local cities such as Nagoya (1989), Hiroshima (1994), and Kumamoto (1996), as well as in suburbs near Tokyo, such as Kichijoji (1980), Chofu (1989), and Utsunomiya (1997).

People no longer needed to go all the way to Shibuya to shop at PARCO. In 2016, the Shibuya PARCO store closed down temporarily so that its aging building could be redeveloped. Since then, the area around the construction site has become a ghost town with little footfall, and in the eyes of the young generation, which does not know the glory of Shibuya, it is the death of Shibuya.

With extensions made to the Saikyo Line (1996), Shonan Shinjuku Line (2001), and Fukutoshin Line (2008), Shibuya has gradually lost its characteristics as a terminal station. It has become just another transit point, losing commuters to Ikebukuro and Shinagawa, and falling to the fifth spot in the ranking of Tokyo's stations.

Sociologist Akihiro Kitada (2002) explained the decline of Shibuya from two perspectives – the Shibuyasation of the suburbs and the suburbanisation of Shibuya. Suburbanisation progressed rapidly in Japan from the 1990s, and stores selling fashionable or chic goods that could once only be found in Shibuya opened in suburban shopping centres and outlet malls. This spread of little Shibuyas was what Kitada called the Shibuyasation of the suburbs. At the same time, the consumption of signs or representations that had reigned supreme in the 1980s gradually waned, and people started to look for more information and lower prices in stores. In place of stores selling cultural goods, those that were once seen in the suburbs, such as convenience stores, drug stores, discount stores, and fast fashion shops, mushroomed in Shibuya as well, with Shibuya becoming just a big suburb. This was what Kitada called the suburbanisation of Shibuya.

The effects of the internet can also be mentioned as a cause of Shibuya's decline. After the launch of Windows 95 in 1995, the internet rapidly spread in Japan; Amazon opened Amazon.co.jp in 2000. Without having to take the trouble of going to Shibuya, people were now able to buy records, books, clothes, and shoes online.

Because of suburbanisation and the development of digital technology, Shibuya lost the privileges it had enjoyed from the 1970s to the 1980s. People were no longer pushing themselves to wear brand-new fashion and walk around Shibuya, which became nothing more than just another one of Tokyo's towns. This kind of change of Shibuya was what Kitada termed 'de-staged'.

On the other hand, today, Shibuya is visited by many foreign tourists, and Shibuya Crossing has become a popular tourist destination that represents Tokyo. As Lonely Planet says, 'Nowhere else says "Welcome to Tokyo" better than this'.

Shibuya as a non-tourist site

Now, I would like to consider the context of Shibuya's reactivation as a tourist town, from three different perspectives.

First, we can point out the Japanese government's tourism policy. For a long time, the government was indifferent to the economic effects of tourism, but in 2003, it developed the Visit Japan Campaign, promoting an inbound tourism policy. According to the Japan National Tourism Organization, the number of foreign tourists, which had been 5.21 million in 2003, grew rapidly, thanks to additional help from the economic development of underdeveloped countries and the expansion of LCC networks, to 10.36 million in 2013, 24.04 million in 2016, and 31.19 million in 2018. Most foreign tourists visiting Japan visit Tokyo, and most of them find their way to Shibuya.

Another important point is that Japan's culture and technology had been reappraised as 'cool' by the rest of the world. Though, in this period, Japan's economy continued to stagnate, and the 1990s were called the Lost 10 decade, Japanese popular culture in the form of animation, comics, computer games, movies, and fashion attracted many fans and types of mania from around the world, and brands like SONY, Honda, Nintendo, MUJI, and UNIQLO, and characters like Hello Kitty and Pokémon, gained worldwide recognition. Chaotic Shibuya, where order and disorder and technology and human activity coexist, became valued as a place symbolic of cool Japan.

A decisively important aspect for Shibuya was the influence of film. In the 2000s, there were many Hollywood movies on the theme of traditional Japan, such as *Last Samurai* (2003) and *Sayuri* (2005), but it was Sofia Coppola who featured contemporary Japan in her film *Lost in Translation* (2003), which also showed Shibuya Crossing. From the late 1990s, numerous digital screens were installed on the walls and rooftops of buildings around Shibuya Crossing, and advertisements were played nonstop. Shibuya Crossing became a world-famous visual space, on par with Times Square in New York and Piccadilly Circus in London. On screen, the advertisements were portrayed as hectic, with pedestrians, vehicles, buses, and motorcycles crossing the intersection every time the traffic lights changed; at night, lights from traffic signals, cars, and neon signs jumbled together. Sofia Coppola felt a glamour of sorts, like that of a sci-fi movie, at this chaotic and busy intersection, and incorporated it into the film as a landscape representative of Tokyo. Later, based on the influence of *Lost in Translation*, this intersection was filmed for numerous hit movies, such as *Babel* (2006), *Tokyo Drift* (2006), and *Biohazard IV* (2010), and Shibuya Crossing came to be 'staged' as something representing contemporary Japan.

From 2003, when Lonely Planet wrote that Shibuya was 'not exactly rich in sights', to today, when it describes Shibuya Crossing as a 'must-visit recommendation', this intersection's landscape has hardly changed at all. The only important change has been that it is now visited by many foreign tourists. There are no temples or national treasures or World Heritage Sites there, nor is there anything exotic or local or traditional. It is not even a public square where people can relax, like at Times Square or Piccadilly Circus. In the conventional sense, Shibuya Crossing is not a tourist site where people gather. It is just an intersection.

French anthropologist Marc Augé (1992) named and analysed the characteristics of places in super-modernity as non-places (*non-lieux*). According to Augé, unlike places until now, for which identities were constructed and relationships built, and those that had history, non-places are spaces that have no connection with identity and history. As concrete examples of non-places, he listed airports, hotels, stations, theme parks, mega stores, resort clubs, and wireless networks.

Japanese critic Koji Taki expressed a kind of rhetoric in which there is an absence of a would-be standard entity as zero – he edited a book titled *Rhetoric of Zero* along with sociologist Ryuzo Uchida (Taki & Uchida, 1992). In another book in which Taki discussed the contemporary city, he stated that the city, in the 19th-century sense (the capital city of Nation State), had already disappeared; he used the word 'zero' in place of 'city' when discussing spaces that represent contemporary society, and listed suburbs, convenience stores, fast-food shops, theme parks, and airports as concrete examples (Taki, 1994).

Shibuya Crossing is a typical non-place or zero place, and could perhaps be called a non-tourist site or zero tourist site in the context of tourism studies. There is no Japanese history, identity, or culture here in the traditional sense, and it is thoroughly lacking in tourist attractions in the conventional sense. Why then do foreign tourists come all the way to this non-tourist site? What do they desire there, how do they perform, and what are they experiencing?

Participatory tourism

The fact that many tourists come to the non-tourist site of an intersection indicates that in some sense, a tourist attraction is being produced. Who is producing a tourist attraction at Shibuya Crossing?

Most of the tourists that come to Shibuya arrive by train or subway. They disembark at Shibuya station and go straight to the intersection, which they can spot right outside the station gates. Tourists first look up at the massive visual screens and then pay attention to the loud sounds emanating. Astonished by the numerous people gathered there, they use digital cameras or mobile phones to photograph people crossing the intersection. Then, when the pedestrian signal turns green, they themselves cross the intersection, taking pictures with their cameras held high. The camera lenses are focusing on the pedestrians passing by, or on their own excited selves. Some even stop in the middle of the intersection to take panoramic shots or group photos. Tourists who have done some research in advance go to the higher levels of surrounding buildings to film the people crossing the intersection. This is their entire tour. There is nothing else in particular to do in Shibuya. They walk through the intersection, view it, take pictures, walk again, and that is all.

At Shibuya Crossing, the tourist gaze and performance shapes the tourism. Like cultivating flowers in the desert, tourist practices have turned a non-tourist site into a popular tourist destination. In this section, I will consider such recursive tourist practices from the perspective of participation.

Conventional tourism is provided by local governments, members of the host community, and the tourism industry, but today, tourists as guests are constructing touristic values. Hiroshi Sudo (2017) called the creative engagement of tourists themselves producing the tourist experience as 'participatory tourism'.

In this chapter, I will examine participatory tourism in three parts. The first has a practical perspective, the second has a theoretical one, and the third involves both.

First, tourist preferences and trends have shifted from 'seeing' to 'doing'. Conventional mass tourism was biased towards 'seeing', with strongly consumptive inclinations and a tendency to cause damage to local community environments and cultures; in contrast, from the 1990s, a new style of tourism has spread in developed nations, called alternative tourism or new tourism. In Japan as well, tourism having keywords such as experience, study, and cultural exchange has begun to gain attention. Various forms of tourism have been observed, such as green tourism in which people stay at private homes in farming villages and actually experience local life, ecotourism in which people enjoy natural attractions through trekking or canoeing with an experienced guide, and volunteer tourism in which people engage in volunteer activities when they visit impoverished areas or areas struck by disaster. Tourists are no longer passive spectators who merely gaze, but participants who use their own bodies to perform aggressively.

Second, there is the theoretical trend called the performance turn in tourism studies. In John Urry's well-known work *The Tourist Gaze* (1990), he applied Michel Foucault's argument asserting the privileged nature of the visual sense in modern consciousness, and proposed a tourism analysis using the concept of the gaze. According to Urry, to travel means to see, and the tourist gaze is framed by social class, gender, nationality, age, and education. With there being no such thing as pure and innocent eyes, the gaze is 'socially organised and systematised'. However, Urry's argument, which overemphasises the visual sense in tourism, was criticised by later researchers. For example, Arun Saldanha (2002) stated, 'Don't tourists swim, climb, stroll, ski, relax, become bored perhaps, or ill? Don't they go [to] other places to taste, smell, listen, dance, get drunk, have sex?', commenting that Urry saw tourists as merely pairs of eyes. Tim Edensor (2000, 2001) applied Goffman's argument clarifying the dramatic nature of social life to tourism research and considered tourism as a form of performance and tourist spaces as stages.

These research trends, called the performance turn of tourism studies, focus on the various senses and body functions, aside from the visual sense in tourism, and place importance on tourists' active and creative participation. Tourism researchers have become inclined to take an interest not only in what tourists gaze at but also what they hear, what they say, and how they perform.

Performativity of tourist performance

The third point of participatory tourism is performativity. Erik Cohen and Scott A. Cohen (2012) explained performance turn in tourism studies by separating it into a moderate mode and a more radical mode. Goffman's research turned its interest towards how behaviour or performance in everyday life preserves the social order, and saw society as something static. And the moderate mode of performance approach, much influenced by Goffman, has a strong tendency to see tourist settings and tourist attractions as a given. Here, what tourists participate in are usually tourist attractions as readymade programmes.

The radical mode of performance approach 'goes a step beyond Goffman' (Cohen & Cohen, 2012). Inspired by the performative speech acts theory by the philosopher of language John L. Austin and by Judith Butler's theory of gender performativity, this mode denies an independent standing to tourist settings, such as destinations, attractions, or events. The keyword here, beyond performance, is performativity. Unlike the tendency of tourism studies to see tourism as a reflection of a social structure, as was found under the influence of Urry, this approach problematises the process in which performative acts by tourists constitute a reality-in-becoming. The programme has not already been constructed; tourist practices construct a programme, and tourists participate in the programming.

Cohen and Cohen stated that the performativity perspective 'has not yet been worked out sufficiently' in contemporary tourism studies, but performative acts by tourists at Shibuya Crossing provide subject matter suited to thinking about the performativity of tourism. The radical nature of tourist performativity at Shibuya Crossing becomes clearer when compared to Harry Potter's Platform 9 3/4 at King's Cross Station in London. At King's Cross station, a fictitious platform that appears in the Harry Potter stories has been recreated, and it is a popular tourist site visited by many tourists coming to London. Tourists watch the performances of other tourists while they pay and wait in line. When their turn comes, staff members lend them a uniform or a hand prop (a wand). As indicated by the staff, they strike standard poses for photographs taken by their fellow travellers or the staff to shouts of 'smile please'. This is naturally not a tourist attraction at which tourists simply gaze as spectators; they themselves are performers. However, their performances are directed according to a script, and everything is planned to fit into a pre-established harmony.

On the other hand, there are no pre-installed programmes at Shibuya Crossing, and there are no official uniforms or scripts. That makes it a non-tourist site. Its tourist attractions and tourist sites do not exist prior to tourist performances; they are the results of tourist performances. Here, the tourist gaze, desire, and performance themselves constitute a tourism programme, and tourists performatively participate in the programming of the tourist attraction.

Participatory turn

This rise in participation is not limited to the realm of tourism but also occurs on the basis of a broader social context. In this section, I will examine the participatory turn in contemporary society.

From the 1980s, state-run businesses in Japan began to be privatised under neoliberal policies, and after the major earthquake in Kobe in 1995, citizen volunteer activities took off. The long-time fact of governments and authorities monopolising social affairs and the public sphere has been critically problematised in recent years, and in the fields of community development and care, education, and risk management, privately owned businesses and citizens have started to participate aggressively.

It would be altogether too naïve to see such participation as the simple democratic delegation of power from government to citizens, brimming with kindliness. Sociologist Toshio Nakano (1999) sounded the alarm bell early on with regard to the rise in volunteer, NGO, and NPO activities in the aftermath of Kobe's major earthquake. Nakano stated that 'volunteers are a requirement of the Nation State system', and that 'voluntary' social engagement by citizens could amount to 'unconscious participation in the mobilisation'. His statements once again take on a realistic persuasiveness ahead of the realities of mobilisation of numerous citizen volunteers for the Olympic and Paralympic Games Tokyo 2020 as cheap labour.

Governments are not the only set-ups that demand participation/engagement. Arlie Hochschild (1983) applied Goffman's performance theory to labour, calling labour that uses emotion as a resource emotional labour, and commented that this is spreading in modern society. Based on Hochschild's theory, Alan Bryman (2004) stated that in service industry workplaces, 'the employee becomes like an actor on a stage' and called their labour performative labour. According to him, organisations try to motivate employees by raising their commitment to a firm or to a team rather than placing an emphasis on control, and 'many consultants and organisations have sought to create high-commitment cultures that draw on employees' emotional resources' (Bryman, 2004). In Japan, performative labour amongst the Tokyo Disneyland staff (who are called the 'cast') is well known, and today, in many restaurants, cafés, and shops that are not leisure facilities, the service staff, including temporary workers, are happily practising performative labour.

Furthermore, not only labourers, but also consumers, are being encouraged to participate. In recent years, many analysts have pointed out that experiences and events are being emphasised in consumption. As seen in the custom of dressing up in costumes (cosplay or kosupure) at Tokyo Disneyland and for Halloween, and in cases of entertainment performances by wedding ceremony attendees, we have come to increasingly wish to be participants and performers rather than spectators in places of consumption.

The thing that may be a primary factor in society's rise in participation, and that made the clearest impression, is the digital network revolution (WEB2.0) of the mid-2000s. Until that point, the majority of the rights and abilities surrounding the transmission and creation of information were dominated by the information industry of major companies, but today, most of that has been transferred to amateur users. Interactive communication through new media, such as YouTube and Instagram, has become ordinary, and users can now easily create and share messages and content. This situation in which ordinary citizens take up 'vernacular creativity' to participate in cultural production was dubbed the 'participatory turn' by Jean Burgess (2007). The structure that invites us into creative participation, and that collects that creativity into the capitalism system, is what Tohko Tanaka (2017) called 'participatory power' and warned against.

Referencing Shannon Jackson, Futoshi Hoshino (2017) discussed the performative turn in contemporary art. Triggered by the end of the Cold War, vision-centric art, which had until then been constructed on the basis of the modern fine arts system, retreated, and social practice emphasising communication, participation, collaboration, and community began to take a striking tone. This change was called the performative turn or social turn in art, and the aesthetic and artistic things that had been tacitly taken for granted in the art world began to be shaken up and questioned again to the point of peril.

In a variety of aspects, such as community development, volunteering, labour, consumption, cultural production, art, and tourism, we are increasingly starting to participate. As Baron de Coubertin, a founder of the International Olympic Committee, described a hundred years ago, the most important thing is taking part. A participatory society simultaneously expands our life chances and encourages us towards expedient participation in society, government, and the market.

Re-staged Shibuya

In this chapter, I have examined participatory tourism and participatory society in the case of Shibuya Crossing. Using keywords like non-tourist site and performative participation, I have explained why an intersection that is not a tourist site in a conventional sense is visited by many foreign tourists. At the end of this chapter, using the stage as a key concept, I would like to further the discussion on the significance of Shibuya Crossing in contemporary tourism and tourism research.

As I have already stated, Shibuya was a town in which young people enjoyed cutting-edge culture in the 1970s and 1980s, and it was a stage upon which they performed, much as actors would. Yoshimi called this 'stageness'. However, from 1995 onwards, Shibuya as a staged city collapsed and became just one massive and ordinary town. This is what Kitada termed 'de-staged'. Sociologist Yoshikazu Nango (2016) said that, today, Shibuya is being born into a circumstance that could be called 're-staged'. Of course, 'stage' here has some differences in meaning from the conventional term on several points. I would like to examine re-staged Shibuya using two perspectives.

First, Shibuya Crossing is being re-staged as a mobile stage in urban life. Sociologist Daisuke Tanaka (2017) said that Shibuya Crossing, after 2000, has been the typical space of 'the urban' in contemporary Japan. On the one hand, Shibuya has been identified as having been de-staged, but on the other, it has acquired a position as an urban stage. Certainly, during the 2002 FIFA World Cup held in Korea/Japan, supporters would gather at Shibuya Crossing whenever the Japan national team won a match, sharing their joy at the centre of the intersection. Since then, this has become an established practice – whenever the Japan national team wins an international match, supporters come to Shibuya Crossing to express their jubilation. Furthermore, during the New Year countdown and Halloween, crossing on bicycles is restricted, and a huge number of people are packed at Shibuya Crossing. The intersection becomes a stage for the countdown and performances. It has often been pointed out that compared to Western countries, Japan has fewer public squares for people to congregate in, but Nango (2016) stated that Shibuya Crossing is a temporary square, only during green lights and special events, and that it is a contemporary form of a Japanese-style square. Certainly, an intersection where traffic lights change between green and red every few minutes, and where vehicles and pedestrians take turns to cross through, could be said to be a space that symbolises a liquid, temporary, mobile society.

Next, Shibuya Crossing has also been re-staged as a tourist performance stage. However, it is vastly different from many other tourist sites and from Shibuya as a staged city of the 1980s; here, there are no directors or producers of performances on stage. The tourists that come to Shibuya Crossing are themselves both objects of the gaze as performers as well as elements of the tourist site. Here, this is a reflexive stage that is staged, gazed at, and performed on by tourists themselves. Furthermore, the tourists' experiences and performances are shared with people around the world through SNS, blogs, and travel sites, calling out to future tourists. Shibuya Crossing is not just an intersection in an urban space; it is a reflexive stage connected to a digital network.

At Shibuya Crossing, locals and tourists cross the intersection at every green light. The fact that it is difficult to differentiate the tourists from the non-tourists is not because the tourists slip into the crowd. Anyone who crosses this intersection knows that many tourists come to Shibuya solely with the goal of visiting this intersection. Whether locals or tourists, all pedestrians are objects of the tourist gaze and, at the same time, subjects of the gaze. Here, everyone is already a tourist. There is no tourist attraction in the conventional sense at Shibuya Crossing. Nevertheless, Shibuya Crossing is a tourist site that is emblematic of modern Japan. In that, the questions of what it means to be a tourist and a tourist site, and what is tourism, start to blur, are re-examined, and are renewed, but only when the pedestrian lights turn green.

References

Asahi Shimbun, 5 March 2016, Tokyo.

Augé, M. (1992). *Non-lieux: Introduction à une anthropologie de la surmodernité*. Paris: Seuil.

Bryman, A. (2004). *The Disneyization of Society*. London: Sage.

Burgess, J. (2007). Vernacular Creativity and New Media. PhD dissertation. Brisbane: Queensland University of Technology.

Cohen, E. & Cohen, S. A. (2012). Current Sociological Theories and Issues in Tourism, *Annals of Tourism Research*, 39(4), 2177–2202.

Edensor, T. (2000). Staging Tourism: Tourists as Performers, *Annals of Tourism Research*, 27(2), 322–344.

Edensor, T. (2001). Performing Tourism, Staging Tourism: (Re)producing Tourist Space and Practice, *Tourist Studies*, 1(1), 59–81.

Hochschild, A. (1983). *The Managed Heart: Commercialization of Human Feeling*. Berkeley, CA: University of California Press.

Hoshino, F. (2017). Gendai bijyutsu no pafoumansuteki tenkai(1): 'Syakaiteki tenkai' no jidai no geijyutsusakuhin [Performance Turn of Contemporary Art(1): Artworks in the Era of 'Social Turn'], *The Bulletin of Kanazawa College of Art*, 61, 103–110.

Japan National Tourism Organization. (2019). Retrieved: 29 October 2019. www.jnto. go.jp.

Kitada, A. (2002). *Koukoku Toshi Toukyou: Sono Tanjyo to Shi [Advertisement City Tokyo: Its Death and Life]*. Tokyo: Kosaido Publishing.

Lonely Planet Publications Pty Ltd. (2003). *Lonely Planet Japan 8th edition*. Lonely Planet website. Retrieved: 29 October 2019. www.lonelyplanet.com.

Nakano, T. (1999). Borantia douingata shiminsyakairon no kansei [The Problem of an Analysis on Civil Society which Mobilises Voluntary Engagement], *Gendai Shisou*, 27(5): 72–93.

Nango, Y. (2016). Syogyoshisetsu ni maizou sareta 'nihonteki hiroba' no yukue: Shinjyuku nishiguchi kouen chika hiroba kara shibuya sukuranburu kousaten made [Whereabouts of 'Japanese Public Square' Built in a Commercial Space: From the Public Square in West Shinjuku Underground to Shibuya Crossing]. In Miura, A., Fujimura, R. and Nango, Y., *Syogyokuukan wa nan no yume wo mitaka: 1960~2010nendai no toshi to kenchiku [What Did Commercial Space dream? City and Architecture from 1960s to 2010s]*. Tokyo: Heibonsya, 67–166.

Saldanha, A. (2002). Music Tourism and Factions of Bodies in Goa, *Tourism Studies*, 2(1), 43–62.

Sudo, H. (2017). Kankosya no pafoumanse ga gendai geijyutsu to deau toki: Aato tsuuri-zumu wo chuushin ni sankagata kankou ni okeru 'sanka' no imi wo tou [When Tourists' Performance Meets Contemporary Arts: Inquiring the Meanings of 'Participation' in Participatory Tourism by Focusing on Art Tourism], *Japanese Tourism Studies Review*, 5(1), 63–78.

Taki, K. (1994). *Toshi no seijigaku [Politics of City]*. Tokyo: Iwanami Shyoten.

Taki, K. & Uchida, R. (1992). *Zero no syujigaku: Rekishi no genzai [Rhetoric of Zero: the Presence of the History]*. Tokyo: Libro Port.

Tanaka, D. ed. (2017). *Nettowaaku sitii: Gendai infura no syakaigaku [Network City: Sociology of Contemporary Infrastructures]*. Tokyo: Hokujyu Publishing.

Tanaka, T. (2017). Kyarakutaa syouhin, syouhigata bunka, sankagata kenryoku [Character Goods, Consumption Cultures and Participatory Power], in Tanaka, T., Yamamoto, A. and Andou, T. eds., *Dekigoto kara manabu karuchuraru sutadiizu [Cultural Studies Learning from Events]*. Kyoto: Nakanishiya Publishing, 93–113.

The Michelin Guide. (2019). Retrieved: 29 October 2019, www.viamichelin.com.

TripAdvisor. (2019). Retrieved: 29 October 2019, www.tripadvisor.com.

Urry, J. (1990). *The Tourist Gaze: Leisure and Travel in Contemporary Societies*. London: Sage.

Yoshimi, S. (1987). *Toshi no doramaturugii: Tokyo sakariba no syakaishi [Dramaturgical Analysis of the City: Social History of City Centre in Tokyo]*. Tokyo: Koubundou.

Chapter 12

Mobilising pilgrim bodily space

The contest between authentic and folk pilgrimage in the interwar period

Masato Mori

Introduction

Research in geography has attended to various aspects of the spatial movement of pilgrims travelling to and around sacred sites. While early studies in geography pursued descriptive research on pilgrimages – for example, Sopher's (1968) spatial analysis of pilgrim circulation in Gujarat or Isaac's (1973) historical analysis of the pilgrimage to Mecca – the turn to representation and discourse in geographical research in the 1990s led researchers to instead emphasise the politics of pilgrimage. These studies demonstrated that pilgrimage is not a simply religious phenomenon but rather a social construct occurring at the interface between sacred and secular affairs, and addressed the contested meanings of pilgrim routes and the social construction of sacred pilgrimage sites (Graham and Murray 1997; Gatrell and Collins-Kreiner 2006). However, with the appearance of the new mobility paradigm (Sheller and Urry 2004), geographers began to demonstrate that the actual movement of pilgrims through space, and not just the architecture of sacred sites, has important political implications. Focusing on the entanglement of movement, representation, and practice, the new mobility paradigm attempts to elaborate the politics of mobility, including the power of motive force, speed, rhythm, route, experience, and friction (Cresswell 2010). Bringing a new mobility perspective to bear on the practices of pilgrimage, Coleman and Eade (2004) differentiate between performative actions, contextualised meaning, metaphor, and embodied experiences to understand pilgrim movements and Scriven (2014) encourages geographers "to find ways to understand how movements, flows and activity shape places and how places in turn shape mobilities" in pilgrimage practice (255).

This chapter aims to further elaborate the mobility of pilgrimage by attending to the ways in which the intersection of speed, transportation technology, representations of pilgrim movement, and experience all combine to mould pilgrim bodily space; what Duncan (1996) termed "BodySpace". The specific focus of the chapter is the 88-temple *henro* pilgrimage of Shikoku Island, a well-known pilgrimage route that became a contested terrain for mobilising pilgrim bodily space during the interwar period. In many ways, these contests were a product of a unique feature of the *henro* pilgrimage; namely, its largely informal structure.

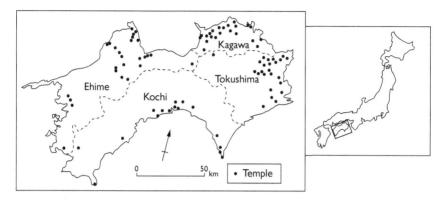

Figure 12.1 Locations of 88 temples of *henro* pilgrimage on Shikoku Island.

- It is associated with no sect and actually often derided as a folk custom.
- A combination of secular and sacred.
- No specific routes or strictures on how to travel.

Accordingly, in the modern period, as transportation networks evolved, pilgrims could choose means of travel, but this became contested by groups attempting to advocate for authentic forms of mobility.

Extending over 1,400 km (Figure 12.1), the pilgrimage entails visiting 88 sacred Buddhist temples connected to Kukai, a folk saint who, despite being a patron saint of the Shingon sect, transcends any religious distinctions (Shinno 1998). As with Kukai's folk image, the 88 temples of the circuit and the pilgrims who travel its circuit are not associated with any Buddhist sect. The 88-temple pilgrimage of Shikoku has no doctrines and holy books, but is rather a symbolic pilgrimage based on a folk religion that believes Kukai is still travelling around Japan. Each temple is numbered from 1 (i.e. Ryozen-ji temple in Tokushima Prefecture) to 88 (Okubo-ji temple in Kagawa Prefecture). Although this sequential ordering does not need to be followed, most pilgrims do follow it.[1]

It is difficult to ascertain when the religious trainings of monks began and why there are 88 temples. According to an entry found in a Buddhist monk's diary from 1653, the pilgrimage system had already been established as a Buddhist pilgrimage by that time. Further, based on dates obtained from pilgrim stickers on the temple walls, the pilgrimage gained popularity not only among monks, but also among ordinary people around the early eighteenth century (Maeda 1972).

Uniqueness found in looseness

For the purposes of this study, three features of the pilgrimage are of particular importance. First, a discrimination towards the poor pilgrims is mapped in new ways in the interwar period. Research has shown that in historical times many pilgrims were poor and travelled the route to receive donations from local people, as evidenced by the fact that the number of pilgrims increased during periods of famine (Maeda 1972). Locals were happy to give but not happy to be begged and even now they are discriminated against. Second, the Shingon sect did not consider such pilgrimage to be part of orthodox religious practice but rather a folk belief (Mori 2005). Accordingly, the uniqueness of the pilgrimage is found in its rather loose and informal system of practices. Since the practices of the pilgrimage were not stipulated by any coherent religious doctrine, and indeed were actually derided by any orthodox Buddhism denominations because of its "folk" status, the pilgrimage was shaped by a unique combination of religious and secular affairs. Thirdly, the informality of the pilgrimage left it to pilgrims to select and establish their own various modes of travelling the route. For example, pilgrimage guidebooks printed between the seventeenth and late nineteenth century, the first appearing in 1687, did not place any constraints on mode of transport, and instead encouraged pilgrims to select any available means of transports: from boats to steam boats, steam trains, and bus services. Likewise, these guidebooks were equally free with their recommendations of routes, only noting the distances between some villages and some of the temples. The guidebooks make no mention of the actual paths to be followed. Pilgrims who travelled on foot followed stone signposts placed by previous generations of pilgrims, not by any Buddhist denomination. It has also been found that poor travellers followed different routes in order to pass through slightly larger villages where they might more readily beg for money and provisions (Asakawa 2008). In addition, it also seems that travellers suffering from Hansen's disease followed different routes from other pilgrims.

This essay examines the mobility of the *henro* pilgrimage, focusing on the interaction between representation and the experiences of pilgrims in the interwar period. During this period, the informal nature of the pilgrimage allowed pilgrims to pursue their journeys via the continually widening modern transportation network. Using modern transport to travel the pilgrimage was represented as a form of modern, rational tourism, and pilgrims enjoyed speedy, comfortable travel that was totally different from pre-modern pilgrimage practices. However, these new modern forms of pilgrimage were harshly criticised by the *Henro-Dogyokai*, an organisation established in 1928 in Tokyo that aimed to hold up the *henro* pilgrimage as an example of the allegedly national spirit of mutual assistance, equalitarianism, and self-sacrifice. As the chairman of the organisation after 1931, Tomita Kojun, a monk of Hosenji-temple, established a nursery school, secondary school, and college, and also organised social activities to enlighten people. The *Henro-Dogyokai* was also founded with this purpose, and furthermore was recognised for its contribution to enlightening "decadent" pilgrims to be more "religious" (Mori 2005). The organisation launched a monthly magazine, *Henro*, held special lectures, and organised annual parades to provide readers with opportunities to become aware of what it framed as authentic religious pilgrimage. Ironically, however, because of the pilgrimage's lack of religious doctrine or rules, its religiousness turned heavily on two non-religious features: forms of transportation between temples and pilgrims' paraphernalia.

This chapter employs qualitative methods to understand how discourses and representational practices shaped the means and experiences of travelling. In addition to examining several guidebooks and related documents, the main source is *Henro*, a monthly magazine published by the *Henro-Dogyokai* and distributed to temples and members of the organisation.[2]

Between modern tourism and pilgrimage: new experiences along the circuit

From 1867 onwards, the newly established Meiji government set out to rapidly develop transport infrastructure (e.g. ports, railways, and roads), and policies concerning the infrastructure were installed by the 1920s (Mizuuchi 2000): large ports, which allowed large ships to dock, were officially rebuilt with the Act of Port of 1873 which promoted rebuilding ports for large steam vessels; the Act of Railway Nationalisation of 1906 propelled an integrating of local private railway companies; construction of roads became financed by the governmental budget under the Act of 1919 and the Ministry of Railways started bus services on the built roads. All of these policies were pursued from Meiji onward but Shikoku was late to the party and railroads did not develop until the 1920s.

Shikoku Island saw the first railroad company in Ehime Prefecture, Iyotetsudo railway, in 1887, and the second in Kagawa Prefecture, Tosan-Denkikido railway, in 1911. After 1914 when Takamatsu city in Kagawa Prefecture and Matsuyama city in Ehime Prefecture were railroaded, Japan National Railway constructed railroads and completed the installation in 1935. The roads' construction enabled the Ministry of Railways to develop lines of bus services to connect local areas on Shikoku Island after 1934. All of this changed the opportunities for pilgrims.

The continually widening modern transportation network enabled pilgrims to travel the pilgrimage fast and comfortably. Table 12.1 shows the number of days that pilgrims from different historical periods spent completing the pilgrimage as well as the forms of transportation utilised. While it took Chozen, a seventeenth-century monk, 91 days to complete the pilgrimage, in 1925, Tomita, a monk and founder of the pilgrimage association, completed the pilgrimage in 35 days. His colleague Miyao circumnavigated the route in nearly half that time. In short, the use of modern transport greatly reduced the number of days spent on the pilgrim trail. During his only 18-day pilgrimage, the famous cartoonist Shigeo Miyao used non-pedestrian forms of transportation a total of 48 different times. Table 12.1 also illustrates a shift in the kind of transportations used: while Seisei Kobayashi, a monk, and Itsue Takamure, a well-known female social activist, mainly used steamships, pilgrims after the 1920s tended to use trains. The shift from steamships to trains and buses further accelerated the speed of pilgrimage.

Table 12.1 Travelling days and usage of transport

Year	Travellers	Days	Number of times of usage of transport				
			Boats	Trains	Cars	Others	Sum
1653	Chozen	91	6	0	0	–	6
1907	Seisei Kobayashi	81	11	2	0	Carriages (6)	13
1918	Itsue Takamure	97	7	0	0	–	7
1926	Kojun Tomita	35	5	10	18	Carriages (1)	33
1932	Shigeo Miyao	18	7	13	28	Cable car (1), carriages (2)	48
1937	Senseisui Ogihara	18	3	16	23	Cable car (2)	42
1938	Yuichi Miyake	36	5	18	19	Cable car (2)	42
1941	Tetsuma Hashimoto	34	6 (5)	19	20	Cable car (2), unknown (1)	45

The development of modern transport drew a new kind of pilgrim to the route. Tsunezo Kadoya (1923, n.p.), the author of a self-printed guidebook, described this phenomenon: "Certain classes of poorly educated farmers and merchants were dominant in the henro pilgrimage, but recently the situation has changed so that many intellectual and wealthy class people are undertaking the pilgrimage". Travelling the pilgrimage via modern transport blurred the boundary between religious route and tourism as it allowed pilgrims to experience enjoyable, comfortable, and speedy travel. In short, it enabled the development of a "touristic" pilgrimage, a new form of travel spurred by the rise of a domestic tourism industry catering to a burgeoning middle class.

The new tourism-oriented pilgrimage was also facilitated by the creation of new institutions, and in particular the formation of the *Nihon-Ryokobunka-Kyokai*, a semi-governmental institution established in 1924 to promote tourism to ordinary people after the Great Kanto Earthquake of 1923 in order to encourage the burgeoning middle class of Japan to travel around Japan via the new railways. They were also interested in controlling the new behaviour to discipline travellers into sophisticated modern urban consumers and whose energy was also restored via getting back in touch with national parks. The fact that the head office of this organisation was located within the headquarters of the Ministry of Railway illustrates the tight relationship between the railway and tourism industries. A tourist guidebook printed by this institution introduces its readers to the increasingly modern and speedy features of the pilgrimage: "Due to the development of public transport, now travellers do not necessarily walk, but instead take steam trains, tram cars and buses. It is said that pilgrims using modern transport complete the journey in twenty-four or five days" (Nihon Ryokokyokai 1941, 46).

The development of a tourism-oriented pilgrimage transformed the nature and experience of the journey – from long and arduous to easy and comfortable. Nagando Murakami, an editor of the journal *Henro* who undertook a pilgrimage in 1928, described how "The hard and difficult pilgrimage derived from dangerous spots on the paths and inconvenient accommodations has now disappeared" (5). Articles in newspapers recommended the new touristic pilgrimage to their readers. For example, in 1934, the *Osaka Asahi News*, a top-selling paper, launched a special series of articles to provide its urban readers with detailed information about how to undertake the pilgrimage using public transport, including steamships, railways, and buses. The series also provided information on how to comfortably enjoy travel on the modern transportation network and advice on finding comfortable accommodation along the route. The authors noted that "[P]eople without strong motivation will be fed up with a long journey staying in uncomfortable accommodation". They also called attention to how this style of pilgrimage was a "combination of belief and tourism for pleasure" and the notion of a "modern henro" received many enquiries from readers (*Osaka Asahi News* 1934).

The development of this touristic form of pilgrimage based on public transport de-contextualised the pilgrimage from its religious and sacred meanings and reshaped it as a new kind of pilgrim experience. For example, the monthly magazine *Travel*, a publication launched in 1924 for the growing Japanese middle class by the *Nihon-Ryokobunka-Kyokai*, featured a series of articles describing the *henro* pilgrimage experiences of a reporter between 1928 and 1930. The articles were compiled into a book and published in 1930. The author of the series of articles, Ijima Minoru, announced his mission to convey information about the pilgrimage to potential middle-class pilgrim-tourists. He provided readers with illustrations meant to help them complete the circuit in the minimum number of days, paying no attention to the sequential ordering of the temples. He noted that "I think we must not force ordinary people to undertake religious travel. I feel a sense of nostalgia but I never want to be a religious pilgrim" (Ijima 1930, 80).

The speedy and rational form of modern pilgrimage established through the development of new transport created a new form of embodied practice. Before the spread of modern transportation, travel on foot required pilgrims to traverse several physically difficult sites, called *henro-korogashi*, and the effort to overcome these sites gave pilgrims a sense of religious achievement. In contrast, pilgrims travelling on bus services enjoyed confronting these difficult sites with only their eyes. One author noted the "drastic change in society that can be observed in Shikoku island. Road construction and transport development allow travellers to enjoy seeing difficult sites from tourist boats and cars parked along prefectural roads" (Murakami 1931, 5). This statement shows how the development of transport transformed pilgrims' practice from challenging physical performance to voyeuristic pleasure.

Shigeo Miyao, a famous cartoonist who used modern transport 48 times during his pilgrimage, wrote about the photogenic scenery between the sacred temples: "We can enjoy panoramic views of the cape between Kashiwasaka slope and Iwamatsu. A pilgrimage path goes through Mount Kannondake, so the landscape from the path will be better than the roadway of coastlines" (Miyao 1943, 100). In fact, however, while Miyao actually travelled via modern transport on the coastal roadway to avoid walking in the mountains and thus missed this panoramic view, he did not conceal his desire for the pleasure of viewing such scenery along the route.

Before the development of modern transport, walking was the principal way of travelling the pilgrimage route, and pilgrims therefore experienced fatigue, toil, and a sense of fulfilment when they overcame the difficult and dangerous sites. Walking over difficult trails required pilgrims to keep their eyes trained on the path below them. On the contrary, however, travellers using modern transport did not exercise their body but rather enjoyed viewing distant landscapes as speed and ease of movement released their eyes from the land at their feet.

Representations of religious bodies and spirituality

In the 1930s, the alleged lack of religiousness of the new pilgrims who travelled the route via modern transport became the target of criticism from the *Henro-Dogyokai*, an organisation established within the offices of Hosenji-temple in Tokyo in 1929. Murakami Nagando, an editor of a monthly journal issued by the organisation, writes,

> I was surprised when I learned that a lot of people were using vehicles, breaking a prohibition on the use of transport. Ship and rail companies sell discount tickets, taxi companies persuade pilgrims to use their services by tugging at their sleeves. Devils are setting up nets of temptations everywhere. I am irritated to know that there are some salesmen lurking in the sites of sacred temples in particular … I believe that undertaking the pilgrimage on foot is important, therefore I want to terminate the unpleasant trend of pilgrimage using transport.
>
> (Murakami 1931, 5)

Although there was no prohibition against using vehicles in any text about the pilgrimage, Murakami describes the transport providers as "devils" and emphasises the importance of pursuing pilgrimage on foot.

This insistence on walking as authentic was prevalent in the literature published by the *Henro-Dogyokai*. They repeatedly emphasised that walking the pilgrimage route was the most valuable practice, and contrasted this authentic form with the modern touristic way of completing the circuit. The discourse of this organisation asserts that the authenticity of pilgrim practice turns on the matter of speed. Walking, they insisted, was a religious way of experiencing the pilgrimage because it demands slow movement, a pace quite obviously at odds with the modern touristic forms of pilgrim movement. The *Henro-Dogyokai* moulded two kinds of rhetoric to justify their notion of proper religiousness. First, they high-lighted the significance of walking the pilgrimage to perform the experience and philosophy of Kobodaishi, the folk saint and imagined founder of the pilgrimage. Murakami, in a text referred to previously, writes that:

> The word "henro" principally means doing training precisely the same as Kobodaishi did, therefore walking on the footpath itself has the same value as visiting the sacred temples. When you see stones on the path, you will imagine that he took rest on them, when you walk on old narrow paths, you will find it difficult to leave that site as you look for his footprints. Keeping this mental-ity and walking on the path lead you to shed tears of penitence and to appreci-ate the companionship of Kobodaishi.
>
> (Murakami 1931, 5)

Further evidence of the shared nature of such opinions among individuals affili-ated with the *Henro-Dogyokai* is provided by Sato, a monk, who suggested in the pages of *Henro* that: "the teachings of Kobodaishi are still available today, these are his teaching of living and working, and thus his teaching of walking step by step. Henro pilgrimage is indeed an incarnation of Kobodaishi's teaching of walking step by step" (Sato 1931, 5).

Another form of rhetoric described the effect of walking the pilgrimage as working to purify the mind spoiled by modern urban life:

> When people remove their self-centredness and start the pilgrimage by going over mountains and crossing valleys in wild nature guided by Kobodaishi, the debris accumulated in their minds is completely cleared and purified as if they are newly born.
>
> (Sato 1931, 5)

It is important to note that the insistence on walking the pilgrimage privileges pilgrims' moving bodies which overcome physical difficulty and improve their spirituality. As explained earlier, speedy modern touristic pilgrimage practices reduced the physicality of traversing dangerous spots on the footpath. The use of vehicles on the roads put vision in transcendent position over other senses in encountering and enjoying the landscape.

It was in the parades initiated in the early 1930s that advocates staged their version of an authentic form of pilgrimage. These annual parades started in 1931, followed by a monthly training programme in 1933. Since both the parades and the trainings were held in sites around Tokyo, they provided opportunities for partici-pants and viewers to see and experience an allegedly authentic form of pilgrimage. Despite the absence of any rules in the old guidebooks of the pilgrimage, the *Henro-Dogyokai* insisted that the authenticity of the pilgrimage turned on foot travel as well as traditional pilgrim paraphernalia, including white robes, a conical sedge hat and a walking stick. While the first annual parade held in 1930 attracted

Figure 12.2 A photo of the *henro* parade in 1931.

Source: *Henro* 1931.

fewer than 200 participants, the number of participants gradually increased to 2,000 in 1940 (Mori 2005). It is important to point out that the organisers' insistence on an authentic form of pilgrimage entailed the mobilisation of pilgrims' bodies. As evidenced by the following detailed description of these parades from *Henro*, walking was sharply contrasted to modern touristic ways of pilgrimage: "all public transports collectively stopped to clear the way for our pilgrim parade" (*Henro* 1931, 3). In this way, pilgrimage on foot was placed higher than pilgrimage using modern means of transport. Figure 12.2 shows that all participants in the parade of 1931 wore white robes and carried the prescribed hats and walking sticks.

With the coming of the Pacific War, the organisation began to insist even more emphatically that walking the route was essential. Pursuing the pilgrimage on foot became increasingly articulated with similar national movements – Kosei-Undo – that encouraged preferred forms of leisure such as drama, chorus, and hiking. In the mid-1930s, it was suggested that hiking both developed a healthy body and released mental stress. However, the toil of the *henro* pilgrimage, and not the joy, was held up as an original form of hiking practice by people affiliated with the *Henro-Dogyokai*. Hiking was selected as one of the important components of Kosei-Undo, and the idea of healthy walking and praying for a victory in the Second World War was developed in the late 1930s. At that time, the *Henro-Dogyokai* urged the idea of healthy walking to contribute to victory and urged pilgrims to undertake the *henro* pilgrimage on foot.

> It is not just meaningless but also apologetic not to undertake the henro pilgrimage on foot, because now in this country people are urged to walk and walk … We absolutely have to undertake the pilgrimage on foot.
>
> (Tomita 1941, 1)

Attempting to walk the pilgrimage became narrated as a necessity by the *Henro-Dogyokai*. It is important to note that while the organisation attempted to restore the authenticity of the pilgrimage, this attempt was a completely modern affair. In a meeting, Murakami, mentioned previously, stated that "it is troublesome when we develop a campaign for the henro pilgrimage, we are often recognised as beggars and discriminated by ordinary people" (*Henro* 1940, 6). As explained before, many conventional pilgrims had survived by begging for food, money, and accommodation from locals. However, the members of the *Henro-Dogyokai* set up a strict split between old pilgrims and themselves, rejecting the legacy of premodern times. Bodies moving in poverty were represented as unpleasant.

Conclusion

This chapter examined the mobility of the *henro* pilgrimage, highlighting the relationship between speed, technology of movement, and representations of modes of travel and experience. Since the pilgrimage was never structured by strict rules, pilgrims could travel the route via means other than walking as the modern transportation network began to develop throughout Shikoku Island. Along with the rise of a domestic tourism industry in the mid-1920s, a form of touristic pilgrimage became popular and accelerated the speed of the pilgrimage, making the journey a sort of leisure activity devoid of physical toil. The spread of a speedy, comfortable, and enjoyable pilgrimage de-contextualised its religiousness: a religious sense of achievement felt when overcoming the dangerous and difficult spots on the footpath was not appreciated by travellers enjoying the views of such spots from vehicles.

The *Henro-Dogyokai* criticised this modern touristic pilgrimage and emphasised the effects of the pilgrimage on bodies instead. The pilgrims' bodily movements between temples became an arena for the inscription of religious meaning. It should be noted that while the organisation emphasised an authentic form of pilgrimage, evidence of such authenticity is difficult to find. Traditional guidebooks hardly mentioned the form of movement of the pilgrimage. Paralleling the rise of a touristic modern pilgrimage, a counter discourse arose that emphasised the bodily practice of undertaking the pilgrimage on foot. The religious meaning and spirituality of the pilgrimage became practised through such bodily walking. This newly emerged meaning stressed the originality of the pilgrimage attuned to a Japanese modernity. This means not only that the religious meaning and spirituality were foregrounded as a counter discourse against a modernised pilgrimage but also that the organisation's statements and attitudes towards the pilgrimage themselves shared in the particularity of modernity.

Notes

1 Each of the four prefectures (meaning four countries) of Shikoku Island assumes a special meaning, and the series of meanings signifies the temporal flow of the pilgrimage.

The flow moves clockwise from the Tokushima Prefecture (called "the training place of awakening faith (*hosshin no dojo*)"), through Kochi Prefecture (called "the training place of religious discipline (*shugyo no dojo*)"), and Ehime Prefecture (called "the training place of enlightenment (*bodai no dojo*)"), and finally to Kagawa Prefecture (called "the training place of nirvana (*nehan no dojo*)" (Tanaka 1977, 1981).

2 All references to and citations from these Japanese-language historical documents are translated into English.

References

Asakawa, Y. (2008). *Junrei no Bunkajinruigakuteki Kenkyu: Shikokuhenro no settaibunka [Cultural Anthropology of Pilgrimages]*. Tokyo: Kokonshoin.

Coleman, S. & Eade, J. (2004). Introduction: Reframing Pilgrimage. In *Reframing Pilgrimage: Cultures in Motion*, edited by Coleman, S. & Eade, J., 1–15. London: Routledge.

Cresswell, T. (2010). Towards a Politics of Mobility. *Environment and Planning D: Society and Space*, 28(1): 17–31.

Duncan, N. (ed.). (1996). *BodySpace: Destabilising Geographies of Gender and Sexuality*. London: Routledge.

Gatrell, J. & Collins-Kreiner, N. (2006). Negotiated Space: Tourists, Pilgrims, and the Baha's Terraced Gardens in Haifa. *Geoforum*, 37: 765–778.

Graham, B. & Murray, M. (1997). The Spiritual and the Profane. *Ecumene*, 4(4): 389–409.

Henro. (1931). Teito no Henro Koshin. *Henro*, 1(7): 2–3.

Henro. (1940). Hayamawari Ohenro no Hanashi. *Henro*, 10(2): 4–7.

Ijima, M. (1930). *Fudasho to Meisho Shikokuhenro*. Tokyo: Hobunkan.

Isaac, E. (1973). The Pilgrimage to Mecca. *The Geographical Review*, 63(4): 405–409.

Kadoya, T. (1923). *Shikokureijo Annai*. Ehime: Self-published.

Kong, L. (2001). Mapping "New" Geography of Religion: Politics and Poetics in Modernity. *Progress in Human Geography*, 25: 211–233.

Maeda, T. (1972). *Junrei no Shakaigaku [Sociology of Pilgrimages]*. Kyoto: Mineruva.

Miyao, S. (1943). *Gatobun Shikokuhenro*. Tokyo: Hobunkan.

Mizuuchi, T. (2000). Kaihatsu Toiu Sochi. In *Ekkyosuru Chi 4: Sochi, Kowashi Kizuku*, edited by Kurihara, A. & Komori, Y., 69–102. Tokyo: University of Tokyo Press.

Mori, M. (2005). *Shikoku Henro no Kin-gendai*. Osaka: Sogensha.

Murakami, N. (1931). Shikoku Junpai Shokan. *Henro*, 1(6): 5–6.

Nihon Ryokokyokai (ed.). (1941). *Tsurisuto Annai Sosho 2 Shikoku Chiho*. Tokyo: Japan Tourist Bureau (first edition 1935).

Osaka Asahi News. (1934). Shikokureijo Shinhenro, *Osaka Asahi News*, March 31.

Reader, I. (2006). *Making Pilgrimages: Meaning and Practice in Shikoku (new edition)*. Honolulu, HI: University of Hawaii Press.

Sato, D. (1931). Henro wa wareara no seishin wo seijomuku ni kaeraseru. *Henro*, 1(1): 5.

Scriven, R. (2014). Geographies of Pilgrimage: Meaningful Movements and Embodied Mobilities. *Geography Compass*, 8: 249–261.

Sheller, M. & Urry, J. (eds.). (2004). *Tourism Mobilities: Places to Play, Places in Play*. London: Routledge.

Shinno, T. (ed.). (1998). *Seiseki Junrei [Pilgrimages for Sacred Marks]*. Tokyo: Yuzankaku.

Sopher, D. (1968). Pilgrim Circulation in Gujarat. *The Geographical Review*, 58(3): 392–425.

Tanaka, H. (1977). Geographic Expression of Buddhist Pilgrim Places on Shikoku Island, Japan. *Canadian Geographer*, 21(2): 111–132.

Tanaka, H. (1981). The Evolution of a Pilgrimage as a Spatial-Symbolic System. *Canadian Geographer*, 25: 240–251.

Tomita, K. (1941). Aruke, Aruke, Aruke. *Henro*, 11(4): 1.

Chapter 13

Digital media as "social spaces" of tourism

The Japanese cases of travelling material things

Hideki Endo

Introduction

We live in "social spaces" to which we attach some meanings as we express various performances and continually engage with others.[1] In this regard, in the present age, "social spaces" have become closely connected to digital media, which is changing the nature of society. In this chapter, we will consider this idea through the example of tourism.

I will first identify how social spaces in the present age are strongly affected by conditions pertaining to mobility. I will then describe how "heterogeneously twisted social spaces" are created in diverse forms by multi-layered mobility flows. On that basis, I will assert that media following the digital revolution has taken shape during an "Age of Mobility" and, at the same time as promoting social mobilization, the "platforms" (which form an element of digital media) have in the Age of Mobility become a form of social space as settings in which various performances can be expressed.

Based on the above, I will investigate how a close connection between "social spaces" in tourism and digital media has come to change the nature of tourism by looking at the example of the travel of stuffed animals. To conclude, I will pose a new question arising from the fact that tourism mobility has started to give rise to phenomena that could not have existed before.

The effect of mobility on "social spaces" in the present age

"Social spaces" in the present age

The spaces in which we lead our lives are always social spaces. Sociologist Erving Goffman uses the concepts of "front region" and "back region" to discuss them (Goffman, 1959).[2]

"Front region" has the meaning of "front stage", where people perform situation-appropriate roles on the basis that they are visible to others with whom one is not familiar. In contrast, the "back region" refers to a kind of "backstage" where people are released from the performance of their roles and can relax. For a waiter at a restaurant, for example, the dining area is the front region and the kitchen is the back region.

A waiter who had been relaxing in the kitchen will assume the anxious demeanour of one attending to their work as soon as they step out into the dining area, where there are customers. This is because the waiter has moved from one space to another, from the "back region" to the "front region". Thinking in these terms, one could say that "front regions" and "back regions" are formed only once given social significance, rather than on the basis of any physical characteristics.

Accordingly, as soon as a customer wanders into the kitchen, although it is physically unchanged, the significance attached to it (the definition of the conditions) changes such that it is no longer a "back region".

The same is true of lecture rooms at a university. A lecture room could be described as a "front region" for both teaching staffs and students. Thus, the teaching staff plays a role appropriate for teaching staff, and the students play roles appropriate for students. If students started a live guitar performance out of nowhere, lectures would never happen. However, a student might sometimes play guitar in a lecture room when there is no lecture and no one is in the room. At such a time, the very same lecture room is no longer a "front region" for that student, but has become a "back region" and it is just as if he were practising guitar in his own room.

We attach many types of significance to social spaces (defining their conditions) as we live in them, including but not limited to "front region" or "back region". The term "social space", as used by Goffman, is a setting in which we carry on with our lives among others and act out roles by conducting various performances. However, Goffman looked at issues concerning "social spaces" that emerge at the micro-level during face-to-face interactions, and hardly ever theorized about "social spaces" as taking shape within a particular social background of the times. Therefore, there has been a trend towards looking at "social spaces" without any connection to the social background. Goffman's discussion of the "social spaces" that can be seen at the micro-level during face-to-face interactions progressed as if "social spaces" would continue to be exactly the same in the context of any time period.

However, all "social spaces" are, without exception, influenced by the social background of the times. Especially in the present age, "social spaces" are strongly affected by the social backgrounds in which human beings, material, capital, information, images and ideas are moving and travelling globally beyond borders. Social spaces in the present age are certainly not unrelated to our conditions of global mobility; indeed, our conditions of mobility play an important role in their formation.

The age of mobility: divergence and convergence of mobility-scapes

According to Peter Adey, "We simply cannot ignore that the world is moving" (Adey, 2017, p. 1). He wrote that, "Maybe, the world is moving a bit more than it did before too. We might even say that mobility is ubiquitous; it is something we do and experience almost all of the time". For Nigel Thrift (2006) even space itself is characterized by this mobility and movement: "every space is in constant motion", he writes. Mobility is not something "very new" as Anthony Giddens (2000, p. 1) comments on globalization, but certainly something "new" is happening in the world.

John Urry sets out the characteristics of this mobility as a "mobility paradigm" (Urry, 2007, pp. 46–54). This global mobility has surely transformed our lives in the present age and will have a significant influence on "social spaces", the settings in which they are managed. Anthony Elliott and John Urry express this as follows in their text, *Mobile Lives*:

> Changes in how people live their lives today are both affected by and reflect the broader changes of global mobility processes. Or, more specifically, the increasing mobilization of the world – accelerating carbon-based movements of people, goods, services, ideas and information – affects the ways in which lives are lived, experienced and understood. ... Our conjecture is that, in the face of a new global narrative of mobilities, the self-fashioning of lives is now recast and transformed.
>
> (Elliott & Urry, 2010, p. x)

So, what forms does mobility take now? Below, I would like to adapt the discussion in Arjun Appadurai's *Modernity at Large: Cultural Dimensions of Globalization*, and describe five dimensions, the "scapes" for the expression of mobility: "ethnoscapes"; "materialscapes"; "financescapes"; "governancescapes"; and "imaginaryscapes" (Appadurai, 1996).[3]

Firstly, the term "ethnoscapes" is a way of referring to global cultural flows observed in the movement of people such as foreign laborers, tourists, migrants, and refugees. Next, "materialscapes" refers to movement of material things such as goods, industrial raw materials, production machinery, and cargo, across borders.

"Financescapes" refers to the continuous movement of global capital across borders, and "governancescapes" to the instability of regional and national institutional authority and sovereignty crossing borders and becoming mobile. Finally, "imaginaryscapes" refers to global cultural flows seen in the movement of information, images, ideas, and thought.

These five mobility-scapes give rise to multilayered mobility flows, sometimes diverging and sometimes converging. As an example, let us consider the "European refugee crisis", with many refugees surging into various European countries since 2015 (Hakata, 2016). More than 1.2 million people have become refugees as a result of civil war, war, sectarian confrontation, terrorism, and conflict occurring in Middle-Eastern states such as Syria and Iraq, in African states such as Libya, Sudan, and Somalia, in South Asian states such as Afghanistan and Pakistan, and in states in the west of the Balkan Peninsula such as Kosovo and Albania. In such circumstances, ideologies calling for the regulation of the movement of migrants and refugees, or their expulsion, cross borders and take a negative form as a result of people feeling that national sovereignty and institutions are being threatened. Indeed, it is ironic that anti-globalist ideologies are circulating in a global fashion. In other words, one could say that mobility is being expressed through the convergence of "governancescapes" and "imaginaryscapes" to one another, while diverging from "ethnoscapes".

One might also think of the referendum held in the United Kingdom in 2016 concerning withdrawal from the European Union (Murakami, 2016). Before the referendum, it was initially expected that the people of the United Kingdom would take a realistic judgement, and that the Remain camp would win, avoiding any radical changes. However, in the end it was the Leave camp that won, and as a result the UK has commenced proceedings to separate from the EU.

Supporters of the Leave camp included comparatively older people who wanted to preserve the "traditional values" of the UK, and low-skilled and low-income working-class people. They harboured beliefs and concerns that they were unable to benefit from global capital, and that their own rights were threatened by the continued influx of migrants and large financial contributions to the EU. It emerged that, among such people, "governancescapes" and "imaginaryscapes" had clearly diverged from the flow in the EU, which was developed by a convergence of "ethnoscapes", "financescapes", and "materialscapes", and Brexit was the result.

Of course, in this same UK, those belonging to the Remain camp saw the situation differently. To them, there was no divergence among "ethnoscapes", "financescapes", "materialscapes", "governancescapes", and "imaginaryscapes"; they were all in convergence. Thus, even within the same country, the UK, differing and multi-layered mobility flows are constantly created as the five mobilities repeatedly diverge and converge in various ways. Thus, "heterogeneously twisted social spaces" take many forms.[4]

Media as social spaces in the "age of mobility"

Digital media as "social spaces"

Following the "digital revolution", media can be said to be playing a significant role in the emergence of social mobility. The term "digital revolution" refers not only to a shift in media towards the use of digital technologies, but also to monumental shifts in social systems resulting from the use of digital technologies for media (Ishida, 2016). Indeed, there is a reflexive and recursive relationship between media and social systems following the "digital revolution".

Taking music as an example, it has now become the norm to listen to music through a streamed digital sound source accessed via music distribution applications on our smartphones. This technology has changed the music market and impacted people's lifestyles, transforming the very nature of music into something that we listen to while being mobile: while walking or running, or travelling by aeroplane, train, car, or bicycle.

The same is true for video. Video, which had formerly been broadcast through analogue televisions and recorded on videotapes, came to be broadcast on digital televisions and recorded on DVD and Blu-ray. And now we have become able to watch video while being mobile, through the Internet on our smartphones. This has affected the film business, and our lifestyles have been significantly transformed through that business. FinTech, as represented by mobile payment and the like, has also encouraged enhanced mobility in people's lifestyles, as well as transforming financial markets (Table 13.1).

Following the digital revolution, media has taken shape within the "Age of Mobility", and encouraged the mobilization of society. At the same time, in the Age of Mobility, media have become "social spaces", settings in which various performances are expressed. As a concrete example, let us consider how people's views concerning the Trump administration's immigration policy have divided and oscillated in the United States of America.

In the United States of America, policies have been put in place to restrict immigration, because it seemed that large numbers of migrants were going to surge in from other countries (predominantly Central and South America). President Trump's supporters supported the President's migration policies on the basis of a belief that migrants were stealing their jobs and violating their rights. For them, the "ethnoscapes" were diverging from the "governancescapes" and "imaginaryscapes". In contrast, there were also people who strongly opposed Trump's migration restriction policies. There is the belief among these people that the global flow of human beings, material, capital, information, images, and ideas is important for the United States of America.

In such circumstances, those who support President Trump's migration policies, and those who are critical of them, have taken to expressing their own opinions, beliefs, and performances in the settings offered by digital media, such as Social Networking Systems (SNS). SNS have become "heterogeneously twisted social spaces", pregnant with varying and different significances (definitions of the conditions) concerning migration policy.

SNS have become "real" settings for human performance, such that there is no comparison between SNS and other mass media. Perhaps it is for this very reason

Table 13.1 Some specific examples of the "digital revolution" in media

	Analogue	Digitization	Digital revolution
Document creation	Paper, pencil	Word processors, personal computers	Cloud computing
Music	Records, tapes	CD, DVD, LaserDisc	Online music distribution
Video	Film, videotapes, analogue television	DVD, BD, digital television	Online video distribution
Finance	In-store transactions	Electronic transactions	FinTech

Source: amended by the author, from Jo (2016).

that President Trump attacks traditional mass media as "fake news", and continues to express political performances through Twitter. In the past there has always been consideration of "social spaces" as connected to physical spaces, with many examples like kitchens and dining rooms, or classrooms and homes. However, as discussed in Joshua Meyrowitz's *No Sense of Place: The Impact of Electronic Media on Social Behavior*, digital media (including SNS), quite distinct from any physical location, have come to play a significant role as "social spaces" in modern society (Meyrowitz, 1985). Our concept of the "real" social world is something that has taken form since the arrival of digital media, which create a "virtual" world, and in this respect "real" and "virtual" are, from the outset, not conflicting concepts.

A focus on "platforms"

When considering the above, it becomes necessary to take a closer look at "platforms", one of the elements that comprise digital media.[5]

Media are formed by four elements: (1) content; (2) devices; (3) infrastructure; and (4) platforms (Tanaka *et al.*, 2014, p. 17). Firstly, "content" refers to the content of the information sent and received through the media. Next, "devices" refers to the material equipment of the media, such as television receivers, mobile telephones, smartphones, and the like. "Infrastructure" refers to the equipment used to transmit information, such as the transportation systems used to deliver newspapers, and optical cables, radio, satellite channels, and Wi-Fi. Finally, the term "platforms" is used to indicate the environments that form the framework, or foundation, on which media content, services, and products can be gathered and exchanged (Lessig, 2006). Web-services such as Google, SNS such as Facebook, Twitter, and Instagram, Internet shopping sites such as Amazon and Rakuten, and Cookpad (in which cooking recipes and videos are gathered) are all positioned as online platforms (Figure 13.1).

When we conduct research into media, we tend to focus on the content expressed there. We do not often direct our attention to devices, infrastructures, or platforms that exist behind such content. When we think about messages exchanged by smartphone, we are conscious of the content of the messages, but hardly notice other elements of the media than the contents.

However, for example, even if the content remains the same, might not devices themselves convey some kind of additional message, such as setting, context, or

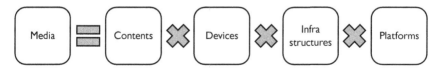

Figure 13.1 Media elements.
Source: created by the author.

atmosphere? Consider when one is arranging a meet-up. The process of meeting up has completely transformed since the appearance of mobile phones; we now exchange messages by asking, "where are you now?" and confirming the location as if it were completely normal, without thinking about it. Devices infiltrate human beings down to the unconscious level, sending us messages outside of the content.

It is the Canadian researcher Marshall McLuhan who made such a claim. Even if the context is romantic in either case, the feel of a conversation by public telephone and of a conversation through lines on one's smartphone will be completely different. On this basis, McLuhan asserts that "the media is the message" (McLuhan, 1964). McLuhan's argument, which focuses more on the characteristics of the devices and infrastructures than of the contents, is extraordinarily insightful.

However, one might think that with his approach, the "devices" and "infrastructures" elements of media are given too much attention. In considering the nature of digital media, and how it simultaneously has a major impact on our thought and behaviour, and is used to express them, might the "platforms" – web services such as Google which use artificial intelligence (AI) technologies, and SNS such as Facebook, Twitter, and Instagram – be becoming more important than "devices" or "infrastructures"? They may not involve physical entities, but countless people are using these platforms as the settings for gathering together and interacting with each other (Hamano, 2015, p. 20).[6] When considering "social spaces" in the present "Age of Mobility", it is essential to direct our attention towards digital media "platforms".

Tourism mobility realized by "platforms"

The significance of "platforms" to tourism

This will become clearer by considering the example of tourism.

It has now become impossible to think about the mobility of human beings, material, capital, information, ideas, and technology without looking at tourism and travelling.

Looking at the situation of tourism globally, in 2011 the number of people travelling abroad globally surpassed 1 billion for the first time, and the number has continued to rise since then (Figure 13.2). If one refers to the trend in international tourist numbers in the most recent ten years as recorded in the Ministry of Land, Infrastructure, Transport and Tourism's *White Paper on Tourism in Japan, 2018*, the number of international tourists rises from 930 million in 2008 to 1.40 billion in 2018 (Ministry of Land, Infrastructure, Transport and Tourism, 2018). Based on the estimate of the United Nations' *State of World Population* that the world population is 7 billion, it can be calculated that approximately one sixth of the world population travels abroad. Even in Japan, the number of people travelling overseas in 2018 was over 15 million, at 18.95 million people. The number

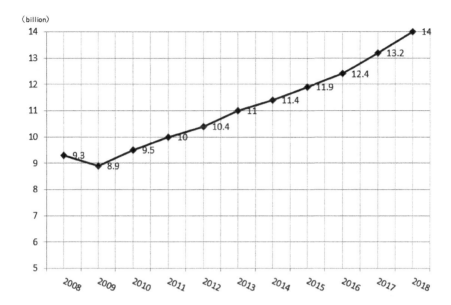

Figure 13.2 Trends in numbers of international tourists from 2008 to 2018.

Source: created by the author with reference to the Ministry of Land, Infrastructure, Transport and Tourism's *White Paper on Tourism in Japan* (2018, p. 1).

of foreign tourists travelling to Japan is also increasing, with the figure going up every year, and reaching 31.19 million visitors in 2018.

Tourism not only refers to the movement of these people, but also to the movement of things such as souvenirs and suitcases. Further, people set out on their vacations after having searched for information and data through media including holiday magazines, the Internet, and their smartphones, and they take a great deal of images relating to their destination along with them. As a result, there is also a movement of information, data, and images. Furthermore, by experiencing various things and events at their travel destinations, people form memories and bring them from destinations to home (the movement of memories). Additionally, as tourism is formed on the basis of many industries (such as travel agencies, transportation industries including the aviation industry and so on, and the accommodation industry including hotels and the like), it goes without saying that it follows a movement of capital.

When considering mobility, it is essential to look at tourism. On this subject, Mimi Sheller and John Urry have presented the concept of "tourism mobilities", stating the following:

> We refer to "tourism mobilities", then, not simply in order to state the obvious (that tourism is a form mobility), but to highlight that many different

mobilities inform tourism, shape the places where tourism is performed, and drive the making and unmaking of tourist destinations. Mobilities of people and objects, airplanes and suitcases, plants and animals, images and brands, data systems and satellites, all go into "doing" tourism. Tourism also concerns the relational mobilizations of memories and performances, gendered and racialized bodies, emotions and atmospheres. Places have multiple contested meanings that often produce disruptions and disjunctures. Tourism mobilities involve complex combinations of movement and stillness, realities and fantasies, play and work.

(Sheller & Urry, 2004, p. 1)

When tourists set out to visit their destinations, media will be important. They will depart with travel information and images of their destinations. The destinations chosen and the tourist activities undertaken are often determined on the basis of such information and images. The same is true for foreign tourists visiting Japan. The information and images displayed by the media they encounter will have a significant influence on the places within Japan that they visit, the tourist activities that they participate in, and the souvenirs that they purchase.

According to the Ministry of Land, Infrastructure, Transport and Tourism's *Consumption Trend Survey of Foreigners Visiting Japan 2017 Results Report*, when foreigners were asked, "Which source(s) do you feel were helpful in obtaining information about your destination prior to coming to Japan?", the source that received the most responses was "personal blogs" (31.2%). Next was "Social media" with 21.4%; in contrast, 14.6% of persons responded that "Travel guide(s)" were helpful, and 9.4% that a "TV program" was helpful (Ministry of Land, Infrastructure, Transport and Tourism, 2017). When one looks at such data, one can see that the role of travel guides and TV programmes is declining. Formerly, such media played a significant role. Tourists travelling around with a *Rough Guide* or *Lonely Planet* guidebook in hand was a common sight. Or, programmes broadcast on televisions provided them with tourism information and images.

Now, however, it is digital media "platforms" such as blogs, SNS, and video-sharing sites that are playing an increasingly large role in tourism. In this process, it is irrelevant whether the "devices" or "infrastructures" are smartphones and Wi-Fi. They are unimportant; what is important is the "platforms". The expression of one's thoughts and performances in the settings (social spaces) provided by social media platforms has become an essential part of tourism.

When material things go on holiday

As society becomes mobile in this way, the performances, information, images, and ideas expressed in the digital media platforms as "social spaces" transform as they enter a new phase. At the same time, this is causing the digital media platforms as a "social space" to encourage the various phenomena associated with tourism mobility to become something new (Figure 13.3).

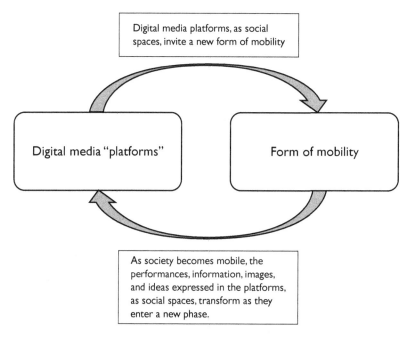

Figure 13.3 The reflexive and recursive relationship between platforms and mobility.

Source: created by the author.

In order to bring into relief what I mean here, let us focus below on the mobility of material things that is realized by "media as platforms". "*Nui-dorī*" (a phenomenon involving taking photographs of stuffed toys) at the Tokyo Disney Resort is one specific example of this.

"*Nui-dorī*" refers to having fun by making stuffed animals the stars of photographs. At Tokyo DisneySea, the characters "Duffy", "ShellieMay", "Gelatoni", and "StellaLou" are gaining popularity, but tourists come with their own stuffed animals and deliberately bring those into DisneySea to enjoy "*nui-dorī*".[7] The main objective is to put the stuffed toy in a performative pose, and upload photographs of this to SNS using a digital device.

With such tourism, the mobility of human beings is not in the foreground. It is, rather, the mobility of material things that is brought to the fore by uploading photographs of the material things recorded to "platforms" such as Instagram, Twitter, and Facebook through digital media. In such circumstances, stuffed animals that can be easily posed so as to make "*nui-dorī*" easier have started being sold at Disney Resort.

The case of Japanese travel agencies specializing in stuffed animals can be offered as a similar example. Among travel agencies in Japan nowadays, companies have appeared that coordinate holidays not for people, but for their stuffed animals. These companies are entrusted with the customers' stuffed animals, which their employees take around with them as they visit various destinations, spend the night at hotels, and eat their meals. They provide the service of showing the customers photographs and making it look like their stuffed animals are really enjoying the trip, by uploading them to SNS with digital devices. Thus, a mobility of material things has emerged in modern tourism, brought about by digital "media as platform".

After such circuits, "emotions" and "affections" that form an indispensable part of tourism, such as "joy" and "happiness", are induced in the stuffed animals' owners. The expression of the travel of material things through digital devices on platforms (such as Instagram, Twitter, and Facebook) as "social spaces" has become an objective of tourism, through which the owners of the stuffed animals are able to satisfy the emotional and affectional part of tourism (happiness, joy, etc.).[8]

In this process, the "subject" of the tourism is not human beings, but rather stuffed animals (non-humans). Non-humans are the "subjects" of tourism mobility. According to Bruno Latour, in modern times non-humans (or nature) have been separated from humans (or society), and have come to be regarded as simply objects that humans act upon (Latour describes this as "purification"). However, the human (society) and non-human (nature) are deeply intertwined, bound to each other in a network in "subjects" (that is to say, "agents") (Latour calls this "translation") (Latour, 1991).

It would seem that these travelling stuffed animals have also gone beyond simply being objects owned by human beings and have become subjects with agency, giving rise to emotions and affections in people. People's emotions and affections are not the product of their actions as subjects, but a hybrid product woven together by humans and non-humans.

An anecdote provided by Latour himself allows this concept to be easily understood. It goes as follows. There was a hotel manager who became angry about the never-ending number of customers who would leave without returning their room key. He reminded customers orally, "Please return your room key to the front desk" when handing over keys, and put up a written sign, but to no avail. Then, the manager decided to attach key-chains to the room keys. In this anecdote, once key-chains were attached, customers would notice them when they put them in their pocket and started returning them to the front desk. What we see here is that what triggered the behaviour of returning room keys to the front desk was not the customers themselves, but the non-human key-chains (Latour, 1993).

Be that as it may, perhaps it is still not proper to state that "people's emotions and affections are a hybrid product woven together by humans and non-humans". It would be more accurate to state that humans have become "objects" whose emotions and affections are induced. The "subjects" of the tourism are not humans but stuffed animals (things). If that is the case, one could say that with the travel of stuffed animals it is material things that are the "subjects" of tourism mobility.

While detaching and nullifying the human movement ethnoscapes, the stuffed animal movement, materialscapes based on digital media "platforms" are simultaneously forming "social spaces" as they converge with the financescapes of the tourism and media industries and the governancescapes of governments and communities; this is giving rise to diverse mobility "lines" centred around material things (Ingold, 2007). The arrangements of, and relationships between, material, capital, and power also create a flow of human emotions and affections (an imaginaryscape). Thus, as much as they may be "interpellated" as "subjects" with emotions and affections, human beings are transforming more into "objects" (Althusser, 1995).[9]

Concluding remarks: remaining questions

As has been seen above, digital media (such as SNS), which are separated from any physical locality, are taking shape in the "Age of Mobility" as "heterogeneously twisted social spaces", pregnant with varying and different significances (definitions of the conditions). The performances, information, images, and ideas expressed there are transforming as they enter a new phase not seen in society before this point, which itself encourages the various phenomena associated with tourism mobility to become something new. This can be seen clearly in the movement of tourism, or tourism mobility.

For example, the "emotions" and "affections" created by tourism can now be induced without human mobility through digital media "platforms". As was seen when looking at the example of exchanging photographs of travelling stuffed toys on Instagram, various mobilities (materialscapes, financescapes, governancescapes, and imaginaryscapes) centred around things are intertwining on digital medial "platforms". This will allow us to experience happiness and joy without the involvement of human movement (ethnoscapes).

Nowadays it has become possible for us to take digital Augmented Reality (AR) technology with us during tourism, and to take souvenir photographs together with anime characters at sites that feature in anime programmes. There are even hotels where AI-equipped robots work at the front desk or as concierges. Accordingly, I would like you to imagine the following scene: a customer in his/her own home using Instagram to look at photographs of stuffed animals taking souvenir pictures together with anime characters through AR at locations that appear in anime programmes, and at photographs of stuffed animals receiving their hotel check-in forms from AI-equipped robots. When a customer smiles, alone in his/her room, because of the emotions and affections brought about as he/she thinks, "my stuffed animals look like they're enjoying themselves", then perhaps something completely new and unprecedented will have started to emerge.

As digital media "platforms" are treated as settings (social spaces), and tourismscapes are realized through the use of digital media technologies such as AR and AI, this kind of scene will be possible. However, could we call this tourism?

Perhaps this should no longer be called tourism, and should be described as "the demise of tourism".

On the other hand, perhaps this could be described as a "complete tourism" in which the tourism conditions are taken to nullify human mobility. It is possible that this "complete tourism" referred to as the "the demise of tourism" is starting to be realized by treatment of digital media "platforms" as "social spaces". What might the significance of this situation be? I would prefer not to write an answer to this without serious thought. Rather, for the time being I will leave this chapter "hanging" with the following question:

Given the above, what is the essential meaning of "tourism"? This question ought to result in the radical deconstruction of tourism mobilities critically.

Supplementary note

This chapter is a revised version of a paper originally published in *Tourism Studies Review*, and was written with the assistance of JSPS Grant-in-Aid for Scientific Research 17H02251, "*Gendaishakai ni okeru tsūrizumu mobiriti no shintenkai to chiiki* (New developments and regions in tourism-mobility in modern society)" (Principal Investigator: Kanda Koji).

Notes

1 "Social spaces" can be defined as the fields of meanings where varieties of social realities are generated while people interact with the others.
2 As is well known, Dean MacCannell used the concepts of "front region" and "back region" when thinking about social spaces in tourism (MacCannell, 1999).
3 Appadurai refers to "ethnoscapes", "technoscapes", "financescapes", "mediascapes", and "ideoscapes". "Ethnoscapes" and "financescapes" are as described above. "Mediascapes" and "ideoscapes" correspond to the term "imaginaryscapes" as used in this chapter. Of these, "mediascapes" in particular refer to forms of expression in global culture that can be seen in the movement of various images and symbols in popular culture through media including newspapers, television, and the Internet. "Ideoscapes" more specifically refer to the unstable situation of more ideological images such as values and world-views crossing borders and becoming mobile. Additionally, Appadurai's "technoscapes" refer to the situation of technology (whether mechanical or information technology) moving across various borders.
4 Scott Lash also talked about "platform capitalism", focusing on the "platform" element of digital media, at a lecture held at Ritsumeikan University's Hirai Kaichiro Memorial Library conference room on Friday June 22, 2018.
5 The term "platform" used in this chapter could be said to have considerable overlap with the term "architecture" as used by Lawrence Lessig and Hamano. Nevertheless, the word "platform" is used here instead of "architecture" in order to express with greater emphasis the nuance of "social spaces" formed by digital media.
6 Reflexivity can also be seen in the relationship between social mobility and digital media. In that sense, the concept of "reflexivity" (Nakanishi, 2013) is important when considering modern tourism, together with "mobility", "digital media", "platforms", "materiality", and "emotions/affections".
7 "Duffy" is a teddy bear originating from Tokyo DisneySea boasting extraordinary popularity, and "ShellieMay" is a teddy bear said to be Duffy's girlfriend. "Gelatoni", another

DisneySea-originated character, takes the form of a pale-green male cat, and is supposed to be good at painting and aiming to become a painter. "StellaLou" is another DisneySea-originated character, a lavender-coloured female rabbit stuffed animal that dreams of being a dancer.

8 In future, it will be necessary to incorporate "emotion" and "affection" into the "mobility turn" and "tourism turn" in media studies (Ito, 2013; Kitano, 2018).

9 On this point, this chapter accepts Alexander Galloway's discussion relating to protocol after decentralization (Galloway, 2004).

References

Adey, P. (2017). *Mobility (second edition)*, Oxford: Routledge.

Althusser, L. (1995). *Sur la reproduction*, Paris: Universitaires de France.

Appadurai, A. (1996). *Modernity at large*, Minnesota, MN: University of Minnesota.

Elliott, A. (2018). *The culture of AI: Everyday life and the digital revolution*, London: Routledge.

Elliott, A., & Urry, J. (2010). *Mobile lives*, Oxford: Routledge.

Endo, H. (2011). *Gendai bunkaron: Shakai riron de yomitoku popyura karutya [Contemporary cultural studies: Social theories to read popular cultures]*, Kyoto: Minerva Publishing.

Endo, H. (2017). *Tsurizumu Mobirities: Kanko to ido no shakai riron [Tourism mobilities: Social theory of tourism and mobility]*, Kyoto: Minerva Publishing.

Galloway, A.R. (2004). *Protocol: How control exists after decentralization*, Cambridge, MA: MIT Press.

Giddens, A. (1990). *The consequence of modernity*, Cambridge: Polity Press.

Giddens, A. (2000). *Global capitalism*, London: New Press.

Goffman, E. (1959). *The presentation of self in everyday life*, New York: Doubleday & Company Inc.

Hakata, K. (2016). *Nanmin mondai: Isuramuken no doyo, EU no kuno, Nihon no kadai [Refugee issue: Fluctuation of Islamic world, anguish in EU, and Japanese challenge]*, Tokyo: Chuoukoron Publishing.

Hamano, S. (2015). *Akitekutya no seitaikei: Joho kankyo ha ikani sekkeisaretekitaka [The ecology of architecture: How the information environment has been designed]*, Tokyo: Chikuma Publishing.

Hannam, K., & Knox, D. (2010). *Understanding tourism: A critical introduction*, London: Sage.

Hannam, K., Butler, G., & Paris, C.M. (2014). Developments and key issues in tourism mobilities, *Annals of Tourism Research*, 44(1): 171–185.

Hattori, K. (2018). *Makuruhan ha meseiji: Meseiji to tekunoroji no mirai ha dokoe mukaunoka [McLuhan is message: What future will we face in message and technology]*, Tokyo: East Press Publishing.

Ingold, T. (2007). *Lines: A brief history*, Oxford: Routledge.

Ishida, H. (2016). *Otona notameno mediaron kogi [Media theory for adult people]*, Tokyo: Chikuma Publishing.

Ito, M. (2013). *Jyodo no kenryoku: Media to kyoshinsuru shintai [The power of affection: Embodiment resonating with media]*, Tokyo: Serika Publishing.

Ito, S. (2016). *EU bunretsu to sekai keizaikiki: Igirisu ridatsu ha naniwo motarasunoka [Disunity of EU and world-wide economic crisis: What impacts does Brexit bring]*, Tokyo: NHK Publishing.

Jo, H. (2016). *Nihon niokeru dejitaru kakumei [Digital revolution in Japan]*, retrieved: January 6, 2019, www.eyjapan.jp/industries/technology/column/2016-04-25.html.

Kitano, K. (ed.) (2018). *Materiaru seorizu: Aratanaru yuibutsuron nimukete [Material theories: Toward a new materialism]*, Tokyo: Jinbun shoin Pubushing.

Larsen, J., & Sandbye, M. (2014). *Digital snaps: The new face of photography*, London: I. B. Tauris.

Lash, S., & Urry, J. (1994). *Economies of signs and space*, London: Sage.

Latour, B. (1987). *Science in action: How to follow scientists and engineers through society*, Cambridge, MA: Harvard University Press.

Latour, B. (1991). *Nous n'avons jamais ete modernes: Essai d'anthropologie symetrique*, Paris: La Decouverte.

Latour, B. (1993). *La clef de Berlin et autres lecons d'un amateur de sciences*, Paris: La decouverte.

Lessig, L. (2006). *Code version 2.0*, New York: Basic Books.

MacCannell, D. (1999). *The tourist: A new theory of the leisure class*, Los Angeles, CA: University of California Press.

McLuhan, M. (1964). *Understanding media: The extension of man*, New York: McGraw-Hill.

Meyrowitz, J. (1985). *No sense of place: The impact of electronic media on social behavior*, Oxford: Oxford University Press.

Ministry of Land, Infrastructure, Transport and Tourism (2017). *Consumption Trend Survey for Foreigners Visiting Japan Heisei 29nen*, retrieved: September 17, 2018, www.mlit. go.jp/common/001230775.pdf#search='%E5%B9%B3%E6%88%9029%E5%B9%B4 %E7%89%88+%E8%A8%AA%E6%97%A5%E5%A4%96%E5%9B%BD%E4%BA %BA%E3%81%AE%E6%B6%88%E8%B2%BB%E5%8B%95%E5%90%91'.

Ministry of Land, Infrastructure, Transport and Tourism (2018). *White Paper on Tourism in Japan Heisei 30nen*, retrieved: September 17, 2018, www.mlit.go.jp/statistics/ file000008.html.

Murakami, N. (2016). *EU ha dounarunoka: Brexit no shogeki [The futures of EU: The impacts of Brexit]*, Tokyo: Heibonsha Publishing.

Nakanishi, M. (2013). Saikisei no henka to aratana tenkai: Lassyu no saikiseiron wo kijikuni [The transformation of reflexivity and for the future: Lash's perspective on the transformation of reflexivity], *Japanese Sociological Review*, 64(2): 224–239.

Nanba, K. (2011). *Mediaron [Theories of media]*, Tokyo: Jinbun shoin Publishing.

Sheller, M., & Urry, J. (2004). *Tourism mobilities: Places to play, places in play*, London: Routledge.

Stiegler, B. (2004). *De la misère symbolique 1: L'époque hyperindustrielle*, Paris: Éditions Galilèe.

Sudo, H., & Endo, H. (2018). *Kanko shakaigaku 2.0: Hirogariyuku tsurizumu kenkyu [Sociology of tourism 2.0: Develops and transforms of tourism studies]*, Tokyo: Fukumara Publishing.

Tanaka, H. *et al.* (2014). 2020nen no media to komyunikeshon [Media and communication in 2020], *AD STUDIES* Special Issue, 50: 6–21.

Thrift, N. (2006). Space, *Theory, Culture and Society*, 23: 139–146.

Urry, J. (1990). *The tourist gaze: Leisure and travel in contemporary societies*, London: Sage.

Urry, J. (2000). Mobile sociology, *British Journal of Sociology*, 51(1): 185–201.

Urry, J. (2007). *Mobilities*, Cambridge: Polity Press.

Urry, J., & Larsen, J. (2011). *The tourist gaze 3.0*, London: Sage.

Index

Page numbers in **bold** denote tables, those in *italics* denote figures.

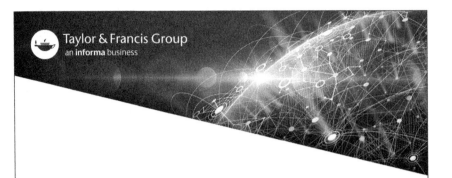

Printed in the United States
By Bookmasters